Modern Scandinavian Prints

Modern Scandinavian Prints

Frances Carey

Published for the Trustees of the British Museum
by British Museum Press

The Trustees of the British Museum gratefully acknowledge the generous donation from Dr Birgit Rausing towards the acquisition by the Department of Prints and Drawings of work by Scandinavian artists and towards the production of this catalogue.

Front cover *Skaugum*, 1933/4 (cat. 81, detail), by Rolf Nesch

Back cover *An artist's wife*, 1913 (cat. 11), by Carl Larsson

Frontispiece *Self-portrait with skeleton arm*, 1895 (cat. 51), by Edvard Munch

Page 6 *Herring catch*, 1938 (cat. 83, first of six parts), by Rolf Nesch

Published to accompany an exhibition at the British Museum from 24 January to 20 April 1997

First published in 1997 by British Museum Press A division of The British Museum Company Ltd 46 Bloomsbury Street, London WC1B 3QQ

ISBN 0 7141 2605 5

A catalogue record for this book is available from the British Library

Photography by the British Museum Photographic Service

Designed by James Shurmer

Typeset in Photina and printed in Great Britain by BAS Printers Ltd, Over Wallop, Hampshire

Contents

Preface

The British Museum's links with Scandinavia go back to the very beginning of its institutional history when the young Swedish botanist and favourite pupil of Linnaeus, Daniel Solander (1736–82), was appointed assistant librarian in 1763. His memory is kept alive among Print Room curators because of the folio document boxes he devised which bear his name and form the basis of our storage system. They were originally made to preserve the papers accumulated on Captain Cook's first voyage on the *Endeavour* from 1768 to 1771, for which Solander was engaged as a companion by another eminent naturalist, Joseph Banks (1743–1820), whose personal librarian he subsequently became in tandem with his duties in the Museum. Banks, who was *ex officio* a Trustee of the British Museum from 1778 until his death, not only had connections with scientific circles in Scandinavia, particularly in Sweden, but also became deeply involved in the affairs of Iceland, a colony of Denmark, during the Napoleonic wars from 1801 to 1813. Together with Solander, Banks had visited Iceland in 1772, bringing back a collection of books which he presented to the British Museum, and it was to him that the Icelanders appealed when the British embargo on Danish vessels from 1801 onwards (because of Denmark's alliance with France after Nelson's attack on Copenhagen) threatened the population with starvation.[1]

The collection of Scandinavian prints and drawings is of more recent creation, stemming in the first instance from a group of 143 etchings by Danish artists of the first half of the nineteenth century, the so-called Golden Age, that was bought by the Museum in 1859. For material of the late nineteenth century onwards, the contacts and generosity of a former Keeper of the Department of Prints and Drawings, Campbell Dodgson (1867–1948), were the determining factors; the gifts during his lifetime, followed by the bequest of his entire private collection of approximately five thousand items, made him the Department's most notable modern benefactor.[2] His Scandinavian material, which was largely of Swedish origin, included four hand-coloured etched views of Stockholm by Johan Fredrik Martin (1755–1816), who published these with his brother Elias (1739–1818) after the latter's return to Stockholm in 1780 from an eleven-year sojourn in London.[3] For the most part it consisted of the work of contemporary printmakers, much of which came via his subscription to the Swedish Graphic Society (Föreningen for Grafisk Konst), from *c.* 1906 until his death. His predilection for the etchings of Carl Larsson (p. 20) and Anders Zorn (p. 30) was fostered by the example of the museum collections he admired in Germany, particularly that in Dresden built up by Max Lehrs, whose taste in modern prints was so influential on Dodgson's own. He visited Sweden on two occasions in 1927 and 1933: the first time was in connection with an Anglo-Swedish print exhibition under the patronage of Prince Eugen, when Dodgson took the opportunity to admire 'the really beautiful modern museum of art' in Gothenburg and to buy 'a good deal of modern Swedish glass, which we like very much'[4] in Stockholm, as well as reviewing the exhibition itself.

After the Dodgson Bequest, which with its various supplements was registered between 1949 and 1953, the next phase of acquisition of Scandinavian material did not begin until 1989, with the exception of the prints by the German-born artist Rolf Nesch (p. 97). The first example by him, *Black chorus line* (1930), was purchased in 1980, followed by a large group in 1983 which included *Herring catch* (1938, cat. 83), made after his departure from Hamburg to Norway at the end of 1933. Further acquisitions of his work have continued up to the present, making the British Museum's holding one of the few serious representations outside Norway and Germany.

In 1989 the British Museum purchased a number of prints by Danish artists of the late nineteenth and early twentieth centuries, building upon the etchings of their predecessors that came to the Museum in 1859. Thereafter the real stimulus to extend collecting activity came from the knowledge and enthusiasm for Scandinavian culture of all periods possessed by Sir David Wilson, then Director of the British Museum. In 1990 work was acquired by some of the leading postwar printmakers in Sweden from the Saga Gallery, which for ten years until its closure towards the end of 1990 was the only gallery in London to handle modern Scandinavian art. At the same time, the acquisitions policy was put on a new footing through the intervention of the Swedish art historian Birgit Rausing, who instigated a fund for the further improvement of the collection of works on paper by Scandinavian artists of the past hundred years, and from this both prints and drawings have been purchased.

In the interests of creating a visually coherent exhibition, much that is in the British Museum's collection has had to be omitted, including the Department's holding of drawings. This contains some good examples by two important Swedish artists from the end of the nineteenth century, Carl Fredrik Hill and Karl Nordström; drawings by the Surrealist sculptor Eric Grate, one of many Swedes to spend the formative years of his career in Paris; work by artists who came to maturity after the Second World War such as the Danes Palle Nielsen (p. 91) and Jørgen Rømer; and examples by two of the proponents of abstraction in Sweden, Rune Jansson and Pierre Olofsson, with those of a more recent generation, Claes Eklundh, who works in Sweden and New York, and Olav Christopher Jenssen from Norway, who has lived in Berlin since 1982. There are also good printmakers for whom no space could be found or who are not yet properly represented in the Museum's collection. One principal example is the Danish Surrealist/Concretist artist Richard Mortensen, who lived in Paris between 1947 and 1964 and was quick to perceive in the early 1950s the possibilities of silkscreen printing for the translation of the hard-edged abstract style he developed in his painting; the Department owns a *pochoir* of 1953 from a mixed portfolio published on the occasion of an exhibition at the Galerie Denise René,[5] which will be included in the Department's forthcoming exhibition, Printmaking in Paris 1905–1970.

This exhibition, however, is the first in London to deal with Scandinavian printmaking in general since one sent in 1938 to the Victoria and Albert Museum by the Nordic Graphic Union. Munch (p. 60) is a colossus who bestrides many borders, but apart from his prints the material is largely unfamiliar to a British or American audience. The exigencies of time and resources have limited the survey primarily to Denmark, Sweden and Norway, with Finland and Iceland represented only by a few artists who have spent most of their working lives elsewhere.

Neither the selection nor the arrangement of the entries within the text was ever intended to defer to individual national identities, or to adumbrate precisely the history of art in the respective countries; printmaking is in any case too capricious a vehicle for the latter exercise once it is divorced from a purely reproductive role. The purpose of the exhibition and more particularly of the catalogue is to illuminate some of the issues common to all the Scandinavian countries, both social and artistic, and to demonstrate their relationship to the rest of Europe. Artists of non-Scandinavian origin such as Rolf Nesch, or those who spent much of their careers outside their native countries, such as Munch and Asger Jorn (p. 108), have been among the most influential in establishing the concept of a 'Nordic sensibility'. For this reason the last pan-Scandinavian exhibition in London, held at the Barbican in 1992, was called Border

Crossings and referred to Asger Jorn's quotation from *Alfa and Omega* of 1963/4: 'Thus it is not a matter of standing guard over Nordic art but of throwing it into the scales, of opening chests and drawers and buying our freedom with its help.'[6]

None of the recent acquisitions for the collection or the research and execution of the catalogue could have been accomplished without the unstinting help of many people in Scandinavia who have shown commendable patience towards a novice in their field, whose imperfect grasp of their languages must at times resemble the opening credits of the film *Monty Python and the Holy Grail* – into which Swedish words and references are oddly interjected. Despite many other calls upon their time they have shown a warmth of hospitality that is certainly not attributable to 'a fondness for social pleasures in which the mind not having its proportion of exercise, the bottle must be pushed about', the stricture levelled by Mary Wollstonecraft in her eloquent but severe account of *A Short Residence in Sweden, Norway and Denmark* (London, 1796).[7]

My greatest debt is to Birgit Rausing and her husband Gad, to whom I owe the fund at my disposal for the past six years which has supported the acquisitions and helped to subsidise this catalogue. They have given much more besides in kind and in spirit: their knowledge, contacts, hospitality and friendship have been a constant boon. Through them I have also benefited from the intelligent understanding and exemplary efficiency of Birgitta Olofsson at the Tetra Laval headquarters in Lund, and the hospitality of their son and daughter-in-law in Stockholm, Finn and Cecilia Rausing.

Museum colleagues, artists, their families and dealers have all contributed to the enterprise. Where they have assisted with specific information or commented on particular entries they have been acknowledged in the appropriate places, but I would like to thank further the following people whose co-operation has been beyond the call of duty. In Denmark Chris Fischer and the staff of the Kongelige Kobberstiksamling at the Statens Museum for Kunst in Copenhagen have dispensed professional advice and tea in equal measure; Troels Andersen of the Silkeborg Kunstmuseum has provided information, hospitality and some very welcome additions to the British Museum's collection; Lis Clausen of Clausens Kunsthandel in Copenhagen, one of the most agreeable printshops I know, has been indefatigable on my behalf; Erik Hansen has been the kindest of friends in offering help in connection with Aksel Jørgensen (p. 81); finally, 'the cordial reception which strangers receive from the inhabitants of small towns' mentioned by Mary Wollstonecraft was well and truly extended to me by Chris and Dorte Page of Roskilde and Ragnhild and Per

Christensen from Hjørring in Jutland, whose lives show no 'want of scientific pursuits' as suggested by Wollstonecraft.[8]

In Norway my overwhelming debt is to Sidsel Helliesen, Curator of Prints and Drawings at the Nasjonalgalleriet in Oslo from whom I have learnt so much, and to Eivind Otto Hjelle, the son-in-law of Rolf Nesch. Gerd Woll of the Munch Museum has advised on matters of substance in relation to Munch; Ben Frija of Galleri K, Mette Spendrup and Espen Ryvarden of Galleri Riis, the Galleri Kaare Berntsen and the two collectives for the sale of artists' work, Norske Grafikere and Kunstnerforbundet, have all supplied material and information. Eve Uthaug, the widow of the sculptor Jørleif (p. 135), has been a generous hostess together with her son and daughter-in-law, Geir and Marianne, and her brother in England, Harald Christopherson, to whom I owe the introduction.

Returning to Sweden there are Jane Rothlind of the Maps and Prints collection of the Royal Library (Kunglige Bibliotek) in Stockholm, whose excellent survey of Swedish black and white printmaking has been indispensable; Ragnar von Holten, Senior Curator at the Nationalmuseum, has been a valuable source as an expert on Surrealism, an artist himself and friend of many others in the catalogue; Magdalena Gram and the staff of the Art Library of the Statens Konstmuseer in Stockholm extended their assistance well beyond official opening hours; Pontus Grate, formerly Deputy Director of the Nationalmuseum and son of the sculptor Eric, has unwittingly brought home to me how provincial the English can be in comparison with cultivated Scandinavians, while his father's widow, Ann-Mar, has cheerfully acted as a courier on my behalf; the artist Gunnar Norrman (p. 56) and his wife Ulla have also made me welcome in their beautiful home, as has the dealer Ann Westin, now head of contemporary art exhibitions at Sotheby's in Stockholm. The Grafiska Sällskapet, which like its Norwegian counterparts mentioned above acts as an outlet for printmakers in Sweden, was equally helpful.

Within England I want to thank Samuel Josefowitz for his ready co-operation and Fiona McIntyre for permitting me to read her transcript of interviews conducted in 1994 with a number of printmakers in the Malmö/Lund area of Sweden; Michael Snodin of the Victoria and Albert Museum for help with Carl Larsson and some questions of translation, and Jane, Lady Abdy for her knowledge of Peter Ilsted (p. 78). My family and my colleagues at the British Museum have borne the brunt of my preoccupation with things Scandinavian and I am grateful for their support. I should specifically like to thank Jean Rankine, the Deputy Director, for checking final proofs and Märit, the wife of David Gaimster in the Department of Medieval and Later Antiquities, for translating a problematic passage; Nick Williams and

Ben Johnson, both formerly of the Department of Prints and Drawings, who helped me to organise some of the practical details for the exhibition in the early stages, Graham Javes and Bill Lewis, who have been responsible for all the photography, and Annette Pinto and Victoria de Korda for the mounting of the work. Conventional expressions of gratitude to the editorial and production staff of British Museum Press are never sufficient return for the multitude of sins they have to endure from their authors, so I would like to offer especial praise to my editor, Nina Shandloff, and to Julie Young, in charge of production, as well as to the copy editor John Banks and the designer James Shurmer, who have all contributed to the making of a 'silk purse'.

Finally, none of this would have been possible without the initial enthusiasm of Sir David Wilson or the continuing support of his successor as Director, Dr Robert Anderson, and of the Keeper of Prints and Drawings, Antony Griffiths. The most rewarding aspect of any collecting policy and its subsequent exhibition and publication is working within the context of the British Museum as a whole, where in this case Scandinavian archaeological material, the Lewis chessmen, modern applied art and design and the graphic arts are all part of the same infinitely various institution.

1. For full details of Banks's dealings over Iceland see Harold Carter, *Sir Joseph Banks* (London, 1988), pp. 458–70.

2. An essay on Campbell Dodgson as a collector by Frances Carey has been published in *Landmarks in Print Collecting*, ed. Antony Griffiths (London, 1996), pp. 211–35.

3. These joined two others purchased by the Department in 1915 during Dodgson's keepership. Two large watercolour views of Stockholm by Elias Martin have just been presented to the Department of Prints and Drawings as a part gift in honour of Joseph and Lisbet Koerner.

4. Both quotations are taken from Dodgson's private correspondence with his niece, Eveline, for 30 March and 13 April 1927, belonging to the Department of Prints and Drawings.

5. See Jan Würtz Frandsen, *Richard Mortensen: L'Oeuvre Graphique 1942–1993* (Copenhagen, 1995), no.15.

6. Barbican Art Gallery, London, *Border Crossings* (1992), p. 92.

7. 'Hospitality has, I think, been too much praised by travellers as a proof of goodness of heart, when in my opinion indiscriminate hospitality is rather a criterion by which you may form a tolerable estimate of the indolence or vacancy of the head' (Penguin edition, 1987, p. 73).

8. Ibid.

Introduction

The crucial period for the development of the principal modern Scandinavian states was between the mid nineteenth century and the early 1930s, when the attitudes and institutions of social democracy that have characterised the political climate of these countries for the remainder of the twentieth century were firmly in place. The mutuality of their small-scale, homogeneous communities was held up for admiration everywhere by social commentators such as the American journalist Marquis Childs, whose book *Sweden: The Middle Way* was published in 1936. It permeated all levels of cultural life, as reflected by the many societies for the appreciation and propagation of the fine and applied arts that burgeoned from the end of the nineteenth century onwards.

Scandinavian art of this period is sometimes defined in terms of a few Nietzschean supermen, namely Zorn (p. 30), Munch (p. 60), Vigeland (p. 68) and Willumsen (p. 73), but collectivism rather than individualism was the more typically Scandinavian approach to artistic activity in the widest sense. This was exemplified by the associations that enabled artists to assume control of their own exhibitions and sales outside the confines of the academies or the commercial world, to act as pressure groups and even to influence the acquisition policies of their national collections. They varied from bodies that existed purely for exhibition purposes such as Den Frie in Copenhagen, established in 1891 as the earliest of the Scandinavian secessionist movements in protest against official Academic prescription, to 'artists' houses', for example the one in Oslo founded in 1930 (Kunstnernes Hus) which provided communal facilities for the practice, discussion and display of local work and a lifeline to the outside world through an adventurous policy of loan exhibitions from abroad.

Another influential factor was the belief in the educational role of art as a vehicle for social improvement in the home, the workplace and many other contexts. 'Beauty for all' (*Skönhet för Alla*) was the credo declaimed in 1899 by the Swedish reformer Ellen Key (1849–1926), based on the ideals of the Arts and Crafts Movement in Britain, a credo she propagated in her lectures to the Workers' Institute (founded 1880) and at evening readings among a circle of cultivated families in Stockholm. Carl Larsson's subject matter and illustrational style (p. 20) captured her enthusiasm as a means for the general improvement of domestic visual culture when she saw the first of his watercolours of his family displayed at the Stockholm Art and Industry Exhibition in 1897. The reproduction of his work in book form and as single-sheet images as well as a small number of original lithographs printed in large editions made Larsson into the bourgeois artist *par excellence*, whose colourful evocations of an idealised family life were to be seen in homes and schools throughout Scandinavia and Germany by the beginning of the First World War.

The social purpose of art was reinforced by private and public patronage for mural decoration in schools, workers' clubs, libraries and community halls, starting with organisations such as Konsten i Skolan (Art in Schools), founded in Sweden in 1897 with the support of the King's brother, Prince Eugen (1865–1947). He was a key figure in the nation's cultural life, as a practising painter who had studied in Paris and as a patron with liberal artistic and political views; for example, he supported Norway's claim to independence even when, in 1905, Sweden was on the verge of invasion in an effort to preserve the union. His home and its contents at Waldemarsudde in Stockholm were bequeathed as a museum, which opened to the public in 1948.[1] Munch, who worked on a number of large decorative schemes – the *Frieze of life* for the University Aula (reception hall) in Oslo (1914–16), followed by a decoration for the dining hall of the Freia Chocolate Factory in 1922 and an unfinished canvas representing workers building the new Oslo Town Hall – wrote to Ragnar Hoppe of the Nationalmuseum in Stockholm in 1929:

I'm well aware that many here in the Scandinavian countries have been opposed to my approach to painting – its large format and also the way I have tried to treat psychological problems. The new realism with its attention to details, its smooth execution and limited format has penetrated everywhere. It would not surprise me, however, if this type of painting soon will vanish. With its small canvases and large frames it's a bourgeois art intended for living room walls. It's an art dealer's art which rose to prominence after the victory in the French Revolution. We live in the era of the workers. I wonder if art won't become everyone's property again and take its place in public buildings on large wall surfaces.[2]

In 1937 the Swedish government made it a rule that one per cent of the construction cost of every public building was to be reserved for artistic decoration; similar policies were carried out in Norway, while in Denmark this became common practice without any statutory requirement as such. To this day public commissions provide a significant means of expression and support for Scandinavian artists, whose work has become embedded in the life of many local communities.

Ellen Key's doctrine was of particular relevance to the applied arts, where Scandinavian manufacture was to become a byword for collaborative effort between artists, craftsmen and industrial processes in the creation and execution of socially responsible design – the dominant theme of numerous exhibitions, starting with the one devoted to the home held at Liljevalchs in Stockholm in 1917. By the early 1930s Scandinavian functionalism commanded an international reputation; it combined traditional craftsmanship with the techniques of mass production in the expression of a modernist aesthetic which transformed living rooms from Gothenburg to New Canaan, Connecticut[3] over the next thirty years, gaining an even greater ascendancy in the powerful American market after the Second World War. The integration of democratic values into the concept and execution of design was eventually epitomised by products such as the inexpensive daily wares devised by Kaj Franck (1911–89) in the 1950s for the Finnish china manufacturer Arabia, or the 'Super Ellipse' table of the same period by the Danish polymath Piet Hein (1905–96); he adapted a shape originally created for a Stockholm motorway intersection in order to impose a non-hierarchical seating arrangement conducive to the harmony he wished to see instilled in all aspects of life.

Artistic printmaking had a less coherent trajectory than the evolution of Scandinavian design and, with a few exceptions, never gained an equivalent degree of self-confidence or the exposure abroad that a well-coordinated promotional strategy achieved for the products of the latter. The market for the prints made by the great majority of artists in these countries was close to home, an essentially uncompetitive one with the philanthropic ideal of 'a cheap, easily distributed, yet high-quality art form which people with smaller incomes could also purchase'.[4] Prints were perceived as a valuable part of the visual context of daily life, whether as images to hang on the walls in both private and public spaces or in book form. Woodcut or wood-engraved illustration became a distinctive feature of the thriving Scandinavian book culture of the twentieth century, promoted across a broad spectrum by the principal publishing houses, including Gyldendal of Copenhagen, founded in 1772, as well as by more ephemeral concerns. Access to prints was not necessarily through individual ownership but often existed via the widespread lending schemes operated by local art societies that were at first

derived from the German Kunstverein model of the early nineteenth century. These societies acted as cooperatives, using their members' joint subscriptions for the purchase of pictures that could be circulated and shared like books. They appear to have been particularly effective in Denmark, where the Rector of Århus University explained in 1962:

In most countries it is only the 'collectors' who have original works of art in their homes. It may be a sign of their special love of art or it may be the desire on the part of the rich to display their wealth. The middle classes are satisfied with or actually prefer reproductions of old masters or copies of famous sentimental scenes. The man in the street is not usually concerned with art at all. But things are very different in Denmark. In a normal Danish home, whether that of labourer or peasant, craftsman or smallholder, up to the level of professor or company director, everyone has paintings on his walls.[5]

The heyday of such organisations was during the twenty years immediately after the Second World War, which prompted a desire for the reaffirmation of social democratic principles as expressed in initiatives such as the prints both chosen and commissioned for the Good Art in the Home and Public Places exhibition at the Nationalmuseum in Stockholm in 1945 (see cat. 121), the establishment of the Workers' Art Association in Denmark in 1946 and two societies established in Sweden in 1947 and 1949, Folkrörelsernas Konstfrämjandet (Society for the Public Encouragement of Art) and Folkets i Bild Konstklubb (Pictures and the Community Art Club); the latter bodies were concerned on the one hand with encouraging a rising generation of painters to venture into colour lithography and on the other with the more traditional styles of the older black and white printmakers. Programmes were also introduced for the purchase and distribution of prints to places of employment, stimulated by publications such as the Norwegian book *Kunst på Arbeidsplassen* (Art in the Workplace) by Harry Fett, published in Oslo in 1946 and 1948. Similar schemes for schools had existed since the turn of the century, but they too received renewed impetus from the egalitarianism of the postwar years. In the latter context organisations were set up in Norway in 1948 and in Sweden in 1953 to promote art in schools; the circulation and distribution of original prints was an important part of their activity.

This prodigality of 'public spirit'[6] can be traced back to the romantic nationalism born of the Napoleonic wars and the ensuing redistribution of territory, which altered the balance of relations between the Scandinavian countries and the neighbouring powers. The uneasy proximity of Denmark to the German states (most notably Prussia), Norway's resentment of the mere exchange of Danish for Swedish rule until full independence was achieved in 1905, and Finland's mounting bitterness against annexation by

Russia, tended to foster separatist feeling at home rather than a sense of a common Scandinavian cause during the nineteenth century. This was reflected in cultural attitudes, focusing on language, literature, archaeology, music, craft and the visual arts, which entailed the rediscovery (and sometimes the invention) of traditions whose emphasis on individual national identity contrasted with the later internationalism of Scandinavian design in the twentieth century. Transcending these divisions, though, was the growth of liberal institutions in Denmark, Sweden and Norway which paved the way for the greater consensus of the next century. Foremost among them were the improvements in educational provision leading to the introduction of universal elementary education to Denmark in 1814, Sweden in 1844 and Norway in 1860 (it was not achieved in England until 1870).

A further development of unique value to the predominantly rural population of the Scandinavian countries was the folk high schools, started in Denmark by the charismatic theologian Bishop N. K. S. Grundtvig (1783–1872) to instil patriotism (as a bulwark against the Germans) and a liberal Christian outlook. The first folk high school was founded in northern Slesvig in 1844; within twenty years they had spread throughout the country, reaching Norway in 1865 and Sweden in 1868, catering to the needs of young adults who attended residential courses during the winter months. In place of conventional 'book learning' they offered instruction by 'the living word', involving debate, the transmission of oral history, folklore and poetry, and community singing. The movement drew attention generally to rural traditions such as wood-carving, which became the focus of national revival during the latter half of the nineteenth century; at the same time the gathering pace of archaeological excavation was establishing the historical antecedents of 'indigenous' motifs, and concerted efforts were made to preserve peasant culture, such as the foundation of the Nordiska Museet (Nordic Museum) in Stockholm in 1873, followed in 1891 by Skansen, the world's first open-air museum, which fulfilled the same purpose for rural buildings.[7]

All concepts of 'national schools' of art are artificial constructs, the outcome of particular historical circumstances and expedients which choose to ignore the role of cultural influences that defy political exclusion. Denmark was the first of the Scandinavian countries to formulate such a concept for the visual arts, in reaction to the encroachments of German nationalism, though in reality the work of artists of Danish and German origin coincided to a large extent during the first half of the nineteenth century; Copenhagen provided the nearest source of academic training for many north German artists, while Italy and the notion of a

Wanderjahr through different towns and scenery en route was as familiar a pattern for the Danes as it was for their German contemporaries.[8] Foremost among the proponents of a 'Danish School' was the art historian Niels Lauritz Høyen (1798–1870), who in 1829 was appointed a professor at the Danish Royal Academy (founded 1754). In 1853, together with a number of artists, two copper-plate printers and a museum curator, he became a founder member of Den Danske Radeerforening (DDRF, The Danish Etching Society),[9] which at first used the publication of subjects drawn from the architecture, antiquities and landscape of Denmark to foster a consciousness of national identity. The early plates were the work of Jørgen Roed (1808–88), Vilhelm Kyhn (1817–1903), Jacob Kornerup (1825–1913) and Johann Thomas Lundbye (1818–48),[10] whose extensive visual records of his travels in Denmark and Italy in the 1840s were a constant source of inspiration to future Danish artists, including Per Kirkeby (p. 166); impressions from the plates he executed before his untimely death were issued in several editions starting in 1855, then again in the 1870s, and were still being printed in 1913. The mood and sense of place so keenly felt in many of the early Danish etchings were indebted to the example of contemporary German landscape printmaking, with which they shared a common source in seventeenth-century Dutch and Flemish etching – well represented in the Kongelige Kobberstiksamling (Royal Print Collection) that was eventually incorporated into the Royal Museum of Fine Arts in 1874.

Similar influences were at work among Norwegian artists of the same period such as Johan Christian Dahl (1788–1857), who studied at the Copenhagen Academy before going on to Dresden, and Thomas Fearnley (1802–42), who was also a member of the English Etching Club from its foundation in 1838. Their pervasive effect continued well into the twentieth century among a later generation of Swedish artists who came to maturity after the First World War and were the first to develop a recognisably 'national' identity as printmakers. These included the etchers from Falun (see p. 35) – a region notable among Romantic authors for the sublimity of its copper mines (for example, E. T. A. Hoffmann's short story 'Die Bergwerke zu Falun' (The Mines at Falun) – and others who produced detailed transcriptions of the rural landscape or more closely focused studies of plants recalling the Linnaean tradition of botanical illustration. All this took place in Sweden against a background of rapid industrialisation and the expansion of Stockholm (its population doubled between 1890 and 1930), whose urban landscape became another focus for intaglio printmakers; they saw it through the medium of Meryon's views of Paris or of the British 'architectural' style of printmaking epitomised by Muirhead

View of the Old Town in Stockholm from the south side (1923–5) by Sir Muirhead Bone (1876–1953). Drypoint, third state.

Bone, who executed a number of views of Stockholm himself during a visit in the summer of 1923.

Scandinavian artists were compelled by their relative isolation to seek training, sometimes patronage and, in the case of printmaking, the necessary technical expertise on the European mainland. Throughout the nineteenth and much of the twentieth century Copenhagen served as the artistic capital of Scandinavia, to which Norwegians gravitated at first because of their history of Danish rule prior to 1814; Swedes also went there, particularly from southern Sweden, which retained close cultural as well as geographical ties with Denmark, its former overlord prior to the Treaty of Roskilde in 1658. Apart from Copenhagen itself, Düsseldorf, Munich, Berlin, Paris and London were the principal centres to which the Scandinavians headed,

establishing above all in Berlin and Paris veritable colonies of writers, artists and musicians. Scandinavian artistic life was later sustained in Paris through government subsidies for artists' houses (a Danish one was opened on the Champs Élysées in 1934) and more ambitious centres such as the Swedish Institut Tessin (founded 1935), which firmly entrenched the francophile bias of much of the visual culture of the respective countries. The artists' sense of both individual national identity and a broader Scandinavianism often crystallised away from home, where the radical modernists more readily found an audience. Munch's reputation was made after the scandal attendant upon the closure of his exhibition in 1892 at the Verein Berliner Künstler (Berlin Artists' Association); he was immediately signed up by the dealer Eduard Schulte to show the exhibition in Düsseldorf and Cologne, eventually touring it to Copenhagen, Breslau, Dresden and Munich after it had re-opened at the Equitable Palace in Berlin.

One of the most outspoken critics of the initial closure of the Munch exhibition was Karl Köpping (1848–1914), a former chemist as well as painter and reproductive printmaker, and an influential teacher at the Berlin Academy. Johan Nordhagen (1856–1956) was sent to him in 1898 on a stipend from Norway in order to develop his technical expertise so that he could effectively run the first engraving class at the School of Arts and Crafts in Oslo. Köpping did not himself teach Munch but he contributed to the climate of interest in Berlin, aided by the presence of professional printing firms including Felsing and Lassally, which must have encouraged Munch to make his first attempts at printmaking while he was living there in 1894/5 (see p. 60), as did the Finnish artist Akseli Gallen-Kalléla (1865–1931), who exhibited with Munch in Berlin in 1895. Attention was shifting from reproductive to original printmaking and it was the example of Max Klinger (1857–1920), whose reputation soared in the 1890s, which convinced Munch among many others of the imaginative possibilities of original expression through graphic means.[11]

Paris from the 1880s onwards was an equally important catalyst for some of the Scandinavian artists who were to give serious attention to printmaking. Once again the presence of experienced professional print workshops, the requisite commercial structure for the sale of prints, the specialist societies and journals which promoted them among their subscribers, and a broadly cosmopolitan clientèle created propitious circumstances for the efforts of the Norwegian Frits Thaulow (1847–1906) and the Swede Anders Zorn (p. 30). An early supporter of Munch, Thaulow (whose first wife was Gauguin's sister-in-law) achieved considerable success with his series of colour etchings based on his landscape paintings, which he executed in Paris in the 1890s and published from 1903 through the dealer Georges Petit as well as exhibiting them at the Autumn Exhibition in Christiania (Oslo). The aquatinting of the plates was carried out by the intaglio printer Eugène Delâtre, then they were coloured individually à la poupée.

One of the main markets for Thaulow's prints was in the United States, where Zorn also made a huge impact after the 1893 Columbia World's Fair in Chicago, from which he received $10,000 worth of commissions for paintings and prints. The American Midwest was the focal point for successive waves of Scandinavian emigration, mainly from Sweden and Norway, between 1870 and 1914. The Norwegian population tended to regard Minneapolis as its cultural centre, while by 1893 Chicago's Swedish population was second only to Stockholm's and a significant element in the cultural life of the city. One of the most prominent writers on the American scene was the radical Swedish poet and columnist Carl Sandberg (1868–1967), whose *Chicago Poems* were published in 1914, followed in 1918 by *Cornhuskers* (for which he won the Pulitzer prize), *Smoke and Steel* in 1920 and *Slabs of the Sunburnt West* in 1922. The expatriate communities helped to shape the perception of national identity in the United States and Scandinavia by asserting their cultural heritage through religious and educational institutions; Scandinavian studies came to occupy a strong position in many midwestern universities, starting with a chair founded at the University of Wisconsin in 1875.

No other Scandinavian artist, painter or printmaker, ever achieved within their lifetime the almost universal success of Anders Zorn, whose prices continued to rise exponentially until some seven or eight years after his death in 1920; Zorn's etching of his mother, *Mona*, fetched prices far in excess of those paid for Rembrandt's portrait of his mother. Zorn's introduction to etching was in London in the 1880s under the tutelage of another Swede, Axel Hermann Haig (1835–1921),[12] whose architectural subjects such as *The vesper bell*, inspired by Nuremberg, commanded a ready market in Britain and America. Zorn honed his eye through the study of Rembrandt prints before moving in 1888 to Paris, where his career as a painter-etcher was well and truly launched.

The latter part of Zorn's career was largely spent in Sweden, where he was able to find a technician capable of working to his satisfaction in the person of A. G. Lundin (1882–1948), who printed his first plate for Zorn in 1900. Lundin first worked for a commercial printing firm in Stockholm, travelling in 1906 to Berlin, where for three years he profited from the vastly greater range of experience and equipment available in his field. Upon his return to Sweden he offered valuable assistance to the students at the school of etching and engraving which had in 1909 just been established by Axel Tallberg on a more secure basis at the Academy's premises in Stockholm. Tallberg (1860–1928) had lived from 1886 to 1895 in England, where he was a member of the Royal Society of Painter-Etchers, and had been struggling to gain the support of the Swedish Academy for 'a school of black art' since 1893; he returned to Sweden in 1895 in order to put this into practice, including among his earliest pupils Prince Eugen and Carl Larsson (p. 20). Lundin perceived the need for specialist printing facilities for artists' work and accordingly founded his own workshop in 1918, a business involving his wife and daughter that was continued at different locations until the latter's decision in 1972 to close it down. She transferred the largest of the presses to Nils Stenqvist (p. 151), who in 1973 took over the professorship in graphic art at the Academy that had been created ten years before for his predecessor, Philip von Schantz (p. 148). The intervention of new techniques did not make the future for a traditional copper-plate print-er look propitious at this point, but until the 1960s the Lundin workshop had made a major contribution to the practice of printmaking in Sweden.[13]

Tallberg's influence and that of his successor at the Graphic School from 1926, Emil Johanson-Thor (p. 48), ensured that a whole generation of printmakers until the 1950s was brought up on the techniques, style and subject matter of the artists Tallberg had first encountered in England, namely Meryon, Whistler, Seymour Haden, Frank Brangwyn and Frank Short, later to be joined in popularity among Swedish collectors by Muirhead Bone, D. Y. Cameron, James McBey and Joseph Pennell. Swedish artists and public alike were very much dependent on the manuals, art periodicals and print auction guides ema-nating from Britain, which also set the agenda for much of the appreciation of prints in Germany and the United States during the first part of the twentieth century.[14] Bukowski's, the main auction house and dealer in Stockholm who con-trolled the sale of Zorn's prints from 1909, did business with print dealers worldwide, including Colnaghi and Obach in London and Connell in Glasgow. The important collector Thorsten Laurin (1875–1954) certainly evinced this taste in the acquisition of his material, to which many artists had access. Laurin, together with his older brother Carl (see cat. 8), came from the family that owned the publishing house P. A. Norstedt & Söner, specialising in art books. His collection was in many ways comparable to that of Campbell Dodgson (see p. 7), with whom he was in contact, and Laurin displayed a similar sense of public duty in presenting about a thousand of his prints by foreign artists to the Nationalmuseum in 1937. He was a key figure in the encouragement of Swedish printmaking, principally through the Föreningen för Grafisk Konst (F.f.G.K., Society for Graphic Art) founded in 1887 to commission annual portfolios of prints for its subscribers; the society continues to this day, closely linked to the prints and drawings depart-ment of the Nationalmuseum.

The other main Swedish society dedicated to the pro-motion of graphic art was the Grafiska Sällskapet (Graphic Union), which started in 1910 with artists as active mem-bers and collectors as the passive ones for whom annual portfolios of prints were produced whenever possible from 1914 onwards. Its membership was open to artists from other Scandinavian countries and it was instrumental in arranging many exhibitions within Scandinavia and fur-ther afield, thus establishing links with printmaking bodies throughout the rest of Europe and America; one of the first major events was the Nordic print exhibition in 1924 at Liljevalchs Konsthall, the exhibition hall built in the centre of Stockholm in 1916 with money from a private bequest. The Grafiska Sällskapet was involved with the Anglo-Swedish print exhibition in 1927 that brought Campbell Dodgson, then Keeper of Prints and Drawings at the British Museum, to Stockholm, and played a key part in the formation of the Nordic Graphic Union in 1937; nearly thirty years later it instigated the graphic triennials that continue to rotate between different cities in Sweden. In 1948 the society inaugurated an annual stipend to be awarded to a young printmaker each year, and ten years later acquired prem-ises for a permanent showroom for the members' work or that of guest artists from outside; workshops for intaglio printing and lithography followed in 1962 and 1983.[15]

Stockholm was, of course, in all respects a major centre for artistic patronage in Sweden, where aside from Prince Eugen's constant involvement there was also the impressive collection built up since the 1890s by the banker Ernst Thiel (1859–1947). He acquired the work of many Swedish artists and, in keeping with his intense admiration for Nietzsche, sought out that of others whom he regarded as isolated geniuses, including van Gogh, Rodin, Vigeland, Willumsen, Hammershøi and Munch; the house he had built from 1904 to 1907 to house this collection was sold to the Swedish state in 1924, when it was turned into a public art gallery. Out-side Stockholm the most important city was Gothenburg, whose commercial wealth helped to support the fine arts and some interesting modern architecture such as the new art gallery built in the 1920s. There was no graphic school as such until 1947 when Endre Nemes (p. 119) arrived at the Valand School of Art (though printmaking classes were held at the School of Arts and Crafts prior to this date), but Axel Romdahl (1880–1951), Director of the Gothenburg Museum from 1923 to 1947, who published the first cata-logue raisonné of Carl Larsson's prints (see p. 22), was intent on turning the collection into one that could offer an out-standing representation of Scandinavian art as a whole. The holding of predominantly Swedish graphic material that he and his successors acquired now amounts to approximately 60,000 prints and 9000 drawings.

Norway, having come late to nationhood, did not acquire a fine arts academy until 1909. Printmaking, however, tended to be seen as the province of the schools of applied arts, starting with Johan Nordhagen's classes in Christiania from 1899. Although a lithographic press had been set up as early as 1823, Norway was very slow to develop specialised print workshops, relying heavily on technical expertise abroad in Denmark and particularly Germany, where the plates were first printed for the Norsk Forening for Grafisk Kunst, founded in 1908. Expertise gradually accumulated among the staff attached to the schools with their own equipment; communal facilities were also eventually avail-able at the Kunstnernes Hus, but the prevailing tradition in

Norway to this day is for artists to print their own work, with the exception of lithography and screenprinting which require more specialised intervention. The first 'black and white' exhibition, with a mixture of reproductive and original contemporary prints from Sweden, Denmark and Germany, was held in 1893 at Blomqvist's gallery, the main commercial venue for prints outside the artists' exhibiting societies. Norske Grafikere (the society for Norwegian printmakers) was founded in 1919 to fulfil the same purpose as its Swedish counterpart, Grafiska Sällskapet, holding its first exhibition in 1922 which included the work of Munch and Pola Gauguin, the youngest son of Paul. The latter's role in Norwegian artistic life was to be more important as a critic and writer than as an original artist; his interest in Munch, of whom he published a biography in 1932 as well as writing about his prints, was a natural outcome of his family history. In 1919 he had purchased in Stockholm the surviving blocks from his father's *Noa Noa* suite of 1894, which Munch would have encountered at the home of Gauguin's friends in Paris, William Molard and his Swedish wife, the sculptress Ida Ericson, where many of the Scandinavian community congregated. Pola proceeded to print a new edition in 1921 at Christopher Cato's workshop in Copenhagen; his own son Paul René Gauguin (1911–76) became a leading exponent of large colour woodcuts, which achieved some popularity in Norway in the 1940s and 1950s.

The importance of Munch's printmaking so far as Scandinavian as well as German artists were concerned lay in the high status it was accorded by the artist and collectors alike in relation to his creativity as a whole. Munch's graphic work was certainly an inspiration to the man who was to direct the course of printmaking in Denmark for nearly forty years from 1920, the date of his first teaching appointment at the Academy. This was Aksel Jørgensen (p. 81). A remarkable figure whose early woodcuts were very much influenced by Munch, he combined a mastery of the craft and discipline of etching and relief printing with tolerance towards the work of others that might differ quite drastically from his own; this generosity of spirit earned him the respect of even the most anarchic of his former pupils, Asger Jorn (p. 108). Copenhagen remained the most populous city in Scandinavia until overtaken in the 1930s by Stockholm as a direct result of Sweden's rapid growth in industrial and commercial prosperity, but by virtue of its geographical position Copenhagen always had readier access to avant-garde movements elsewhere in Europe, from French Impressionism onwards. Between 1912 and 1918 the Danish public were introduced to Futurism, Expressionism and Cubism via travelling exhibitions from Herwarth Walden's Sturm gallery in Berlin, which helped to inspire *Klingen*, a monthly magazine started in October 1917 to present international modernism in literature and art.[16] It included both reproductions and original prints tipped into the main issues, publishing articles by, among others, Kandinsky, who had spent the winter of 1915/16 in Stockholm where his second series of drypoints was printed in 1916.

The First World War – or more particularly the period 1914–16, prior to the anxiety engendered by the Russian Revolution in 1917 and the American entry into the war, which severely restricted transatlantic supplies – was in many ways a time of great prosperity for the three Scandinavian kingdoms, which all maintained neutrality. It produced a number of speculative fortunes which fed into the art market and brought an influx of foreign nationals – 'there are a great number of French, Germans, Russians and Austrians residing here at present' (Axel Tallberg, 12 December 1915, published in the 1996 calendar of the archive of the Royal Society of Painter-Printmakers) – who contributed to a more cosmopolitan atmosphere. The situation was very different during the next war, which imposed a real isolation on Scandinavia; most of it came effectively under German hegemony, including neutral Sweden, although only Norway and Denmark were actually occupied from 1940 to 1945.

In Denmark the enforced return of many artists from abroad and the need to preserve national self-respect helped to focus attention on forms of artistic activity and expression that were innately subversive of the occupying power.[17] Surrealism and abstraction were one route to this end; out of the atmosphere of clandestine association came the germ of Cobra (see p. 108), one of the liveliest of all the internationally collaborative experiments of the immediate postwar period, which included graphic art as an integral part of its programme. Lithography, which hitherto in Scandinavia had been inhibited by the relative lack of facilities, came to the fore from the mid-1940s as an experimental and inherently 'democratic' medium because of the ease of multiplication. A specialist workshop was opened in Copenhagen in 1944 by J. Christian Sørensen, who had trained under Mourlot in Paris (it later moved to Hjørring in Jutland). This was followed in 1947 by that of Permild and Rosengreen, thereby providing the necessary conditions for the production of the large editions of colour lithographs distributed throughout Scandinavia under the aegis of the two Swedish schemes, Folkrörelsernas Konstfrämjandet (see p. 139) and Konst i Skolan. They were also essential to the more casual efforts of Asger Jorn and his associates until the former transferred his work to another Danish lithographer, Peter Bramsen, who had joined the Clot atelier in Paris in 1963 and subsequently became a full partner in Clot,

PLATE I

121 Lennart Rodhe, *Greenhouse*, 1945

PLATE 2

Above and right   84   Rolf Nesch, *St Sebastian* triptych, 1941

PLATE 3

PLATE 4

PLATE 5

Left, above
122 Lennart Rodhe,
Sawmill, 1947

Left, below
95 Asger Jorn,
*Council for the
Propagation of Danish
Beauty in Foreign
Lands,* 1952

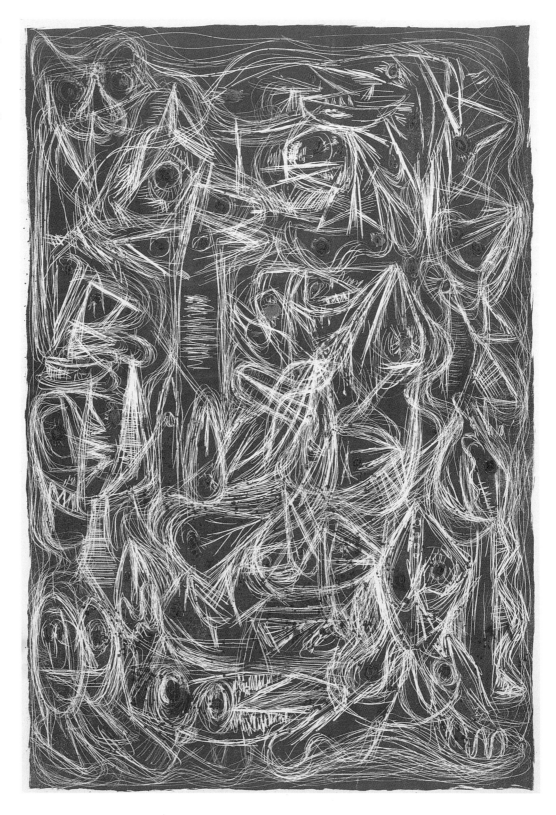

92 Asger Jorn, *ARS-Portfolio* (VIII), 1945

PLATE 6

115 Nikolai Astrup,
The wood, 1957

114 Inger Sitter,
Granite II, 1955

PLATE 7

138 Helmtrud Nyström, *Harvest celebration*, 1985

PLATE 8

141 Olle Dahl, *Sombre*, 1989

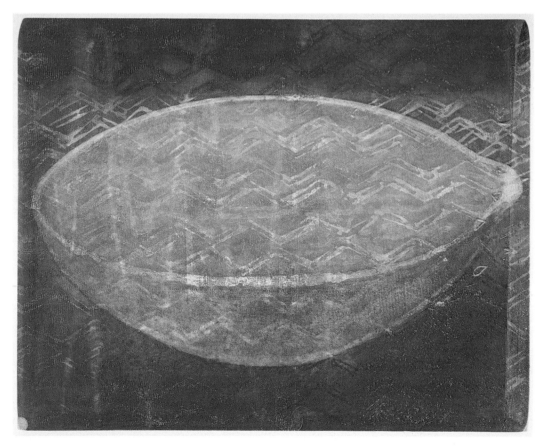

140 Mariana Manner, *Blue Nile*, 1992

Bramsen and Georges, which continues as a major establishment of its kind.

For intaglio printmaking after the Second World War, the main route to liberation for Scandinavian artists who wanted to resist being locked into the academic drypoint tradition was via the open studios run in Paris by S. W. Hayter from 1927 and by Johnny Friedlænder from 1950. Hayter's overthrow of the traditional orthodoxies, as declared in his book *New Ways of Gravure*, published in 1949 just before he returned to Paris permanently after spending the 1940s in New York, transformed the outlook for printmaking in Norway and Sweden to a greater extent than elsewhere. Artists from these countries paid both intermittent and extended visits to the ateliers, whose difference in character Hayter identified in terms of the 'more *picturale* approach' of Friedlænder as compared with his own Atelier 17, 'where the sculptural aspects of printmaking are perhaps emphasized, and where the special characters of the ambiguity of space in the print are being exploited'.[18] The example of Atelier 17 captured the imagination of Jürgen von Konow (p. 131) and through him altered the balance of teaching at the Swedish Academy's Graphic School in the late 1950s, while in southern Sweden Bertil Lundberg (p. 125) from 1964 on sought to create within the Forum School in Malmö a similar environment that would be conducive to free experimentation in black and white and colour. Hayter's influence in Norway accorded well with the highly idiosyncratic approach to intaglio printing taken by the émigré artist Rolf Nesch (p. 97), who had settled in Oslo in 1933 after leaving Nazi Germany and whose work became much better known throughout Scandinavia during the 1950s. Norway also acquired its own version of Atelier 17 under the title of Atelier Nord, set up in 1965 by Anne Breivik (born 1932) and funded by the state from 1978.[19]

The opportunities for printmaking have greatly expanded in the past twenty-five years with the establishment of new departments within higher education (at Trondheim in Norway, for example, and Umeå in the far north of Sweden) and of professional print workshops such as those run by Thormond Larsen in Helsingborg in southern Sweden (founded 1972) and by Niels Borch Jensen in Copenhagen (founded 1979) for intaglio work,[20] both catering to an international clientèle. The work carried out on these premises and by Peter Bramsen in Paris represents in many respects the aristocracy of the printmaking and print publishing world. Alongside such streamlined establishments the more 'domestic' forms of printmaking still flourish, typified by the activities of Clausens Kunsthandel in Copenhagen, the printshop started by Viggo Clausen in 1953 and developed over the years to unite the functions of gallery, studio space and social meeting place. The special quality of this enterprise, which has sustained a whole community of artists in Denmark, has been summed up by one of its regular contributors, Svend Wiig Hansen (p. 161):

There are many houses – one of them was something special – Clausens Kunsthandel at Toldbodgade 9 – that was the name – but it was also the place where people came to talk and see with Clausen – some believed it to be vital to pay a visit – an oasis – some of the callers were us – we who had our exhibitions there – to us that place became home and place of learning – here we met without prior arrangement – for festive and serious conversations and discussions around Clausen – convivial gatherings that could interrupt dark days. But the very best times were those when one was alone with him, preparing an exhibition – the first day of excitement when all the works were laid out on the floor – his scrutinizing gaze, these long seconds of silence – waiting for acceptance – all that amounted to time that was worth remembering – right to his words of relief and his conviction that everything would work well – then you could leave the place at ease.[21]

1. See Inga Zachau, *Prins Eugen*, 2 vols (Lund, 1994).

2. Rolf Stenersen, *Edvard Munch: Close-up of a Genius*, translated and edited by Reidar Dittman (Oslo, 1994), pp. 147–8.

3. Osbert Lancaster in the 1952 edition of *Homes Sweet Homes* caricatured the owners of 'the logical living rooms of Gothenburg and New Canaan' for their 'desperate attempt to modify the machine-turned efficiency of the "planned" interior by the introduction of innumerable exotics from jungle and swamp . . . conceived on the Amazon and nurtured in the hothouses of Copenhagen' (p. 80).

4. Quotation from the catalogue for the exhibition on the fiftieth anniversary of the Nordic Graphic Union, 1987.

5. Quoted by Guy Atkins in *Jorn in Scandinavia 1930–1953* (London, 1968), p. 114.

6. Mary Wollstonecraft, with reference to Norway in 1795, had expressed the view that a growth in public spirit would be the natural outcome of the heightened sense of political engagement and consequent 'enlargement of humanity' brought about by the French Revolution. See *A Short Residence in Denmark, Sweden and Norway* (Harmondsworth, 1987), p. 103.

7. Although the Scandinavian countries were at the forefront of this ethnological interest in rural customs and artefacts, it was a widespread phenomenon of the period, informing projects such as Sir Benjamin Stone's *National Photographic Record* of 1897–1904. *The Studio* (ed. Charles Holme) in 1910 devoted a special issue to 'Peasant Art in Sweden, Lapland and Iceland'.

8. For an account of the genesis of the definition of a Danish national school see the preface by Chris Fischer and introductory essay by Hans Edvard Nørregård-Nielsen in *The Golden Age of Danish Art: Drawings from the Royal Museum of Fine Arts, Copenhagen* (Copenhagen, 1995).

9. The Society is still in existence and continues to offer members specially commissioned prints as well as new impressions

from older plates belonging to the Society. The recent work is not confined to Danish artists; for example, in October 1995 the DDRF was offering an etching by the German artist Günther Förg.

10. Many of these plates were acquired by the British Museum as part of the group of Danish etchings purchased in 1859.

11. For a discussion of the Berlin print world of this period see the introduction to Frances Carey and Antony Griffiths, *The Print in Germany 1880–1933* (London, 1984, reprinted 1993).

12. See J. Mordaunt Crook and C.A. Lennox-Boyd, *Axel Hermann Haig and the Victorian Vision of the Middle Ages* (London, 1984). Haig presented many of his trial proofs to the British Museum in 1903, and more were given by his widow in 1922.

13. For a fuller account of the role of Lundin's workshop see chapter 16 of Jane Rothlind, *Hans Norsbo och Falungrafikerna* (Uppsala, 1986), pp. 210–26.

14. See the introduction to Frances Carey and Antony Griffiths, *Avant-Garde British Printmaking 1914–1960* (London, 1990), pp. 11–15.

15. A chronological table of the history of the Grafiska Sällskapet was published by Lennart Forsberg on the occasion of its seventy-fifth anniversary in 1985.

16. See Inge Vibeke Raaschou-Nielsen, 'Storm over København', *Kunstmuseets Årsskrift* (1992), pp. 90–111.

17. For a discussion of all aspects of Danish artistic life during the war see Eva Friis (ed.), *Kunst under Krigen* (Copenhagen, 1995).

18. *About Prints* (London, 1962), p. 94.

19. See Anthony Christie, '25 Years of Atelier Nord', *Printmaking Today* (winter 1990/1), pp. 29–30.

20. See *Made in Denmark: Kobbertryk fra Niels Borch Jensen's værksted*, Lommebog 65, Statens Museum for Kunst (Copenhagen, 1994).

21. Quoted from a letter to the author from Lis Clausen, 4 September 1996.

Notes to the Catalogue

The work of the artists represented in the catalogue has been loosely grouped according to historical and visual affinities within a generally but not invariably chronological sequence. Titles of works of art are given in translation but those of books and articles are given in the original language as are, for the most part, the names of institutions and organisations, with an English translation provided after the first text reference.

The type of paper used for particular prints is only described where the impression is a proof or when some other distinction can be conveyed by noting such information.

The individual bibliographies following each artist's biography do not include references to the relevant entries in the standard dictionaries of artists, listed in the general bibliography on pages 174–5; these are implicit as a source for all the artists except those excluded by virtue of the publication date of a particular dictionary. An alphabetical index of the artists included in the catalogue, with an indication of their respective nationalities, is provided on page 176.

Carl Larsson (1853–1919)

In contrast with the idyllic vision of his later family life, Larsson grew up amidst poverty in the slums of the Old Town of Stockholm. At first he could afford to attend the Stockholm Academy only part-time, otherwise working as a retoucher in a photographic studio and an occasional illustrator for the comic paper *Kasper*. He quickly demonstrated a facility for draughtsmanship which brought him promotion to the Academy's painting school and a regular income as a contributor to *Kasper*, the start of a lifelong career as a successful illustrator which was always to be at variance with Larsson's grander artistic aspirations. From 1877 to 1889 he spent extended periods of time in Paris or its environs where he frequented the colony of British, American and Scandinavian writers and artists at Grèz and began to paint watercolours *en plein air*, as well as meeting his future wife, Karin Bergöö, a fellow artist whom he married in Stockholm in 1883.

Larsson continued to support himself through illustration, collaborating with the dramatist August Strindberg,

1

whom he first met in 1879, on the latter's text *Svenska Folket* published in two volumes in 1881 and 1882. This proved to be a controversial account of the Swedish people because it eschewed the conventional chronicle of kings and nobility for a history told 'from below'. Two years later Strindberg was proposing a further collaboration to depict the life of rural Europe which would not be an inventory of quaint curiosities but would capture something more essential, the way in which the peasant 'lives and what he thinks, about his situation and what he and his part of the country and his fields and meadows look like …' (*Strindberg's Letters*, vol. I, ed. and translated by Michael Robinson (London, 1992), p. 129). Such an approach was important for Larsson's own interest in the depiction of rural life and his portraits of local artisans at the beginning of the twentieth century. His relationship with Strindberg endured until 1906–8, when it dissolved in bitter recrimination on both sides arising from Strindberg's character assassinations in his *roman à clef* of 1907, *Svarta Fanor* (Black Banners), followed by his personal attack on Larsson and his wife in *En Ny Blå Bok* (A New Blue Book) for 1908.

The intimacy and naturalism of Larsson's watercolours executed in France achieved success in Sweden, where he attracted the attention of the Gothenburg financier Pontus Fürstenberg, who secured him a teaching position in 1886 at the Valand Art School attached to the Gothenburg Museum. Fürstenberg's support gave Larsson his first opportunity to paint on a monumental scale: this remained the ultimate focus of his ambitions for the rest of his life. From April 1888 to December 1889 Larsson lived at his patron's expense in Paris, where he executed the decorative triptych *Renaissance, Rococo and modern art* for Fürstenberg's private gallery (see cat. 1), which was awarded a first-class medal at the 1889 Exposition Universelle. Back in Sweden he completed a mural for a girls' school in Gothenburg in 1891 and won the design competition for the frescoes intended to decorate the main staircase of the Nationalmuseum in Stockholm. The first of these were finished in 1896 but the decoration of the remaining panels around the staircase was to prove to be the great frustrated purpose of Larsson's career, culminating in the Nationalmuseum's refusal in 1916 either to purchase the oil painting for *Midwinter sacrifice* or to accept Anders Zorn's offer to pay for the execution in fresco of this subject and the earlier composition of *Gustaf Vasa's entry into Stockholm on Midsummer Day, 1523*. (The controversy was revived in 1987 when the painting of *Midwinter sacrifice* was sold at auction to a Japanese buyer.)

The vicissitudes of the Nationalmuseum scheme reflect to a degree the incommensurability of the scale of Larsson's ambition with the true nature of his talent as an illustrator, which brought him increasing international fame during the years from 1899 onwards. The principal vehicle for this fame was the series of watercolours and their related publications which Larsson executed as a 'souvenir' of the life of his household and small farm at Sundborn, the summer

2

colours for *Ett Hem* were bought for the Nationalmuseum from Larsson's publisher in 1900, but also in Germany, where the watercolours were widely exhibited and the books soon appeared in translation in a reduced format; between 1909 and 1919, the year of Larsson's death, *Das Haus in der Sonne* (The House in the Sun), a selection of the watercolours from *Ett Hem* and *Larssons* (1902), sold nearly 200,000 copies rising to 336,000 by 1940 (later editions included watercolours from *Spadarvet* and *Åt Solsidan* as well). The watercolours and vignettes of the Larsson books represented a personalised development of the vein of sentimental illustration associated with the woodcut designs of Ludwig Richter (1803–84) published in Leipzig by Georg Wigand in the latter part of the nineteenth century, with titles such as *Der Familien-Schatz* (The Family Treasury), and the comic sketches of Wilhelm Busch (1832–1910).

Larsson's prints often repeated the subjects of his watercolours pared down to their essential linear components because, as C. R. Ashbee said of Walter Crane, he had 'a sort of linear memory' (quoted by Isobel Spencer in *Walter Crane* (London, 1975), p. 188). His first experience of etching was at classes briefly held in Stockholm in 1875 by a Dutchman,

3

cottage near the town of Falun in the province of Dalarna which Larsson received as a gift from his father-in-law in 1888. The house, which became the main family home in 1901, was developed during the preceding decade by Larsson and his wife as a consciously artistic interior imbued with the aestheticism they had encountered in Paris in the 1880s, and through reproductions of the work of English architects, designers and illustrators such as Walter Crane, Randolph Caldecott and Kate Greenaway. Larsson's ambition was to achieve the kind of unstudied visual harmony that he attributed to the Japanese: 'Among us Europeans, art is just something affected, endeavoured, snobbish; among the Japanese a sense of art is common and imparts to everything they do, even the merest trifle, a tasteful style' (quoted from *De Mina* (My Family) (1895) in *The World of Carl Larsson* (La Jolla, 1982), p. 53).

The first of these series of domestic scenes, reproduced in the same format as contemporary photograph albums, was published in Stockholm by Bonniers (who were also Strindberg's publishers) in 1899 under the title *Ett Hem* (A Home), followed by four others, ending with *Andras Barn* (Other People's Children) in 1913. In both moral and aesthetic terms these watercolours became central to an intensely nostalgic idealisation of bourgeois family life for several generations to come, not only in Sweden, where the water-

Leopold Lowenstam, where Larsson produced three prints, but his interest in the medium was not really kindled until 1888/9 when he was in Paris. Later on, in the winter of 1895/6, he returned to the Academy in Stockholm to attend classes run by Axel Tallberg where he experimented with soft-ground etching and mezzotint, working from nude models (see cat. 4). On 15 March 1896 Larsson wrote to Pontus Fürstenberg: 'And now I'm part of an etching club along with the Prince (Eugen), Björk, Bob and young Wennerberg, led by Tallberg, who, although a bit of a suspicious character, is an excellent engraver' (see H. H. Brummer's introduction to the Hjert and Hjert *catalogue raisonné*, p. 14). Many of his prints, which amounted to 112 etchings and four colour lithographs, were commissioned and published by the Society for Graphic Art (F.f.G.K.) under the chairmanship of two notable collectors and champions of Larsson's work, Mårten Sondén and Thorsten Laurin (see p. 15). Outside these editions he was responsible for his own printing; after 1908 this was carried out in a cottage near the school hall that he built in Falun. His etching studio formed the subject of one of the watercolours published in 1910 as part of the album *Åt Solsidan* (On the Sunny Side), the original of which belongs to the Helsingborg Museum. He is shown in the background at work on a print, watched by his youngest son, Esbjörn, while the prominent figure in the foreground is that of a local man, Hans Fröjd, who is operating a small hand-press; a print hanging on the wall can be identified as Dürer's engraved portrait of Erasmus of 1526.

Larsson's prints fall into two categories: the etchings produced for a discerning body of private collectors and art-lovers, and the small group of colour lithographs published in far larger editions of up to a thousand which were intended to have a wider currency in schools and homes. Outside Sweden, the main market for Larsson's prints was once again in Germany, where dealers including Emil Richter and the Galerie Ernst Arnold in Dresden stocked them and they were acquired by the print rooms of the Berlin, Dresden and Munich museums, among others. Hans Singer of the Dresden Print Room praised the etchings in his conservative account in *Die Moderne Graphik* in 1914, evidently finding them more sympathetic than the work of Munch which he felt indulged in subjectivity at the expense of skill.

The British Museum's holding of forty-five etchings and one colour lithograph, containing several particularly rare subjects as well as those published in proper editions, was largely assembled by Campbell Dodgson for his private collection prior to 1913, the date of publication for Axel Romdahl's *catalogue raisonné*, with the exception of one work acquired directly for the Department of Prints and Drawings in 1906 (cat. 7) and two later purchases made by Dodgson in Frankfurt in 1931. Dodgson's introduction to the work may have been via the article published in the Viennese periodical *Die Graphischen Künste* in 1905 by John Kruse of the Stockholm Print Room, who sent Dodgson an offprint by way of thanks for the latter's hospitality to him in the summer of that year when he had been doing research in London on the Nationalmuseum's collection of Rembrandt drawings (letter dated 8 August 1905, among Dodgson's personal correspondence in the Department of Prints and Drawings; Kruse's catalogue of the Rembrandts eventually appeared in 1920). In another letter of April 1906 Kruse offered to make available either the complete run of all the F.f.G.K.'s print publications (he was the current secretary) or a selection of the best issues at a reduced price, according to Dodgson's wishes. In 1910 Dodgson's acquisition of seventeen of the etchings excited the attention of the Swedish newspaper *Svenska Dagbladet*, followed in 1913 by a further notice in the magazine *Idun* (I am indebted to Dr Cecilia Lengefeld for drawing these to my attention). An important stimulus to Dodgson's interest would no doubt have been his many contacts in Germany, where much of his professional research and private collecting of prints by contemporary artists took place before the First World War, particularly in Dresden where his colleague Max Lehrs was a major influence on his taste. (See Frances Carey, 'Campbell Dodgson (1867–1948)' in *Landmarks in Print Collecting*.)

The collection of prints bequeathed by Dodgson to the British Museum in 1949 is the only one in Britain, where Larsson received little attention apart from a few articles (for example in *The Studio* in 1906 and *The Craftsman* in 1912), and some of his watercolours were included in a Swedish Art exhibition organised by the collector Thorsten Laurin, which travelled to Brighton and Liverpool in 1911. The principal concentrations of his work are inevitably to be found in Sweden: at the Nationalmuseum, to which he presented a large body of material in 1908 and where the plates acquired by the F.f.G.K. are also kept, and at the Gothenburg Museum, whose director Axel Romdahl was his first cataloguer. The house with its contents at Sundborn has been preserved as a museum open to the public under the direction of Larsson's descendants.

Bibliography

The literature on Larsson is considerable, though little of any substance has appeared in English apart from a translation of the artist's autobiography, *Jag* (I) (Stockholm, 1931), edited by John Z. Losgren, entitled *Carl Larsson: The autobiography of Sweden's most beloved artist* (Iowa City, 1992). Revealing of the insecurity engendered by the hardship of his early youth, it was completed in 1917, when Larsson was cast down by the disappointments associated with the Nationalmuseum's decorative scheme, his deteriorating eyesight and a general sense of alienation from the prevailing trends in modern art. *The World of Carl Larsson*, translated by Allan Lake Rice from the original Swedish text of Görel Cavalli-Björkman and Bo Lindwall (La Jolla and London, 1982), and the catalogue for an exhibition at the Brooklyn Museum also in 1982 are the fullest accounts of

7

his work in English, but the most comprehensive survey with an exhaustive bibliography is to be found in the catalogue for the Nationalmuseum's exhibition in 1992, which has only a Swedish text. The best interpretative study of Larsson's reputation and his influence, with particular reference to Germany, is Cecilia Lengefeld's *Der Maler des Glücklichen Heims* (Heidelberg, 1993). In 1997–8 the Victoria and Albert Museum will be mounting an exhibition on Carl and Karin Larsson and their home at Sundborn, with a catalogue edited by Elisabeth Hidemark and Michael Snodin, to which Dr Lengefeld will contribute an essay on Larsson's wider influence. John Kruse's article referred to above, 'Carl Larsson als Maler, Zeichner und Graphiker' in *Die Graphischen Künste*, XXVIII (1905), pp. 53–77, was the first proper discussion of his prints, followed in 1913 by Axel Romdahl's full catalogue of all the prints to 1912. In 1923 E. L. Allhusen included a supplement to Romdahl's catalogue with his article 'The Etched Work of Carl Larsson' in *Print Collectors' Quarterly*, x, pp. 197–218; Campbell Dodgson also published a notice, 'Carl Larsson's Lithographs', in the same issue, p. 220. The standard work of reference now for the prints is Hjert and Hjert, *Carl Larsson: A complete catalogue* (Uppsala, 1983) with parallel texts in English, French, German and Swedish. However, as Romdahl's catalogue contains some information that does not appear in Hjert and Hjert, the entries below quote the relevant numbers from both publications.

1 *Profiles*, 1888

Etching. Signed in ink. 239 × 160 mm

R.8,II; H.9,2

1949-4-11-4742. Bequeathed by Campbell Dodgson

This subject was executed in Paris and printed there by Delâtre for publication by the F.f.G.K. for their first portfolio in 1888, one year after the Society's foundation. Twenty-five copies were signed by hand and a further edition of 300 unsigned copies was published with an address. According to Romdahl the plate was purchased by the F.f.G.K. for 150 kronor; it is now in the collection of the Nationalmuseum.

The etching is composed rather like one of his earlier wood-engraved title-page designs for Hans Christian Andersen's *Sagor och Berättelser* (Fairy tales and Stories) of 1877 (see Küllicke Montgomery, 'Grafikern Carl Larsson' in the 1992 Nationalmuseum catalogue, p. 281, for an account of this print, and her essay 'Carl Larsson som illustratör' in the same publication, pp. 305–34). It is an elaborate *trompe-l'oeil* conceit closely related to the painted triptych and its surrounding wood reliefs, *Rococo, Renaissance and modern art*, that Larsson was working on at the time for Pontus Fürstenberg. He has incorporated the symbols of the artist's trade like a *Vanitas* composition, using the profiles with their references to marriage, friendship and patronage to create a visual autobiography. The profiles in question

can be identified as follows: those at top and bottom left, superimposed on a panel taken from the frame for the triptych, are of Strindberg and a caricatural self-portrait of the artist; in the centre on the artist's easel is an image of his wife Karin, wearing a hat, while flanking the motto of the Swedish Artists' Union, *Arte et Probitate* (the Union was formed in 1886 by Larsson and other Swedish artists with French connections in reaction to the Academy, following the success in Stockholm the previous year of their exhibition, From the Banks of the Seine), are medallions of the painters Carl Skånberg and Hugo Birger; in the lower portion of the sheet is a woman's head and shoulders from Larsson's relief sculpture in wood under the painting of *Modern art* in the Fürstenberg triptych (Larsson also made a drypoint engraving of the same motif, H.8), and to her right is a bust by Per Hasselberg of Fürstenberg himself.

In 1895 Larsson produced an etching in only five proof copies of the triptych as a whole. This plate was subsequently reused for two further prints, *Brita and I* (R.32; H.37) in 1896 and *Suzanne*, in 1901 (R.39; H.44).

2 *Graziella*, 1888

Etching. Signed and dated 'Paris 1888' within the plate. Signed in ink and inscribed by the artist on the recto 'Graziella Argeangelo frågar "Si vous avez besoin de modèle?"'. Inscribed in pencil on the verso by Campbell Dodgson 'Graziella' and '£9 (the sum for which Larsson has bought this back from a collector) Kr175:-'. 141 × 99 mm

R.9,I; H.10

1949-4-11-4743. Bequeathed by Campbell Dodgson

Larsson's inscription refers to the young girl's impromptu visit to his studio in Paris when she asked if he could use her as a model. The subject, one of the rarest of his prints, is based on a preparatory pencil drawing now in the Gothenburg Museum; Romdahl in 1913 estimated there were no more than ten impressions, of which those belonging to the Berlin and Dresden Museums, the Bibliothèque Doucet in Paris and Campbell Dodgson were the only ones outside Sweden. Dodgson's own inscription on the verso implies that his impression had been of particular importance to the artist from whom Dodgson may have secured it directly, through the good offices of a contact such as John Kruse.

3 *Empire*, 1891

Etching. 200 × 138 mm

R.12,II; H.13,2

1949-4-11-4744. Bequeathed by Campbell Dodgson

The standard edition size for some of the plates published by the F.f.G.K. was twenty-five signed copies and 425 unsigned. The British Museum's impression in this case belongs to the latter category, which appeared in the Society's annual

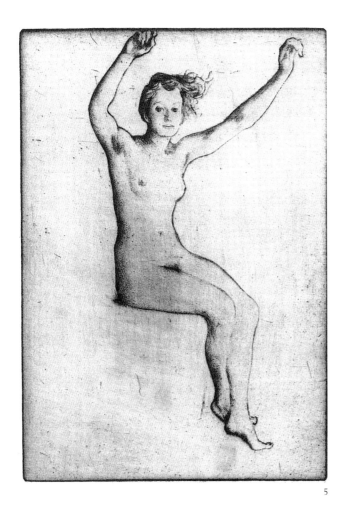

5

4

6

portfolio for 1891. The subject was a dancer at the Gothenburg Theatre, and the print is again based on a pencil drawing now in the Gothenburg Museum. The plate was bought by the Society, duly passing to the collection of the Nationalmuseum.

4 *Standing model*, 1896

Soft-ground etching. Signed in pencil. 239 × 164 mm

R.17; H.20

1949-4-11-4746. Bequeathed by Campbell Dodgson

This and the following subject, cat. 5, were among a small number of studies of nude female models made at Axel Tallberg's engraving course at the Academy of Fine Arts where Larsson attempted his first exercises in soft-ground etching. They are rare because they were practice works, never editioned, and the plates were subsequently destroyed; Larsson's friend and contemporary Anders Zorn also owned impressions of them. The drawings on which both prints were based belong to the Nationalmuseum.

5 *Seated model*, 1896

Soft-ground etching. Signed in pencil. 236 × 165 mm

R.19; H.22

1949-4-11-4747. Bequeathed by Campbell Dodgson

6 *The guardian angel*, 1898

Etching. Signed in pencil. 157 × 197 mm

R.36,IV; H.41,4

1949-4-11-4750. Bequeathed by Campbell Dodgson

This belongs to the twenty-five signed copies issued by the F.f.G.K. prior to the fifth and final state which was published in an edition of 425 unsigned copies. It was later republished as part of John Kruse's article in *Die Graphischen Künste* (1905, p. 75). The composition reflects Larsson's increasing preoccupation with domestic subject matter. In 1895 he published the first of his books about his family, *De Mina* (My Family), illustrated with line drawings amongst the text; the watercolours which eventually appeared in *Ett Hem* in 1899 were begun in 1894, and twenty of them were exhibited at the Art and Industry exhibition in Stockholm in 1897. The colour etching of his daughter Lisbeth eating porridge, in 1894, was the first of his prints in this vein, followed by the large plate *Brita and I* in 1896, based on a watercolour now in the Gothenburg Art Museum. After 1900 their incidence increased as his professional and domestic life became so closely entwined at Sundborn.

7 *Karin and Kersti*, 1904

Etching. Printed in brown, before text. 266 × 184 mm

R.42,II; H.47,2

1906-4-19-370. Purchased

The subject is the artist's wife and the seventh of their eight children (there were four daughters and four sons), who draws while her mother combs her hair. In the third and final state this was printed as part of John Kruse's article in *Die Graphischen Künste* (1905). Romdahl describes the second state as very rare, listing this impression as being in Campbell Dodgson's collection, but in fact it was bought by the Department of Prints and Drawings in 1906 as part of a large miscellaneous group of mainly nineteenth-century prints from the London dealers Messrs Dulau, at the same time as volumes I–IV of *Die Graphischen Künste* for 1905 were purchased. The print is based on a drawing in the same direction belonging to the Gothenburg Museum, where there is also a corrected proof of the first state (see *Från Grafikerns Verkstad: Provtryck fyra århundraden*, Gothenburg Museum, 1984).

8 *Gunilla and Erik*, 1909

Etching. Signed in pencil. 146 × 198 mm

R.59; H.64

1949-4-11-4762. Bequeathed by Campbell Dodgson

The etching is based on Larsson's watercolour of 1905 depicting Mrs Carl G. Laurin and her youngest son on a settle belonging to the Larsson family, designed by the Swedish architect Carl Westmann (1866–1936). Her husband Carl Gustav Laurin (1868–1940), the brother of Thorsten Laurin, was a drama critic, writer and lecturer on art history and founder of the 'Art in Schools' Society. He published a number of articles on Larsson between 1903 and 1932, including one in the *American–Scandinavian Review* in 1925 (no. 13, pp. 747–59). Larsson made an etched portrait of him in 1906. The plate for this study of his wife and child is in the Carl Larssongården at Sundborn.

Dodgson purchased this print on 29 April 1931 from H. Trittler in Frankfurt for 65 Reichsmarks together with one of Larsson's youngest son, *Esbjörn*, of 1911 which cost Rm. 85.

8

9

10

9 *Kersti in black*, 1909

Etching. Signed. 148 × 199 mm

R.63,II; H.68,2

1949-4-11-4765. Bequeathed by Campbell Dodgson

In the second state described here this print was one of 500 unsigned copies published by the F.f.G.K. in 1910. The subject, like the preceding one, is taken from a watercolour of 1905, which showed Larsson's youngest daughter in mourning for her eldest brother Ulf, who had died of appendicitis at the age of eighteen. This was one of the darker events to overshadow Larsson's later years, reflected in the pessimistic tone of some of his introductory remarks to *Åt Solsidan* in 1910, notwithstanding the book's apparently blithe title.

10 *Lisbeth and Pontus*, 1911

Etching. Signed in pencil; inscribed on verso 'Girl seen from behind 2£'. 157 × 120 mm

R.79; H.84

1949-4-11-4755. Bequeathed by Campbell Dodgson

Pontus and Lisbeth were the third and fourth of Larsson's children. This is another rare subject among the etchings which Romdahl cites in his catalogue as belonging to Dodgson.

11

11 *An artist's wife*, 1913

Etching. Signed in pencil. 224 × 294 mm

H.99,2

1949-4-11-4780. Bequeathed by Campbell Dodgson

The portrait of Larsson's wife is one of 165 copies published by the F.f.G.K. before the address; the plate belongs to the Nationalmuseum.

Prior to meeting Carl Larsson in the summer of 1882, Karin Bergöö (1859–1928) had spent four years at the Academy in Stockholm, going to Paris in 1881 in order to study at the Académie Colarossi. Larsson in general opposed the extension to women of a formal fine art education; after their marriage in 1883 and their return to Sweden in 1889 following a second sojourn in Paris, her artistic talents were channelled into the creation of Sundborn, where her role as wife, mother and homemaker were clearly essential to the realisation of Larsson's artistic vision. Her

contribution to the whole conception of Sundborn was every bit as important as that of her husband; her contacts in England, where on several occasions she visited a sister living in Wimbledon, helped to reinforce the influence of the English aesthetic movement; in practical terms she proved an inventive weaver and textile designer (Larsson's watercolours often show her at work on her loom), drawing upon a diverse vocabulary of ideas which accommodated the patterns of the Navajo Indians and the Vienna Secessionists.

Anders Zorn (1860–1920)

Zorn, like Carl Larsson, projected a carefully crafted artistic persona; his painting and printmaking adumbrated the taste of those with newly acquired wealth in Europe and America, and his reputation acted as a fulcrum for the operations of the commercial art market worldwide. He was born the illegitimate son of a German master brewer and a Swedish mother in Mora, at the northern end of Lake Siljan in Dalarna, but attended technical school in Stockholm followed by the Academy in 1875, beginning his artistic career as a painter of portraits in watercolour. From 1881 until July 1885 Zorn was based in London, with frequent visits to Paris, Rome and Spain, then from 1888 to 1896 he kept a studio in Paris, where he developed his reputation as an oil painter, achieving his first critical success with *Fisherman, St Ives* (Musée des Beaux Arts, Pau) when it was exhibited at the Paris Salon in 1888 and purchased by the French state. He was an imposing presence even as a young man, when he was described by an American painter whom he met in St Ives in 1887 as 'a man with great hypnotic quality, who did not talk much, but dominated without speaking' (quoted in Michael Jacobs, *The Good and Simple Life: Artist colonies in Europe and America* (Oxford, 1985), p. 161). His technical brilliance, playing with convention but never wholly flouting it, soon ensured him a fashionable audience which included Sir Ernest Cassel, friend and financial adviser of the Prince of Wales, later Edward VII: 'For there's nothing the bourgeois likes better than being stroked when he thinks he's being manhandled' (Emile Zola, *L'Oeuvre*, 1886, English edn 1993, p. 184). This was extended to North America when Zorn was appointed chief commissioner for the exhibition of Swedish art in Chicago as part of the Columbia World's Fair in the spring of 1893. It proved to be an exceptionally rewarding experience for Zorn, in terms of both his sales from the exhibition and the value of the further commissions for portraits he received from some of the wealthiest families in American society – the Boston heiress Isabella Stewart Gardner and the Chicago financier Charles Deering became two of his most supportive patrons, the latter assembling the largest private collection of his etchings. His commissions kept him in the United States until January 1894, and his numerous repeat visits in 1896, 1899, 1900, 1901, 1903 and 1911 testify to the power of the American market. Zorn not unnaturally felt a considerable loyalty to this transatlantic audience, comparing it favourably with the English, of whom he wrote: 'Art with them is a question of fashion. Their interest in it is only for the sake of good form. They go through a gallery paying more attention to the catalogue than to what is on the walls' (quoted by G. van Rensselaer in 'A Swedish Etcher', *The Century Illustrated Monthly Magazine*, XLVI, 4 (1893), p. 584).

His last visit to Paris occurred in 1906 when his exhibition at the Durand-Ruel Gallery of paintings, watercolours, sculpture and etchings once again confirmed his success on an international scale. Thereafter he spent an increasing amount of time in Mora as well as maintaining an imposing studio in Stockholm. This was accompanied by a corresponding change in the subject matter of his compositions: among the portraits of men of the world, society beauties and winsome female nudes, motifs from the regional life around Mora were more in evidence. From 1889 to 1910 Zorn and his wife Emma (née Lamm) developed their own 'artistic home' on land adjoining the church in Mora, incorporating a medieval log cabin transported from its original site to serve as Zorn's studio. It became a focal point for the preservation of local traditions and the celebration of local festivals, for which the Zorns kept an entire wardrobe of peasant costume to supply their guests. In 1908 Zorn drew up plans for his house and studio at Mora to become a memorial to his life and work: this eventually opened to the public in 1942 after his widow's death.

In addition to his home, the Zorngården, he provided through various bequests for an open-air museum at Gopsmor on Lake Siljan, the third of his painting retreats, a craft centre and folk high school in Mora and the Zorn Museum, which opened in 1939; this was planned by Emma Zorn with Gerda Boëthius, the curator of the collections, and built to a design by Ragnar Östberg, the architect of Stockholm's City Hall (see cat. 19), incorporating a reconstruction of his studio in Stockholm.

Zorn's first period as an etcher was in 1882–9, culminating in his self-portrait, *A painter-etcher* of 1889 (published in the annual portfolio for the F.f.G.K.), which was a measure of the assurance he felt in this field. He learned the rudiments of the medium from a fellow Swede and long-time resident in England, Axel Hermann Haig, who specialised in 'vast plates of cathedrals, every inch conscientiously filled with detail' (from Campbell Dodgson's review of the Anglo-Swedish print exhibition in Stockholm in 1927). Zorn, however, was interested not in laborious architectural compositions but in acquiring a means for the effective translation of his painterly style:

I began to etch in 1883 in London. ... Instead of photographing a picture as a souvenir, I etched it. I etch directly on the plate from nature, and generally do but one biting. I very rarely have more than one sitting. ... I can do an etching from nature, like the portrait of myself and my wife, in three hours. This was retouched with a graver a couple of times. I never use anything but the graver to retouch a line; I never use the drypoint and am almost alone in this. (van Rensselaer, p. 589)

Rembrandt was his immediate model or, more especially, the interpretation of Rembrandt advanced by contemporary artists and writers such as Seymour Haden and P. G. Hamerton, whose study was published in 1883, emphasising the essential spontaneity of the etching medium. Zorn's first visit to Amsterdam took place in 1883, and he had ample opportunities for seeing Rembrandt prints at first hand in commercial galleries and private and public collections, both in London where he visited the Print Room of the British Museum (his name appears in the visitors' book, for example, on 14 January 1885) and in Paris. Among other influences upon Zorn's etching style was the work of Albert Besnard (1849–1934), who had studied under Legros in London from 1879 to 1883, later becoming a close friend of Zorn's in Paris (see Zorn's print of Besnard etching a model, 1896, A.105; H.70).

Zorn's visit to the United States in 1893/4 excited as much interest in his etching as it did in his painting, the article by van Rensselaer quoted above being the first in English to appear on this aspect of his work. Charles Deering's collection of his prints was begun in 1893 (see Zorn's study of Deering and his wife, *Reading*, A.78; H.55); it was eventually given to the Art Institute in Chicago in 1927, joining that of another Chicago collector, Wallace De Wolf, presented in 1913, which together make up the largest concentration of Zorn's graphic work outside Sweden. Another of Zorn's etched portraits on his first visit to North America was of Isabella Stewart Gardner; Zorn wrote to her during his voyage back to Europe to say that it required further work as 'they cannot print nicely in New York' (quoted by H. H. Brummer, *Anders Zorn* (Stockholm, 1994), p. 297). Zorn used a number of different printers in Paris for his earlier plates, then from 1900 to 1920 they were consistently handled by the Stockholm printer A. G. Lundin, whose expertise transformed the technical possibilities for Swedish artists (see p. 14). The year 1905 saw the publication of the first *catalogue raisonné* of Zorn's prints by F. von Schubert-Soldan, soon to be superseded by Loys Delteil's issued as volume IV in his series *Le Peintre-Graveur* (1909). Bukowski's, the Stockholm dealers and auction house, immediately perceived the commercial advantage to be reaped from this indispensable guide for collectors, and concluded a contract with Zorn for exclusive rights worldwide over the sale of his prints (there was no equivalent monopoly over the sale of his paintings). They helped to fuel the market by supplying Frederick Keppel and Arthur Hahlo in New York, Commeter in Hamburg, Artaria in Vienna, Colnaghi and Obach in London and Connell in Glasgow. Edition sizes escalated, requiring steel-facing for both new plates and reprints of those previously published in smaller quantities, although Zorn was not always prepared to agree to the latter. The buoyant level of his print prices, which sometimes exceeded those for Rembrandt, was well established by the early years of the twentieth century; John Kruse of the Nationalmuseum wrote to Campbell Dodgson on 15 January 1906: 'The Zorn etchings are also very expensive at Stockholm. I know they cost about 100 crowns = £5 and 5 shillings. How much in London, by Keppel isn't it?' (from Dodgson's personal correspondence in the Department of Prints and Drawings). Hans Singer in *Die Moderne Graphik* of 1914 commented that competition was so great among American collectors that prices could be as high as 600–1000 marks for his prints. During the war they became valuable securities, and the seemingly inexorable rise in the demand for his etchings

continued after his death – to the extent that Dodgson in 1925 described them, together with the work of the Scottish artists Cameron, Bone and McBey, as having 'ascertainable values like stocks and shares and are dealt with after the manner of such investments at prices out of all proportion to what they cost when first issued. It becomes a nice point of calculation for financial experts whether they are things to buy, to keep or to sell ...' (Frances Carey, 'Campbell Dodgson (1867–1948)' in *Landmarks in Print Collecting*, p. 217).

Zorn's prints never commanded the same degree of interest among British collectors as among their German and American counterparts, although they were shown at Colnaghi's and at the gallery run by the German dealer Richard Gutekunst, while in 1919 fifty-two of them were exhibited in Edinburgh. The British Museum's collection of forty-nine etchings by Zorn comprises twelve subjects presented by the artist's widow in 1924, with all but five of the remainder coming from the collection of Campbell Dodgson in 1949. The correspondence from John Kruse, quoted above, presupposes some expression of interest by Dodgson in Zorn's prints at this date; information given in Delteil's catalogue of 1909 identifies a number of the rarer Zorn prints as already belonging to Campbell Dodgson, while those published by the F.f.G.K. would have come to him in the same way as he acquired the equivalent works by Larsson. An article by Dodgson for the *Svenska Dagbladet*, published on 18 February 1910 in honour of Zorn's fiftieth birthday, makes it clear that, as in the case of Carl Larsson's work, the Dresden Print Room had been a crucial point of contact:

I made the discovery a good many years ago in the Cabinet of Prints at Dresden, which has the good fortune to possess in its director not only the first authority in the world on the engravings of the 15th century, but also an enthusiastic believer in the engravers and etchers of the 19th and 20th centuries, a director whose zeal and ability have secured for Dresden the finest collection of modern graphic art in Germany if not in the world. The fact was further impressed on my mind when I met in Paris a collector who had presented his fine works of Zorn to the Bibliothèque Nationale and then set about collecting Zorn again for himself, and once more at Budapest, where I found in 1909 the entire exhibition space of the Print Room in the fine new museum given up to the display of a nearly complete collection of Zorn.

Among Zorn's portrait etchings Dodgson singled out for praise those of the Americans Colonel Lamont and Henry Marquand and of the sculptor Rodin but reserved his greatest accolade, with due regard for tact, for the Swedish subjects from Mora.

Bibliography

The bulk of the literature on Zorn was published before 1930, including the first two *catalogues raisonnés* of his prints by Schubert-Soldan and Delteil referred to above. Three authors have been largely responsible for the most

12

13

14

15

thorough treatment of Zorn's work, starting with Karl Asplund, a director of Bukowski's, who published a third, updated *catalogue raisonné* of Zorn's prints in 1920. In 1921 *The Studio* in London published his account, *Anders Zorn: His life and work*, and the history he wrote of his firm in 1945 contains information on the marketing of the paintings and etchings. The Swedish art historian and first curator of the Zorn Museum, Gerda Boëthius, published the standard monograph, *Zorn: Tecknaren, malaren, etsaren, sculptoren* (Stockholm, 1949), and *Anders Zorn, an International Swedish Artist: His life and work* (Stockholm, 1954), while the most recent specialist is Hans Henrik Brummer, who has been responsible for the introduction to the fourth *catalogue raisonné* of the etchings published by Hjert and Hjert (Uppsala, 1980), an edition of Zorn's autobiographical writing, *Anders Zorn: Självbiografiska anteckningar* (Stockholm, 1982), and an artistic biography with a full chronological account of his work which accompanied the Zorn exhibition at Prins Eugens Waldemarsudde in Stockholm in 1994. Elizabeth Broun's catalogue of 1979, *The Prints of Anders Zorn*, for the Spencer Museum of Art at the University of Kansas, is one of the few modern studies in English; this includes a useful account of his etching technique and of his reputation in America.

12 *Antonin Proust*, 1889

Etching. Signed and dated within the plate and signed in pencil below. 159 × 240 mm

A.33.v; H.26,5

1949-4-11-4811. Bequeathed by Campbell Dodgson

The British Museum's impression is a proof printed on the verso of a page taken from an old account ledger dated 1852. Delteil estimated that no more than thirty impressions were printed in all, and Asplund identified the total number of states as five and not three as described by Delteil; the plate itself was presented to the Bibliothèque Nationale.

As critic, art historian and cultural politician, Proust (1832–1905) was a major figure in French public life in the latter part of the nineteenth century, briefly becoming Minister of Fine Arts in 1881 in the government of Léon Gambetta; in 1889 he served as the commissioner for fine art at the Exposition Universelle in Paris. He was a keen proponent of the work of Manet and the naturalist painters Bastien-Lepage and Max Liebermann, who were of great importance for Scandinavian artists at the time, and in 1890 published a history of French art from 1779 to 1889. Zorn's first commission in Paris was to paint Proust's portrait in 1888 and the etching is based on this picture, which formerly belonged to the dancer Rosita Mauri, Proust's mistress. She had been introduced by the composer Gounod to the Paris Opéra in 1878 and painted by Manet the following year; Zorn executed a watercolour of her in 1888 which he also translated into an etching exhibited, like the portrait of Proust, in 1891 at the Société des Peintres-Graveurs Français.

13 *Ernest Renan*, 1892

Etching. Signed and dated within the plate and signed in pencil below. 234 × 338 mm

A.73,v; H.50,5

1949-4-11-4842. Bequeathed by Campbell Dodgson

In the fifth and final state this subject was printed in an edition of 125. According to a statement by the artist, he was requested by M. Armand Dayot, the editor of *L'Art et les Artistes*, to make etchings of the four most celebrated living figures in French culture – Rodin, Berthelot, Anatole France and Renan. Although Dayot later claimed that Renan, who was in very poor health, had agreed on condition there was only a single sitting lasting no more than an hour, Zorn stated that he was allowed three sittings. On the first he made a drawing, then on the other two worked on the plate. Joseph Ernest Renan (1823–92) was an enormously influential author of historico-religious works, the most famous being *La Vie de Jésus*, published in 1863 as one of eight volumes on the history of Christianity, the first study to treat Christ as an historical figure.

14 *Girl with a cigarette II*, 1891

Etching. Signed within the plate. 158 × 119 mm

A.62,II; H.44,2

1949-4-11-4813. Bequeathed by Campbell Dodgson

This impression is one of 425 unsigned copies published by the F.f.G.K. in 1893; the first plate, which was identical in size, was abandoned by Zorn after pulling only three proofs. The subject is an American girl in Paris, whose smoking habit marks her out as one of a new generation of more liberated women.

15 *Emma Rasmussen*, 1904

Etching and aquatint. Signed and dated within the plate and signed in pencil below. 201 × 152 mm

A.183; H.122

1949-4-11-4824. Bequeathed by Campbell Dodgson

Dodgson owned this by 1909, as Delteil refers to the impression as being in his collection.

It was one of Zorn's most popular prints, fetching the considerable price of £168 at auction in London in 1920.

16 *Precipice*, 1909

Drypoint. Signed and dated within the plate and in pencil below. 241 × 161 mm

A.228,II; H.252,2

1949-4-11-4835. Bequeathed by Campbell Dodgson

The subject is one of Zorn's many nude studies on the shores of Lake Siljan, for which he often worked from photographs.

16

17

17 *August Strindberg*, 1910

Etching. Signed and dated within the plate and in pencil
below. 299 × 200 mm

A.231,II; H.149,2

1949-4-11-4846. Bequeathed by Campbell Dodgson

August Strindberg (1849–1913), the most celebrated and
controversial of all modern Swedish writers, was an exceptionally vivid subject for portraiture. By 1910, the date of
this print by Zorn, he had antagonised many of his
former friends by his scabrous attacks in 1907–8 on other
leading Swedish artistic figures (see p. 20) and had been
spurned by the Swedish Academy, who passed him over for
the Nobel Prize for literature in 1909.

Axel Fridell (1894–1935)

Fridell was one of a group of contemporary artists from the
town of Falun in Dalarna who all studied under Axel Tallberg at the Academy in Stockholm; intaglio printmaking
was to become their main form of expression, the other
members being Hans Norsbo (p. 42), Stig Borglind (p. 45),
Bertil Bull Hedlund (p. 47), and David Tägtström (1894–
1981). Their identity as a distinct school of printmaking
was not perceived at the outset but became established
later on, starting with the exhibition Five Falun Printmakers held in their home town in 1942. Fridell, who was
given a memorial exhibition at the Nationalmuseum in
1935, was the most accomplished of them all; despite his
comparatively short life, he executed 388 separate plates,
many of which progressed through several different states.
Although a good part of his income was derived from official
portrait commissions, Fridell's reputation as an original
printmaker has rested principally upon his drypoint etchings of urban architectural subjects, his self-portraits and
studies of his friends and contemporaries.

Fridell attended the Academy from 1913 to 1916; his etchings first received serious attention when they appeared in a
student exhibition in 1917 followed by an exhibition at the
Konstföreningen in 1918. His prints were published regularly by the F.f.G.K. from 1915 onwards, though many of the
plates did not appear in this form until after his death. He
was fortunate to have from the outset the support of a fellow printmaker, Albert Olson, also known as Bert Mesch
(1870–1945), who both lent Fridell money and from 1923
onwards acted as an agent for the sale of his work. Mesch
performed a similar service for Bull Hedlund, Norsbo and
Harald Sallberg (p. 49); Olson's work was largely overshadowed by this role, and he did not receive a one-man show of
his own until 1940/1. Fridell made frequent visits abroad
throughout his career, beginning with Copenhagen in 1914
and 1918, then Germany, Venice and Florence in 1921, Paris
in 1923, 1928, 1930 and 1933 and, most important of all,
London in 1926/7, 1929–31 and 1932–4. His experience of
London and Paris, in both literary and visual terms, lay at
the core of Fridell's work, which was already receptive to
the influence of modern British and French etching as
mediated by his teacher Axel Tallberg and his contact with
the collection of Thorsten Laurin. Laurin made Fridell's first
extended visit to London practically possible by bringing
together a group of ten collectors who would support him
for a year, each supplying him with fifty kronor a month in
return for the production of twenty-four plates.

Fridell arrived in London in October 1926, taking lodgings at no. 7 Bedford Place near the British Museum, where
he went to study what he described as the 'classic English
prints' of Whistler and Haden as well as the work of
Rembrandt (see letter of 10 December 1926, in Haskel,
Axel Fridell, vol II, p. 290). His correspondence, together
with the ledger book he kept for his plates from November

1926 onwards (including a retrospective account back to 1921), has provided a complete record of the progress of his work. By the beginning of January 1927 he had already completed five plates which he proposed to submit for entry in the Anglo-Swedish print exhibition due to take place in Stockholm in April of that year (see Haskel, vol. II, p. 303); a further eleven plates were ready by the following July.

After a few months in Bloomsbury, Chelsea became Fridell's centre of operation for the remainder of this and subsequent visits to London; in March 1927 he moved to Oakley Street, where a Miss Cock took in a number of Swedish lodgers, and rented a studio nearby in Cheyne Walk. At the same time he married a Swedish girl, Ingrid Starck, who had been working for a family in St John's Wood, but she soon returned to Stockholm, several months ahead of Fridell. At the end of May he wrote enthusiastically to his wife of his meeting with Martin Hardie of the Department of Engraving, Illustration and Design at the Victoria and Albert Museum, followed by an even more successful visit to Campbell Dodgson at the British Museum, who would already have been acquainted with Fridell's work via his subscription to the F.f.G.K. (see cat. 18). Dodgson purchased an impression of *Old studio in Chelsea* (cat. 22) for his own collection, later acquiring further

18

examples of plates published by the F.f.G.K. (Haskel, vol. II, p. 325); altogether he either presented or bequeathed twenty-four of Fridell's prints to the British Museum.

Despite Fridell's intense involvement with London subjects and the work of the British etchers, he appears to have had relatively little contact with the artistic community, associating mainly with his compatriots similarly resident in London and catering to a market among his friends and patrons in Stockholm. He did become a member of the Chelsea Arts Club in August 1927, and at various junctures he approached the Fine Art Society, whose expressions of interest did not, however, materialise into anything more concrete, while a similar fate befell the overtures he received from a number of American sources. He only exhibited his work on three occasions in England, once at Chelsea Town Hall in an exhibition of views of old and new Chelsea in 1927 and twice at the Royal Academy, in 1929 and 1934 (cat. 26). Fridell was constantly plagued by financial difficulties because the very modest monthly stipend he received from Sweden was insufficient to pay his living expenses and printing costs, of which he often complained in his correspondence, talking of the need to acquire his own press so that he could proof his plates himself. On his first visit he used the firm of McQueen, but on subsequent occasions he resorted more to Collins, Dear & Co. in Horseferry Road, Westminster (later situated on the Fulham Road), who were copper-plate printers used by a number of British artists including Henry Rushbury and Francis Dodd.

In 1928/9 Fridell was again in London in the same lodgings in Oakley Street, then in Wentworth Studios in Manresa Road behind Chelsea Town Hall. At the same time the Swedish Etchers' Association, formed the previous year, organised an exhibition at the Galerie Moderne in Stockholm with Fridell as the central figure, and the dealer Bukowski's, eager to find another etcher who might repay their investment as Zorn had so handsomely done, concluded a contract with Fridell, negotiated by his friend Albert Olson Mesch; this initially covered the period from 15 May 1929 to 30 June 1931, giving the firm exclusive rights over the sale of his work in return for a monthly income of 750 kronor, which was increased to 1000 kronor when the contract was renewed until 2 June 1932. After the expiry of the second term Nils Palmgren, a specialist in Oriental ceramics who also wrote on contemporary Swedish art, organised another consortium of collectors to support Fridell. He had one-man shows at Bukowski's in Stockholm in 1930 and in 1932 in Gothenburg, where the critics noted his dependence upon English printmakers. His visits to Paris, Rotterdam and Amsterdam in 1929/30 were reflected in the renewed influence of Meryon and Rembrandt on his work; the former's presence was immediately apparent in the plates that Fridell executed on the spot, the *Quai des Orfèvres* and the *Quai de Montebello* (Haskel, 299 and 300), using the facilities of Lacourière's workshop.

19

20

For the last few years of his life Fridell was subject to bouts of depression. He separated from his wife in 1932, moving his studio in Stockholm from Stadsgården to one overlooking Kungsgatan. Some of his most idiosyncratic plates were done during his final stay in London through the winter of 1933/4; these were images indebted not to Whistler and Haden but to the work of Dickens, Cruikshank and Doré, and they evoked the damp chill of the foggy reaches of the Thames where forlorn groups of beggars hovered literally on the margins of life.

Bibliography

The first biography of Fridell was published by Karl Asplund of Bukowski's, *Ett Konstnärsliv* (Malmö, 1937), followed by a *catalogue raisonné* in 1947. Jane Rothlind's book on the Falun printmakers, *Hans Norsbo och Falungrafikerna* (Uppsala, 1986, with a summary in English), contains much that is pertinent to Fridell. The indispensable source, however, is Karl Haskel's two-volume study, *Axel Fridell* (Stockholm, 1986); volume I is the *catalogue raisonné* of Fridell's prints while volume II is a fully illustrated biography drawing on all the existing archival material, which for the most part is to be found in the Nationalmuseum. Haskel had already made a documentary film about Fridell's work for Swedish television in 1980. I am indebted to him for his attentive reading of my text on Fridell as well as for the impeccable scholarship of his publication.

21

18 *Man in a cape (the artist Arvid Knöppel)*, 1915

Etching and drypoint. Signed in pencil; inscribed on verso in Campbell Dodgson's hand 'Föreningen för Grafik Konst 1917' and 'Axel Fridell Mannen i Kappen etching'. 187 × 142 mm

H.33.III

1922-3-11-30. Presented by Campbell Dodgson

The plate was published in this state by the F.f.G.K in 1917 in a signed edition; 130 reprints were issued in 1986 to accompany a special edition of Haskel's catalogue to mark the hundredth anniversary of the F.f.G.K. It was Fridell's second plate for the Society, the first having been a portrait of another artist friend, Alfred Hedlund, which was published in 1915. Arvid Knöppel (1892–1970) was a sculptor, draughtsman and printmaker who studied at the Academy from 1914 to 1919. The British Museum's impression was presented to the Department by Campbell Dodgson in 1922 with a group of other prints published by the F.f.G.K., including a lithograph by Knöppel.

19 *City Hall Stockholm II*, 1925

Etching and drypoint. Signed and dated within the plate and signed in pencil below. 198 × 294 mm

H.223.III

1927-1-31-11. Presented by Campbell Dodgson

Fridell executed a number of views of Stockholm in 1925, which in this case was published in 1926 by the F.f.G.K. in a signed edition of 160 followed by an unsigned one of 345 of the fourth state. The City Hall on the island of Kungsholmen was one of the most important architectural monuments of modern Stockholm. Inspired by Swedish medieval brick buildings, it was designed by Ragnar Östberg and constructed between 1911 and 1923. As a prominent landmark it captured the attention of several artists (see cat. 36) and drew favourable comment from Campbell Dodgson on his visit to Stockholm in 1927: 'I think it a very beautiful building, whatever eccentricities it may be accused of' (letter dated 3 April, among his private papers in the Department of Prints and Drawings).

20 *Falun II*, 1925

Etching. Signed within the plate, signed and inscribed in pencil below with the place name. 149 × 196 mm

H.226.I

1926-3-3-9. Presented by Campbell Dodgson

The F.f.G.K. published a signed edition of the first state of this subject and an unsigned edition of the second state in 1925. Fridell's view of the bridge and 'Fish Tower' in his home town of Falun is indebted to the influence of seventeenth-century Dutch etchers such as Everdingen and Jan van de Velde, which tended to be more explicit in the work of his contemporary Stig Borglind (p. 45) than in his own. The composition is a more detailed version in reverse of another plate he had previously executed in 1924 (H.209) for an album of ten views of Falun published by a local bookseller, containing three etchings each by Fridell and David Tägtström and four by Stig Borglind.

21 *Hammersmith*, 1927

Drypoint. 212 × 170 mm

H.246

1949-4-22-7. Bequeathed by Campbell Dodgson

Fridell's immediate response to arriving in London in the winter of 1926/7 was one of excitement at seeing the views he had hitherto only known from prints: 'And Whistler! And Haden! And the Thames! What fun! All right!' (Rothlind, *Hans Norsbo och Falungrafikerna*, p. 99). His own renderings

of the riverscape were clearly inspired, for example, by Whistler's Thames etchings of 1859–61, first published in 1871, and the later Thames etchings of 1879, but the juxtaposition of an interior and exterior view, in which the landscape becomes a picture carefully framed by the window embrasure, was a device more specific to Fridell's own compositions.

The F.f.G.K. published this plate posthumously in 1948 in an edition of 130.

22 *Old studio in Chelsea*, 1927

Drypoint printed on thin cream-coloured paper. Signed in pencil. 270 × 352 mm

H.253.v

1949-4-11-4723. Bequeathed by Campbell Dodgson

This was the print that Fridell was so proud of having sold to Campbell Dodgson in June 1927, presumably for the

22

equivalent of sixty kronor, the price he quoted in a letter to Sweden at the time (Haskel, vol. II, p. 326). The location was Fridell's studio at 44 Cheyne Walk, not far from Carlyle's House at no. 24. Between the second and fifth states Fridell made several alterations to the view through the window, and the number (44) on the pane of glass above the door was reversed in the final state.

23   Roofs in Stockholm II, 1932

Drypoint. 'F.f.G.K.: 1951' added within the plate.
248 × 176 mm

H.339,II

1989-6-17-280. Presented by Birgit Rausing

This is one of a pair of oval views across the roofs of Stockholm from Fridell's new apartment and studio at Kungsgatan 55, done in 1932 and published by the F.f.G.K. in 1950 and 1951 respectively, in editions of 160. They were both acquired for the British Museum by Mrs Rausing in 1989. Together with cat. 24 they attest to the influence of Meryon's views, which particularly captured Fridell's imagination when he visited Paris in 1930 and again in 1932/3.

24

23

24   Göran Helsinges Alley, 1932

Drypoint. Signed and dated within the plate. 378 × 250 mm

H.343,III

1949-4-11-4719. Bequeathed by Campbell Dodgson

The dramatically high viewpoint is along one of the narrow alleys of the Old Town, the original heart of Stockholm, with the tower of the Great Church (Stora Kyrka) rising above. It was published by the F.f.G.K. in 1936 in an edition of 130.

25   Kitchen II, 1932–3

Drypoint. 'F.f.G.K.1937' added within the plate. 178 × 240 mm

H.346,III

1949-4-11-4724. Bequeathed by Campbell Dodgson

Another aspect of Fridell's draughtsmanship was his interest in caricature, a not uncommon sub-text to more elevated artistic composition among his peers. This type of drawing was always present in his work but did not surface

25

26

in his printmaking until 1932/3, when he executed three plates of Dickensian subjects: the first, *The Old Curiosity Shop* (H.344), was done in Stockholm, and the other two, both depicting Fagin's kitchen in *Oliver Twist*, were made in London in 1932/3. This version was published in the third state by the F.f.G.K. in 1937 in an edition of 160, although *Kitchen I* (H.345) was a fully worked plate.

26 *Mr Simmons*, 1933–4

Drypoint. Signed within the plate and in pencil below.
299 × 240 mm

H.365,v

1949-4-11-4722. Bequeathed by Campbell Dodgson

Mr Simmons is arguably Fridell's finest plate, a bid on the part of the artist to vie with the portraiture of Rembrandt or with *Rotherhithe*, Whistler's most ambitious subject from the first Thames series, whose compositional arrangement *Mr Simmons* broadly resembles. Simmons lodged from 1931 to 1936 with Fridell's landlady, Miss Cock, at 85 Oakley Street, where he received free board and lodging in return for help with the book-keeping for the guesthouse. Fridell had previously used the motif of juxtaposing a figure reading in a darkened interior against a view on to the outside world, for example, *The window*, in 1926/7 (H.243) and *Mr*

27

Foss in 1929–31 (H.295). Hugh Foss (1902–73), a mathematician working for the Foreign Office, was another of Fridell's fellow lodgers and the plate, which was started in London but finished in Stockholm, showed him reclining in front of a window on a sofa, reading a newspaper. The view, added by Fridell at the third state, was the one he saw from his studio in Stockholm.

Mr Simmons is altogether bolder in its execution and the characterisation of the figure. Fridell began (as in Mr Foss) working from the foreground and leaving the view blank. As the states progressed, the view was developed in more detail, with preparatory drawings acting as intermediaries between some of the states. The building to the right of the window in the fifth and final state belonged to the copper-plate printing firm of Collins, Dear & Co., where Mr Simmons was printed in January 1934, two months after Fridell first began work on the plate. An impression of Mr Simmons was included in the Royal Academy's Summer Exhibition in 1934.

27 Albert and William, 1934

Etching and drypoint. Signed and dated within the plate, with 'Albert' and 'F.f.G.K. 39'. 245 × 159 mm

H.367,III

1949-4-11-4721. Bequeathed by Campbell Dodgson

Albert and William were among the vagrants scavenging along the Thames who were the focus of a number of Fridell's plates of anecdotal subjects executed in 1932–4. This example was published by the F.f.G.K. in 1939 in an edition of 160. Some of the last group of London plates were reprinted in 1958 at the instigation of Fridell's family before the plates were deposited in the Nationalmuseum.

Hans Norsbo (1897–1955)

Norsbo, who adopted this surname in 1938 having been born Hans Johanson, was the youngest of the Falun printmakers. After graduating from the Academy in Stockholm he went in 1921 to Italy, where he was part of a Scandinavian artists' colony led by Leander Engström, a former pupil of Matisse, at Settignano near Florence. There he executed prints of Italian hill towns, but painting was of more importance to him at this time. From 1926 to 1929 Norsbo was in Rome, where he met Anders Zorn's widow Emma and the art historian Gerda Boëthius, both of whom were to have a great influence on his career. On the latter's recommendation in 1929 he obtained the post of drawing master at the Mora Folk High School founded by Zorn. Emma and Gerda helped to find him portrait commissions, and through them he met at the Zorn house the politician K. G. Westman (1876–1944), who became another of his patrons. Not until after Fridell's early death in 1935, however, did Norsbo come into his own as a printmaker; in that year his prints received favourable attention in the reviews of an exhibition at the Liljevalchs Art Gallery of work by artists from Dalarna, and all but thirty-seven of the 239 plates ascribed to Norsbo were executed from then onwards.

Apart from portraiture, Norsbo's subject matter was predominantly taken from Stockholm and Dalarna, where he continued to maintain a home. A brief exception to this pattern were the visionary landscapes executed in 1938 under the influence of the Christian moral rearmament group known as The Oxford Group after the High Anglican movement in Oxford in the mid nineteenth century; this attracted many writers and artists in Sweden as well as adherents in Norway and Denmark and politicians such as Konrad Adenauer in Germany.

Norsbo's earliest print is dated 1916. Unlike his fellow printmakers from Falun, he often used photographs as the working basis for his compositions, as had Zorn for some of his later subjects. Fridell (p. 35) preferred to work directly on to the plate in front of the subject and then perfected the

28

composition in his studio; Stig Borglind (p. 45) did meticulous preparatory studies which he translated exactly on to the plate; David Tägtström worked in pencil, charcoal and watercolour, often changing his ideas during the transfer of the composition, while Bull Hedlund (p. 47) started with a rapid sketch and then worked freely on the etching plate. Norsbo was the only one of the group to have his own press, but this was merely a tabletop one on which he made *ex libris* or greetings cards; otherwise he depended on the facilities provided at A. G. Lundin's workshop, the subject of one of his prints in 1944 (Rothlind, 136).

Bibliography
Norsbo is fully discussed within his contemporary context by Jane Rothlind in *Hans Norsbo och Falungrafikerna* (Uppsala, 1986), which includes a checklist of his prints.

29

28 *Asea IV*, 1948

Drypoint. Signed and dated 48 within the plate but signed and
dated in pencil below with 1949; numbered 86/95.
211 × 247 mm

R.173

1989-6-18-284. Presented by Birgit Rausing

From 1947 to 1949 Norsbo executed six prints of this
particular subject, the plant of Sweden's largest electrical
company (Allmänna Svenska Elektriska AB) situated at
Västerås (I am indebted to Jane Rothlind for this information). Together with the six *Domnarvet* plates (cat. 29) done
between 1946 and 1953 they form within his *oeuvre* a distinct group of industrial imagery which Jane Rothlind has
related to the influence of Joseph Pennell, with specific reference to the latter's lithograph *Charleroi* reproduced by
Hans Singer in *Die Moderne Graphik*.

Sweden became a fully industrialised nation between the
wars with an impressive national power system based on
hydro-electricity, for which Västerås was a key source of
supply.

29 *Domnarvet V, Wire-rod mill*, 1952

Drypoint. Signed and dated 1952; numbered 93/100.
248 × 318 mm

R.217

1989-6-17-285. Presented by Birgit Rausing

Domnarvet refers to an iron and steel plant in central
Sweden.

44

Stig Borglind (1892–1965)

Of all the Falun printmakers, Borglind's work was the most strongly influenced by seventeenth-century Dutch artists such as Jan van de Velde and Jacob Ruysdael (see, for example, Borglind's *The town of Lindesberg*, 1925, and the *Watermill* of 1927, both in the British Museum's collection), and the eighteenth-century mezzotints of Richard Earlom after van Huysum's elaborate fruit and flower pieces. He studied the collection in the Nationalmuseum in Stockholm and reproductions of prints in *The Studio* and its associated publications such as Malcolm Salaman's *The Great Painter-Etchers from Rembrandt to Whistler* (1914). His plates became renowned for their exquisite silvery tone and the meticulous skill with which he often combined etching, drypoint and engraving, starting with the contours of his forms. Between 1942 and 1965 Borglind took part in all the main print exhibitions in Sweden after winning the prize at the Venice Biennale in 1942 for the best foreign printmaker (Sweden, a neutral country during the Second World War, submitted entries to the Biennale at this time, but there were many absentees). Immediately after his success in Venice came the exhibition of the five printmakers in Falun, when the avant-garde painter and critic Otto G. Carlsund (1878–1948) hailed Borglind as the best of the group.

Borglind executed approximately 150 prints of which the British Museum owns seven subjects, all acquired through Campbell Dodgson.

Bibliography

The first study devoted to Borglind was R. Zeitler, *Stig Borglind: En svensk grafiker* (1948). Jane Rothlind, who discusses him in *Hans Norsbo och Falungrafikerna* (Uppsala, 1986), has recently published an article on him, 'Falungrafikern

31

32

Stig Borglind', in *Artes I* (1996), pp. 75–80, by way of intro-duction to the monograph she is currently preparing. Almost the only reference to him in English was in a brief note in *The Studio*, XLIV (1926), p. 441, on the Falun print-makers which reproduced his etching *Old water-wheel*.

30 *Jay*, 1935

Drypoint. Second state. Signed in pencil. 257 × 168 mm

1949-4-11-4714. Bequeathed by Campbell Dodgson

Another very similar print to this subject published by the F.f.G.K. is Borglind's etching *Hazel-hen* executed the follow-ing year.

31 *Moonrise*, 1942

Etching, engraving and drypoint. Second state. Signed and dated within plate; signed below in pencil and inscribed with title. 217 × 261 mm

1953-6-25-19. Bequeathed by Campbell Dodgson

This poetic landscape was one of six prints chosen by the jury for the Good Art in the Home and Public Places exhi-bition at the Nationalmuseum in 1945 (see p. 11).

Bertil Bull Hedlund (1893–1950)

Bull Hedlund, who was keenly interested in French art and literature, developed as an illustrator specialising in genre scenes rather than as a landscape and portrait printmaker like his contemporaries from Falun. In 1912 he made his first visit to Paris, and his first print in 1914 had a Paris bistro as its subject. Apart from the influence of nineteenth-century satirical artists such as Grandville, Hedlund was also indebted to the anecdotal style of German artists of the 1920s, exemplified by Otto Dix, whose work he saw during a visit to Dresden in 1922, and to a gentler burlesque manner typified by the work of the American artist Reginald Marsh, which he may have seen in reproduction. The two principal exhibitions of his work were both held after his death, a memorial exhibition at the Nationalmuseum in 1952 followed by another commemoration shared with Hans Norsbo and held in the main art gallery in Falun in 1957.

Bibliography

Nils Lindgren's *Bertil Bull Hedlund* (Stockholm, 1952) is the only monograph, and Jane Rothlind's *Hans Norsbo och Falungrafikerna* (Uppsala, 1986) includes information on Hedlund.

32 *Summer night*, 1934

Drypoint. Second state. Signed in pencil. 194 × 301 mm

1949-4-11-4733. Bequeathed by Campbell Dodgson

Together with another drypoint in the British Museum's collection, *Crabs* (1934), this composition with its odd dis-junctions of scale has a more intensely fantastical quality to it than most of Hedlund's prints. The couple standing before their home in the strange light of a Swedish summer night appear frozen within a waking dream, transfixed by the gigantic grasshopper with its connotations of metamor-phosis.

The plate was purchased by the F.f.G.K. for publication in 1935 but Hedlund experienced some difficulty in the print-ing of an edition, having to rework it in places in order to produce impressions of sufficient strength.

Emil Johanson-Thor (1889–1958)

Johanson-Thor attended Axel Tallberg's course while he was a student at the Stockholm Academy from 1908 to 1912, later succeeding him in 1926 as head of what became the School of Graphic Art. In 1954 he in turn was succeed-ed by Harald Sallberg (p. 49), with whom he had long had an uneasily competitive relationship. Many of his earliest prints were black and white lithographs influenced by the work of nineteenth-century French artists such as Millet, and his first visit to France in 1914, accompanied by the Swedish art historian and later Curator of Prints and Draw-ings at the Nationalmuseum, Ragnar Hoppe (who in 1944 wrote the first biography of Johanson-Thor) appeared to confirm this bias. However, in 1916 he was in Copenhagen, where the collections of the Statens Museum – prints, draw-ings and paintings – made a great impression upon him, especially the work by or after Dürer, Brueghel, and the Dutch seventeenth-century artists from the Moltke collec-tion as well as that by Danish artists. This material had a

33

decisive effect upon the formation of his own distinctive style and subject matter, which from the early 1920s onwards focused on winter scenes of the landscape and rural architecture of southern Sweden (Skåne), where he acquired a residence at Sireköping outside his home town of Landskrona. In both his paintings and his etchings Johanson-Thor chose a deliberately Brueghelesque manner in which to depict the flat terrain with its long, low farm buildings, rendered with an almost childlike clarity that contributes to the deliberate naivety of the whole composition. The comparison with Brueghel was specifically invoked by a contemporary critic at the time of a major exhibition of Swedish painting in Paris in 1929.

From 1909 to 1919 lithography dominated Johanson-Thor's printmaking but thereafter until the late 1940s he favoured drypoint and etching as better suited to his mode of expression. Like many Swedish artists, he greatly admired the work of the modern British printmakers, translating W. P. Robins's *Etching Craft* of 1922 because of the dearth of equivalent literature in Swedish. To further his development as a printmaker he visited England from November 1925 to April 1926, equipped with introductions to Muirhead Bone, the Slade and Central Schools of Art and to Campbell Dodgson at the British Museum, where he studied the work of Old Masters and more contemporary artists. During the course of his stay Johanson-Thor became involved with a proposed exhibition of modern Swedish art at the Whitechapel Art Gallery, to which he submitted twelve of his etchings; the exhibition eventually opened on 11 March 1926 amid some acrimony, since many of those involved, including Johanson-Thor, felt it was unrepresentative of the most important contemporary artists.

After his return to Stockholm and appointment as Tallberg's successor, Thor became increasingly involved in the organisation and politics of the graphic art world, including the F.f.G.K., the Grafiska Sällskapet and the Nordic Graphic Union founded in 1937.

His total graphic production from 1909 to 1957 consisted of 176 etchings, of which the British Museum owns four examples, and 164 lithographs of which the Museum has six, all from the period 1915-45.

Bibliography
The principal source is the monograph by Louise Lyberg, *Emil Johanson-Thor: Målaren, grafikern, konstpolitikern* (Lund, 1990), which includes a checklist of all his prints.

33 *Winter, Torna-Hällestad*, 1935

Etching. Signed, dated and inscribed in pencil with title.
220 × 298 mm
1949-4-11-4808. Bequeathed by Campbell Dodgson

Although this was executed and published in 1935 by the F.f.G.K., it evokes the mood of his studies of the Skåne landscape from the early 1920s onwards; the settlement at Torna-Hällestad became a favourite motif for Johanson-Thor after 1930. There is a painting of almost precisely the same scene dating from 1937.

Harald Sallberg (1895–1963)

Sallberg had much in common with Axel Fridell but was not one of the group of printmakers from Falun. He was born on Södermalm, literally 'the south side' of Stockholm, into a predominantly working-class neighbourhood and joined the Etching School attached to the Academy in 1912 as an apprentice printer and technical assistant, later becoming a student in 1921. He worked closely with Axel Tallberg until the latter's retirement in 1926, and then with Tallberg's successor, Emil Johanson-Thor (p. 48), concentrating on architectural subjects as far as his own work was concerned. This bias manifested itself initially in the hundred topographical etchings of Old Stockholm that he executed in 1917/18 and was reinforced by his first trips abroad in 1920 to London and Paris, where he admired the work of D. Y. Cameron, Seymour Haden, Meryon and Whistler.

In 1929/30 he made further visits to London and Paris, etching portraits of Braque and Léger. His interiors with views through windows at this time were close to Fridell's work of the late 1920s. In the course of the following decade Sallberg's work began to diversify; landscape subject matter began to predominate in his etching, while in 1936 he made his first wood-engraving inspired by Bewick, going on to illustrate Linnaeus's *Fyra Skrifter* (Four Writings) in 1939 in this medium. Much later, in 1955/6, he experimented with a mixture of etching and aquatint in compositions influenced by Surrealist collages. By this stage he had succeeded Johanson-Thor as assistant professor at the School of Graphic Art, becoming Director of the Academy's art school as a whole from 1955 to 1959.

Sallberg was a prolific printmaker whose output exceeded five hundred prints by 1960. His early experience instilled in him the importance of an artist pulling his own proofs and led to the publication of a technical handbook, *Konstgrafiska Metoder* (1927), the principal manual in Swedish until it was superseded by Jürgen von Konow's work in 1955 (see p. 131). In 1957 he was the co-author with Gunnar Jungmarker from the Nationalmuseum of what remained the standard history of Swedish printmaking overall, *Svensk Grafik från Tre Sekler* (Three Centuries of Swedish

34

35

36

37

Bibliography
Sallberg published his personal reminiscences of the Academy's etching school in 'Från Rödbotorget till Skeppsholmen: Minnen från Grafiska Skolan' in *Grafisk Konst i vår tid* (Folket i Bilds Konstklubb, Stockholm, 1958), pp. 20–37. The only monograph on Sallberg was published in 1960 by Åke Meyerson.

34 *Stockholm landscape in winter*, 1927

Etching. Signed and dated in pencil. 191 × 372 mm

1929-2-20-7. Presented by Campbell Dodgson

35 *Roofs of London*, 1929

Etching and drypoint. Signed in pencil and inscribed with title in English. 160 × 247 mm

1949-4-11-4804. Bequeathed by Campbell Dodgson

This plate was published by the F.f.G.K. in 1932.

39

Prints)56, until the publication of Jane Rothlind's book in 1992 (see General Bibliography).

Most of the British Museum's collection of thirteen etchings and three wood-engravings were acquired via Campbell Dodgson who, prior to the first of his prints being sent to him by the F.f.G.K. in 1927, was introduced to Sallberg's work by Gunnar Wengström of the Nationalmuseum. The latter sent him two of Sallberg's prints for consideration at the very end of 1926:

I have sent you some days ago two new prints by Mr Harald Sallberg the assistant of Mr Johanson-Thor at the School of Graphics at the Royal Academy. I will only ask you what is your opinion about them. The one is a drypoint, the other an engraving. The larger one, the drypoint, is sold for 50 kronor, the little one for 40 kr. (letter dated 21 December 1926, among Dodgson's personal papers in the Department of Prints and Drawings).

The artist himself in 1929 presented the British Museum with a proof impression printed on pale blue paper of his etching *Pålsundet in Stockholm*. (Pålsundet is the name of a channel or strait in Stockholm; I must thank Birgitta Olofsson for pointing this out.)

38

36 *Harbour and City Hall, Stockholm*, 1932

Etching. Signed and dated within the plate and signed in pencil below. 296 × 296 mm.

1992-6-20-25. Presented by Birgit Rausing

Sallberg's view provides a closer impression of Stockholm's controversial City Hall of 1911–23, designed by Ragnar Östberg, than the earlier print by Axel Fridell previously discussed (cat. 19). In addition to the remarkable brickwork of the structure, the courtyard and west front were later adorned with four bronze statues executed between 1932 and 1936 symbolising the four Mälaren towns. The plate was published by the F.f.G.K.

37 *Alleyway*, 1933

Etching and drypoint. Signed, dated and inscribed with title in pencil. 277 × 227 mm

1949-4-11-4805. Bequeathed by Campbell Dodgson

The subject is an alleyway in the Old Town, probably just below the Great Church like *Göran Helsinges Alley* by Axel Fridell (cat. 24). It was published by the F.f.G.K. in 1933.

38 *Fisherman with nets*, 1935

Etching and drypoint. Signed and dated in pencil. 248 × 355 mm

1949-4-11-4803. Bequeathed by Campbell Dodgson

The plate was published by the F.f.G.K. in 1938.

39 *The etcher*, 1938

Etching and drypoint. Signed and dated in pencil. 267 × 185 mm

1939-7-30-66. Presented by the Contemporary Art Society

The etcher is a self-portrait that was exhibited in London in 1938 under the auspices of the Nordic Graphic Union.

41

Gustaf Isander (1863–1929)

Isander grew up in a musician's home in Stockholm's Old
Town and had to attend a charity school because of his family's poverty. He was self-taught as an artist and did not take
up art as a career until 1917 when he was fifty-four, having
previously worked as a printer, a pedlar and a waiter, among
other occupations. In his memoirs *Av Jämmerdal* (The Vale
of Tears) he described the life of which he had dreamed:
'Alone in a small, light room facing north or west ... No furniture ... There I would like to paint by day, write in the
evenings and at night dream of nothing and everything'
(Jungmarker, 'Gustaf Isander', p. 276). His work, which he
sold by touting it from door to door in his 'beggar's wallet'
(Jungmarker, p. 285), consisted of pastels, sketches and
etchings of which he made only ten plates between 1917
and 1929, all of Stockholm subjects. The British Museum
owns six of these, all but one of them published by the
F.f.G.K., and acquired through Campbell Dodgson in 1922,
1923, 1930 and 1949. Isander perfected a special use of drypoint, approaching his work with a reverent industry which
imbued even inanimate objects with an intense life of their
own: 'There exists no death; everything lives, even stones'
(Jungmarker, p. 277).

40

54

43

Bibliography
Gunnar Jungmarker, 'Gustaf Isander: A unique figure in Swedish art', *Print Collecters' Quarterly*, XXI (1934), pp. 273–85.

40 *Stigbergsgatan 5*, 1920

Etching. Signed and dated in pencil. 202 × 150 mm

1922-9-7-10. Presented by Campbell Dodgson

This and another plate identified as *Stora Glasbrukgatan 40* were published in 1922 and 1923 by the F.f.G.K. They were conceived as lovingly delineated 'portraits' of buildings that the artist described as being on the one hand like an old and faithful servant, a little reserved and abrupt, but neat, straightforward and honest (*Stora Glasbrukgatan 40*) and on the other as resembling a pretty little housemaid, who is more readily able to make friends (*Stigbergsgatan 5*, Jungmarker, p. 281).

42

41 *The Finnish church*, 1920

Etching. Signed in pencil. 118 × 202 mm

1923-8-28-7. Presented by Campbell Dodgson

The church, which remains in use, is a modest building in the Old Town opposite the Royal Palace, built as a games hall in the seventeenth century before being adapted for worship by the Finnish community in Stockholm in 1727. It is very much overshadowed by the grander structures around it, but Isander, who instinctively identified with the humble and apparently insignificant, was delighted to discover that the early morning sun reached it: 'even on the most forsaken one the sun shines sometimes' (Jungmarker, p. 281). The plate was published by the F.f.G.K. in 1921.

42 *Expansion*, 1922

Drypoint. Signed and dated and inscribed in pencil in Swedish on recto beneath the image: 'Expansion, "Train approaching!" in the tunnel of a wide railway cutting, Stockholm'. Inscribed on verso in pencil in the artist's hand: 'the engraving consists of horizontal lines and it has taken one and a half years to complete.' 220 × 174 mm

1923-11-12-6. Presented by Campbell Dodgson

The artist described the engine as 'something like a primeval animal darting out of its cave'. The original study for the print is in the Nationalmuseum, drawn in the same direction as the etching (see Ragnar von Holten, *Svenska Teckningar 1900–talet* (Stockholm, 1985), where it is reproduced on p. 49 opposite a drawing related to another of Isander's prints).

43 *Birger Jarl Square*, 1927

Etching. Signed and dated in pencil and inscribed with the location. 183 × 261 mm

1949-4-11-4738. Bequeathed by Campbell Dodgson

This was Isander's last print, expressive of the tranquillity of a summer Sunday when many Stockholmers would be out of town.

Gunnar Norrman (born 1912)

Norrman belongs to a tradition of printmaking in the southernmost part of Sweden, Skåne, close to Denmark, which is indebted to the example of the Falun printmakers described above. He was born in Malmö and started his career as a student of natural sciences at the University of Lund, graduating in 1938, and working as a temporary assistant at the Botanical Museum there. In 1934 he had already shown as a painter and graphic artist at the annual exhibition of the Scanian Art Association in Malmö, then in 1941 became a supernumerary student at the Etching School of the Academy in Stockholm where his prints were singled out as the best from a display of student work, which was followed in 1942 by his first one-man show at the Malmö Museum. From 1945 to 1972 Norrman showed regularly in Sweden, then in 1976 he began a collaborative arrangement with the Galerie Leger in Malmö which has led to an increasing number of exhibitions abroad in London, Berlin, Düsseldorf, Neuchâtel, Bologna and Genoa, New York and Boston.

44

45

Although he produced a group of lithographs in 1947–52 (cat. 44), the great bulk of his work, amounting to more than seven hundred plates, is in drypoint. In his diary for 1939 Norrman described his first attempt at the medium: 'Today I completed my first "engraving". I couldn't resist the temptation, and with an ordinary pin I scratched out a couple of small pictures on the bottom of a glue tin. Having studied up on it in Sallberg's "Techniques in Graphics", I went down to the cellar and tried to mix some ink to print with' (Nilsson, *Gunnar Norrman*, p. 20). In July 1949 he spent two weeks in London studying the prints and drawings collection in the British Museum and visiting Axel Fridell's haunts along the Thames. It took him until the end of the 1950s to achieve what he considered to be an adequate proficiency in drypoint technique, and the bulk of his work dates from that time.

Norrman acquired a printing press in the mid-1940s, and since then he and his wife Ulla have printed virtually all his plates, with the exception of five items printed in 1981 at the workshop of Niels Borch Jensen in Copenhagen; since 1976 he has also printed a number of editions at the Druckgraphik Kätelhön in Möhnsee-Wamel in Germany. He works from drawings, often done *in situ* then transferred by

tracing the motif with wax lithographic crayon on to a sheet of paper which is laid face down on the plate; the composition is etched in many cases with the aid of a mirror because Norrman works on such a small and meticulous scale.

Norrman's work, encompassing his prints and his tonal charcoal drawings, is deeply imbued with a sense of the landscape of southern Sweden, in particular the wetlands close to his home at Lomma near Malmö, and, since 1956, the landscape and motifs of the Basque Pyrenees and Charente-Maritime in France which he has visited on an almost annual basis. Proximity to the sea is something which he regards as essential to his imagery and sense of affinity for a locale.

The British Museum owns three lithographs by Gunnar Norrman, two of which were presented by the artist in 1952, nine drypoints and one charcoal drawing (*Evening by the river, Fontaine de Vaucluse*, 1989), purchased directly from the artist in 1991.

Bibliography

Gunnar Norrman has had a number of substantial exhibitions, including two retrospectives in Malmö. The most

46

informative of the catalogues is that for Malmö Konsthall and Galerie Leger, *Gunnar Norrman: Drypoints 1959–1982* (1982) with an introductory text in Swedish, German and English. Professor Sten Åke Nilsson of the University of Lund has written an equally valuable monograph, *Gunnar Norrman: Drawings and graphic work* (Malmö, 1987), with a checklist of the prints and a parallel Swedish and English text.

44 *Meadowsweet and cabbage thistle*, 1950

Lithograph. Signed and dated in pencil, inscribed 'orig.lito' and numbered 16/20.
284 × 185 mm

1952-1-26-6. Presented by the artist

Norrman's studies of Scanian wildlife have often been taken from the claypits at Lomma and the wetlands of that area. Between 1947 and 1959 he made at least twelve lithographs, ten of which (but not this one) are described and illustrated in Nilsson's book. As stated above, two of the British Museum's three lithographs, including *Meadowsweet* (the other is titled *Winterwind*, 1950), were presented by the artist in 1952 in gratitude for kindness shown to him

by Print Room staff on his visit to London in July 1949 when, among other services, someone apparently lent him an etching needle. The third lithograph, dated 1947, came from Campbell Dodgson's collection and was presented by his widow in 1953.

45 *Herring smoke-house*, 1962

Drypoint. Signed and dated in pencil, inscribed with title and numbered 8/12. 173 × 255 mm

1991-6-15-184. Purchased from the Rausing Fund

46 *Evening silhouette*, 1969

Drypoint. Signed and dated in pencil, inscribed with title and numbered 16/20. 120 × 148 mm

1991-6-15-186. Purchased from the Rausing Fund

47 *Squirreltail grass I*, 1973

Drypoint. Signed and dated in pencil, inscribed with title and numbered 14/15. 245 × 172 mm

1991-6-15-188. Purchased from the Rausing Fund

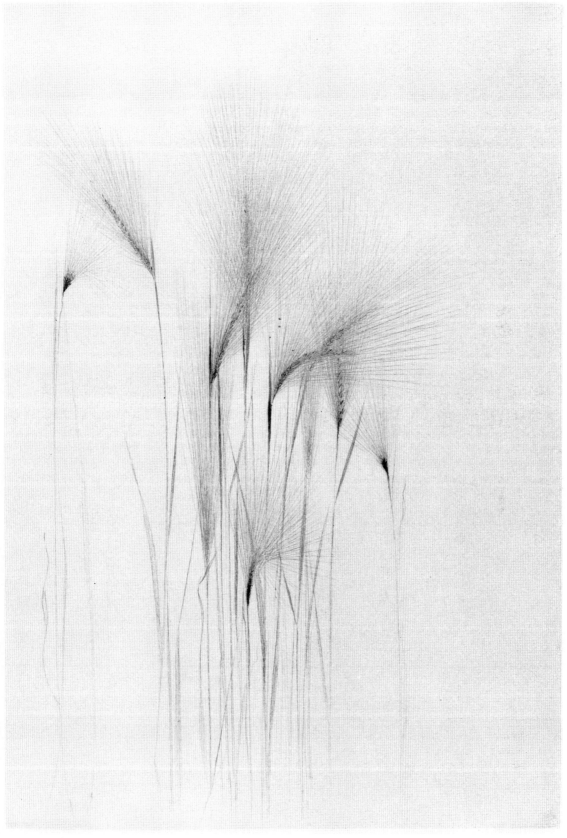

47

Edvard Munch (1863–1944)

Munch is the most famous of all Scandinavian artists. His resonance as a printmaker was in many ways greater abroad than in his native country, but Norwegian financial and critical support was none the less crucial to his career. The son of a doctor in Christiania (now Oslo), he enrolled as an engineering student in accordance with his father's wishes but soon abandoned this in 1880 to become an artist. Through his friendship with the realist painter Christian Krogh he was introduced to a circle of radical artists and intellectuals which gave him a network of contacts elsewhere in Europe. In 1886 he completed the three paintings that established his credentials as an original talent in terms of both imagery and mode of expression: the first version of *The sick child*, *The day after* and *Puberty*. His first one-man show in April 1889, consisting of more than sixty paintings and forty drawings, elicited a clutch of testimonials pressing his claim to state support for study abroad. From the autumn of 1889 until 1892 he spent much of his time in Paris and again from 1896 to 1897; apart from summer visits to Norway and some longer periods from 1897 to 1901 his main base for nearly sixteen years was otherwise Berlin, until his nervous breakdown in Copenhagen in 1908 and return to his native country the following year. His most significant work as a printmaker, which began in 1894, was accomplished during this period, prompted by the presence of the requisite markets and expertise in Berlin and Paris. Between 1894 and 1896 Munch familiarised himself with the main techniques of printmaking, displaying an immediate originality in his grasp of their expressive possibilities even though his motifs were closely allied to his paintings. He was more ambitious with his earliest lithographs (see cat. 51) than he was with the etchings (see cat. 48), both of which were shown for the first time in 1895, in Berlin in March and at Blomqvist in Christiania in October as an adjunct to his paintings. The latter exhibition, which included the prints from the Meier-Graefe portfolio (see cats. 48–50), attracted hostility but some critics rallied to his defence, even calling upon the Nasjonalgalleriet to acquire all of the graphic work as well as some of the paintings, while Thadée Natanson, the editor of *La Revue Blanche*, published a favourable review in the November 1895 issue, reproducing the lithographic version of *The scream* the following month.

By September 1897, when sixty-five of Munch's prints were included in a major exhibition at the Diorama in his home town, his graphic intentions had begun to take shape in his mind in the form of a series to be known as *The mirror*; this in turn was a reflection of the group of paintings, first shown collectively in 1895 under the title of *Love*, which underwent many revisions and additions, eventually to be subsumed within the title *The frieze of life*. The Nasjonalgalleriet in Christiania, which had braved the controversy caused by the 1895 exhibition at Blomqvist to buy Munch's

painting *Self-portrait with a cigarette*, made its first purchase of Munch's prints in 1898, and continued to support his painting and printmaking; then in 1902 sixty of the prints were sold to the University Library. Other early patrons in Norway included a factory owner, Olaf Schou (1861–1925), who gave his entire collection to the Nasjonalgalleriet from 1909 onwards; another was the businessman Halfdan Roede (1877–1963), who was described in 1912 as having a house lined with Munch's prints (see *Edvard Munch/Gustav Schiefler Briefwechsel*, vol. I, p. 423), and there were several others, most notably Rasmus Meyer (1858–1916) in Bergen and Ernst Thiel of Stockholm (see p. 15), whose substantial collections of prints were put together before the First World War. However, the principal market for Munch was in Germany, where he not only fired the enthusiasm of young artists such as the members of *Die Brücke* but attracted a very dedicated clientèle. Of approximately 750 prints that he made overall, a large portion were printed in Germany by Sabo, Angerer and Felsing for intaglio work and Lassally for lithography and woodcuts. In 1901 a further purchase of two of his paintings by the Nasjonalgalleriet in Christiania enabled Munch to return to Berlin, where he had many of his plates, stones and blocks shipped from Norway in order to run off larger editions, because he saw the prints as a source of steady income. Prominent among his patrons was the industrialist and politician Walter Rathenau (later assassinated in 1922) and a number of collectors from north Germany, including Albert Kollmann, a dealer, and the Lübeck doctor Max Linde, who first met Munch through Kollmann in 1902, published a book on him, *Edvard Munch und die Kunst der Zukunft*, in the same year, and commissioned a series of fourteen new etchings and two lithographs; Linde's father-in-law, the Hamburg senator Gottfried Holthusen, also acquired paintings and prints from the artist. Another important new acquaintance for Munch in 1902 was the Hamburg judge Gustav Schiefler, who in his diary for 11 October records his first encounter with Munch's prints at Linde's home: 'These etchings have subjects that arouse the most profound emotions of the heart; they move me particularly through their composition and line. It is the most powerful, I can truly say the most exciting impression that I have experienced from works of contemporary art' (*Munch/ Schiefler Briefwechsel*, vol. I, p. 37).

Schiefler decided in 1904 to take on the task of cataloguing Munch's prints, a task that he performed for several contemporary artists – Max Liebermann, Emil Nolde and E. L. Kirchner, for example – but none of his other subjects required quite the same degree of patience and tenacity as did Munch. Schiefler's accounts of his discussions with Munch in the course of the preparation of the catalogue, of which the first volume appeared in 1907 and the second in 1927, provide some of the most telling insights into the artist's character and also into the demands made upon the cataloguer, who might well have recalled Hamlet's injunction to Horatio to 'absent thee from felicity awhile, And in this harsh world draw thy breath in pain, To tell my story'. Much of the correspondence between the two concerns the marketing of the prints, which was of paramount concern to Munch. In 1904 he entered into a three-year agreement with the Berlin dealer Bruno Cassirer, to whom he assigned control over the sale of his prints in Germany, but within a year he was dissatisfied with the arrangement, complaining that Cassirer was not doing enough. Two important sales of prints to collectors in Scandinavia, Ernst Thiel and Rasmus Meyer, which were not subject to Cassirer's monopoly, enabled Munch to buy his way out of the contract in 1907, while the publication of Schiefler's *catalogue raisonné* made it easier for Munch to arrange the promotion of his prints himself. In 1908 alone, Munch refers to writing to propose exhibitions of his prints to Mannheim, Cologne, Hagen, Coblenz, Düsseldorf, Bremen, Karlsruhe, Wiesbaden, Essen, Jena, Leipzig, Basel and Stuttgart, and a high proportion of these came to fruition. He paid close attention to the pricing of his prints to ensure that certain levels were safeguarded, and keenly analysed the commercial outcome of his exhibitions. The relative lack of success of one held at the Kunstsalon Louis Bock in Hamburg in June 1908 he attributed partly to the fact that no prices had been advertised for the individual prints: 'People make up their minds more readily with prints if they can see the price' (*Munch/Schiefler Briefwechsel*, vol. I, p. 286). Contemporary photographs make it clear that Munch often had his prints displayed unframed: this prompted Max Linde in 1903 to recommend a better presentation in order to enhance their effect (Prelinger, *Edvard Munch: Master printmaker*, p. 111).

The spate of exhibitions continued undiminished after Munch's return to Norway in 1909, with Schiefler acting as the coordinator in Germany, particularly after the death in 1915 of Kollmann, who had previously assumed this role. A new generation of collectors came to the fore, including Curt Glaser, the art historian and curator of modern prints at the Berlin Print Room until 1926, then director of the Kunstbibliothek until 1933; he was the driving force behind the fine Munch collection held by the former institution, amounting to 230 sheets by 1933, as well as forming a considerable private collection of his own which was sold in 1933. Other patrons were dealers such as Hugo Perls, Ludwig Gutbier (who ran the Galerie Ernst Arnold in Dresden and Breslau), J.B. Neumann of the Graphisches Kabinett in Berlin and the business tycoon Heinrich Stinnes, whose massive print collection of 200,000 items was dispersed over three years after his death in 1932. From 1913 the market spread further afield with eight of Munch's prints being included in the Armory Show in New York, followed in 1919 by an exhibition of fifty-seven prints at the Bourgeois Galleries, also in New York. The home market became correspondingly more important after the outbreak of war because Scandinavian neutrality created the conditions for a financial boom, particularly in shipping, and record prices were fetched by Munch's work between 1916 and 1920 when the lithograph of *The sick girl* (1896) sold for 4000 kroner. One of the youngest Norwegian collectors was Rolf Stenersen (1899–1978), a stockbroker and son of a publisher of hymnbooks, who bought his first pictures in 1918 from profits made on the stock market. By 1921 he owned eighteen of Munch's prints, the number rising to four hundred by the time he presented the collection to the municipality of Oslo in 1936 (they are now kept with the rest of his collection in the museum named after Stenersen that was opened in 1994 in the centre of Oslo).

Between Munch's return to Norway in 1909 and the outbreak of the First World War the demand for his prints was such that Felsing and Lassally in Berlin were required to pull new impressions without his supervision, often with correspondingly inferior results. Schiefler, among his many services to Munch, was responsible at first for obtaining the materials Munch needed, for example etching and aquatint ground and copper and zinc plates in October 1912; Munch was also keen to acquire an intaglio press, for which Schiefler consulted Erich Heckel in Berlin (*Munch/Schiefler Briefwechsel*, vol. I, pp. 592 and 595), recommending the purchase of one from Krause in Leipzig. During the war Munch had his woodblocks and lithographic stones sent back from Germany and in 1916, when he acquired his house at Ekely, he set up a press in the cellar where he printed new impressions and transferred earlier drawings to stone with the assistance of a lithographer, Peder Anton Nielsen. This renewed his interest in printmaking in general, which he continued through the 1920s and 1930s, but there was a noticeable diminution in intensity and it did not play the same economic role after the collapse of the German market in the aftermath of the First World War. His own interests had in any case shifted towards large public works of art, starting with his murals for the Aula at Oslo University which were accepted in 1914. At his death in January 1944 Munch bequeathed to the city of Oslo 1008 paintings, 4443 drawings and 15,391 prints with permission to sell ten copies of each of his later graphic works.

Bibliography
There have been several biographies of Munch, including one published in 1932 by Pola Gauguin (1883–1961), son of Paul and art critic for the main Oslo newspaper, *Dagbladet*; he also wrote on Munch's prints. Munch reputedly preferred Gauguin's book to that written in 1933 by Jens Thiis, Director of the Nasjonalgalleriet (1909–41), because it was 'written by a painter'. Rolf Stenersen, *Edvard Munch: Close-up of a genius*, first published in Stockholm, 1944 (Oslo, 1945, translated into English by Reidar Dittmann, Oslo, 1969), is interesting for the information it provides on the market for Munch's work, written from the perspective of a man who was a collector and the artist's financial adviser.

The standard biography, however, is Reinhold Heller, *Munch: His life and work* (London, 1984).

There is no catalogue of Munch's paintings, and that of the prints by Gustav Schiefler, *Verzeichnis des graphischen Werkes Edvard Munchs*, vol. I (up to 1906) (Berlin, 1907) and vol. II (1906–26) (Berlin, 1927), is very out of date. Sigurd Willoch's *Edvard Munch: Etchings* (Oslo, 1950) is useful for this aspect of his printmaking. A new *catalogue raisonné* of Munch's prints by Gerd Woll of the Munch Museum in Oslo is in preparation; I am grateful to her for supplying me with drafts of the entries relevant to the prints in the British Museum and for providing careful assistance with the text for my catalogue. Munch's correspondence with Schiefler, *Edvard Munch/Gustav Schiefler Briefwechsel*, 2 vols, ed. Arne Eggum (Hamburg, 1987), is an invaluable quarry for information which goes beyond the details of their relationship, including a full list of Munch's exhibitions from 1903 to 1943. Two important critical studies are *Edvard Munch: Symbols and images* (National Gallery of Art, Washington, DC, 1978) and Elizabeth Prelinger, *Edvard Munch: Master printmaker* (New York, 1983), which, apart from a thorough discussion of his printmaking techniques, incorporates information on his print production into the chronology adapted from Johan Langaard and Reidar Revold, *A Year by Year Record of Edvard Munch* (Oslo, 1961). Sarah Epstein's *The Prints of Edvard Munch: Mirror of his life* (Allen Memorial Art Museum, Oberlin, Ohio, 1983) provides an account of Munch's printmaking from beginning to end. Some of the prints described below were published in the British Museum's exhibition catalogue by Frances Carey and Antony Griffiths, *Printmaking in Germany 1880–1933* (London, 1984, reprinted 1993). The major prints in the British Museum's collection not mentioned below are the lithograph *Jealousy* (1896, the large version, Sch.58), the woodcut *The old fisherman* (1899, Sch.124) and *Vampire* (1902, Sch.34), a combination of woodcut and lithography.

Of the more recent catalogues three important ones are *Munch et la France* (Musée d'Orsay, Paris, 1992), with an essay by Gerd Woll on the prints, *Edvard Munch: The Frieze of Life*, ed. Mara-Helen Wood (The National Gallery, London, 1992) and *Munch und Deutschland* (National Gallery Berlin, Stuttgart, 1994), which contains another essay on the relevant aspects of Munch's printmaking by Gerd Woll, who has published a catalogue for the Munch Museum, *Edvard Munch 1895: First year as a graphic artist* (Oslo, 1995) with text in Norwegian and English.

48 *The sick child*, 1894

Drypoint. Signed and annotated '10' in pencil. Printed on Japan paper. One of ten impressions printed by Angerer before steel-facing from the Meier-Graefe portfolio. 390 × 293 mm

Sch.7, fifth state b

1949-4-11-4792. Bequeathed by Campbell Dodgson

Some of Munch's most powerful images of the 1880s and 1890s were rooted in the traumas of his childhood and the deaths from tuberculosis of first his mother when he was four, then his nearest sibling, Sophie, in 1877. He painted four versions of the composition on which this print is based as well as executing another closely related etching, *The head of the sick child*, and a colour lithograph, *The sick girl*, in 1896. The first of the paintings, which was the model for the etching of 1894, was exhibited in 1886 with the title *Study* and remained of particular significance to Munch, despite his successive repetitions; when the Nasjonalgalleriet in 1931 wanted to sell the second version, dated 1896, in order to raise the money for the original one, Munch wrote to the owner, the lawyer Harald Nörrgård: 'I am certain you will understand me when I think that my first sick child ought to go to the National Gallery – It is perhaps my most important picture and at any rate my breakthrough into expressionistic painting' (Arne Eggum in *Edvard Munch: Symbols and images*, p. 152).

By the end of 1894 Munch's financial position in Berlin was apparently verging on destitution, which may have provided the impetus for him to try his hand at printmaking as a way of finding a wider currency for his work. In a letter to his aunt written at this time, Munch referred to having begun to work with prints 'with the possibility of publishing a small collection – intaglio prints' (Gerd Woll, *Edvard Munch 1895*, p.9), while Eberhard von Bodenhausen, a member of the literary and artistic association subsequently responsible for the magazine *Pan*, commented: 'It seems to me that printmaking is your true domain and I have no doubt that pecuniary results will come when you achieve even greater technical perfection' (*ibid.*, p. 14). The 'small collection' materialised in June 1895 in the form of a portfolio of eight prints, all but one of which were restatements of earlier paintings, published at the expense of the critic Julius Meier-Graefe (1867–1915), who wrote the introduction. The British Museum's impression of *The sick child* purchased by Campbell Dodgson in August 1911 from J.B. Neumann's Graphisches Kabinett in Berlin for 180 marks, together with *The girl at the window* (1894, Sch. 5), for 80 marks and *Dr Max Asch* (1895) (cat. 49) for 100 marks, came from the same copy of the set of ten printed on Japan paper, which was followed by an edition of fifty-five on wove paper printed in brown ink after the plates had been steel-faced; the remaining subjects were: *The lonely ones, Moonlight night in St Cloud, Tete-à-tete, Christiania Bohème* and *The day after* (cat. 50).

The prints in the Meier-Graefe portfolio represented what

would now be called a 'learning curve' for Munch in terms of his induction into the various intaglio techniques; four were done in pure drypoint and the remaining four in combinations of etching and drypoint, etching and aquatint, and drypoint and aquatint. They all went through several states, which in the case of *The sick child* amounted to six (including two not described by Schiefler). The landscape, which does not appear in any of the painted versions, first occurred like an elaborate remarque in the third state; then much later, after the publication of the portfolio, in the sixth and final state the plate was cut down to eliminate the space for the landscape altogether. Despite the valuable experience gained through this group of prints, Munch did not really build upon it to any great extent as far as intaglio printmaking was concerned, because lithography captured his imagination as a more flexible medium. Neither was the portfolio a commercial success: its sales were perhaps partly inhibited by Meier-Graefe's insistence that it must remain as a single entity. The market for original prints in Germany was only in its infancy at this time, when even established artists such as Max Liebermann met with no great result until the turn of the century. Thereafter the situation changed; 1901/2 was a watershed for Munch, when the

sales of his prints really gained momentum, and Schiefler estimated that they brought him an income of four to five thousand marks a year between 1902 and 1904.

49 *Dr Max Asch*, 1895

Drypoint. Signed and annotated '10' in pencil. Printed on Japan paper. One of only ten impressions prior to steel-facing, from the Meier-Graefe portfolio. 267 × 189 mm

Sch.27.II

1949-4-11-4790. Bequeathed by Campbell Dodgson

Dr Asch was a Berlin gynaecologist and patron of modern art who introduced Munch to Stanislaw Przybyszewski (1868–1927), a former medical student who became one of the most controversial figures in the bohemian life of Berlin. After writing an essay 'On the Psychology of the Individual' in 1892, Przybyszewski went on in 1894, to be one of four authors (together with Meier-Graefe, Franz Servaes and Willy Pastor) of the first study on Munch. (For a discussion of the literary and artistic environment inhabited by Munch in Berlin in the 1890s see Carla Lathe, 'Edvard

49

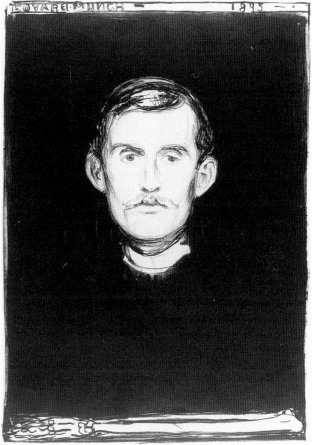

51

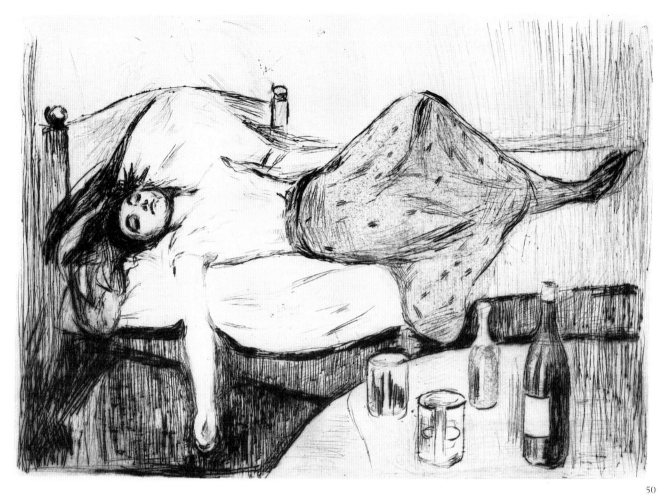

50

Munch and Modernism in Berlin 1892–1903', *The Frieze of Life*, pp. 38–44).

According to Gerd Woll there are three states of this portrait done from life, the only one of the Meier-Graefe plates not to be derived from an earlier painting.

50 *The day after*, 1895

Drypoint and aquatint. Printed on buff paper by Angerer for the ordinary edition of the Meier-Graefe portfolio.
210 × 285 mm

Sch.15

1982-7-24-1. Purchased

The contrast in texture between this impression and the two preceding examples from the Meier-Graefe portfolio demonstrates the superior quality of printing prior to the steel-facing of the plates. The original version of the painting of this motif was exhibited in 1886, then destroyed by fire; a second version shown in Berlin in 1892 is now lost, but the surviving example of 1894/5 is in the Nasjonalgalleriet, Oslo.

51 *Self-portrait with skeleton arm*, 1895

Lithograph printed on off-white wove paper. Signed and dated in pencil and inscribed 'No 11', with figure of '350-' below.
456 × 320 mm

Sch.31,1

1949-4-11-4872. Bequeathed by Campbell Dodgson

From the outset Munch achieved a freedom of expression through black and white lithography which was to make it his preferred graphic medium for the rest of his career. Gerd Woll identifies twelve subjects as having been executed in Berlin, prior to his move to Paris from February 1896 to April 1897 where he had access to the facilities of Auguste Clot's workshop and the added advantage of a sophisticated interest among artistic circles in original lithography. Berlin could not offer the same stimulus, but the lithographs he made there showed considerable daring and mastery in his use of the medium, working directly on the stone, although later he practised transfer lithography as well. The subjects included *Vampire I*, *The scream*, *Madonna* and this haunting and subversive form of self-portraiture; Munch's insertion of his name and the date into the main composition has been compared with Vallotton's similar positioning of his titles within his woodcuts and lithographs. The skeleton arm introduces a more sinister dimension which had previously appeared in an unfinished portrait of Stanislaw Przybyszewski of about 1894 (see *The Frieze of Life*, cat. 76, p. 120), to be compared as well with the foetus and spermatozoa framing Munch's *Madonna* of 1895. *Self-portrait with skeleton arm* is now known in four states, of which the version here is the second (according to Gerd Woll there is only one impression of the recently identified first state). It was reprinted in 1913 by Lassally, with the upper and lower borders containing the artist's name, date and the skeleton arm painted over, then probably transferred to a new stone before being printed again in Norway about 1916.

The British Museum's impression was purchased by Campbell Dodgson from Ernst Arnold in Dresden for the equivalent of £20 in July 1921. The exact number printed is not known, but Gerd Woll's draft entry notes that other examples in Bremen and in the Nasjonalgalleriet, Oslo are numbered '33' and '41'.

52 *Melancholy (On the beach; Evening)*, 1901

First version 1896; Sch.82. Woodcut printed in grey, beige, blue and black on thin Japan paper from two blocks, one sawn into three sections. Signed in pencil. 374 × 470 mm

Sch.144

1980-12-13-19. Purchased

Munch's stay in Paris from 1896 to 1897 was an intensely productive one, which fired his interest in new techniques including woodcut and colour printing. Within the latter context his early woodcuts were developed as planar, pictorial compositions using a jigsaw-puzzle method for simultaneous printing in different colours; Munch experimented

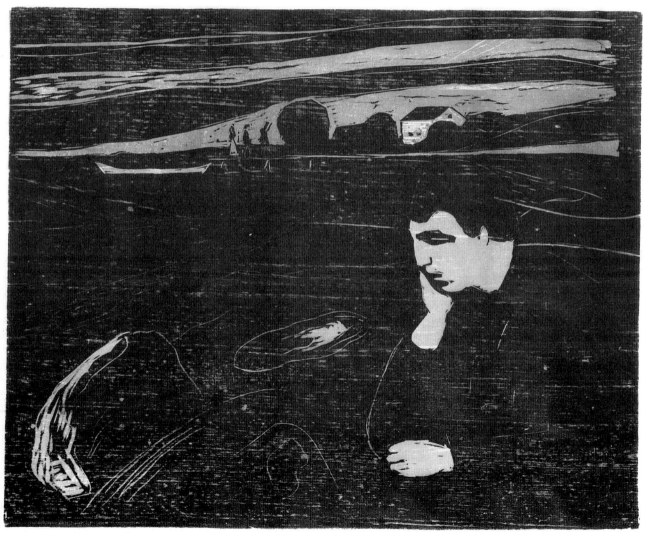

52

53

with a huge variety of colour combinations, thereby often varying the mood of his compositions from one impression to another. His later black and white woodcuts were more consciously sculptural images which had a greater influence on the development of Expressionist printmaking.

Melancholy was one of Munch's favourite compositions which he included among the twenty-five prints exhibited as *The mirror* at the Diorama in 1897. It was derived from a painting of 1891/2 by Munch called *Jealousy* but now known as *Melancholy* or *The yellow boat* (in the Nasjonalgalleriet, Oslo; an early version of the composition belonging to a private collection is on loan to the National Gallery in London). It was the subject of a famous article by Christian Krohg called 'Thank You for the Yellow Boat' (*Dagbladet*, 27 November 1891) in which he described the resonance of its colour and declared that, because it bordered on music more than on painting, Munch deserved a civil list grant as a composer. Krogh himself appeared in the painting with his wife Oda as the people on the pier in the

background, while the Norwegian writer and critic Jappe Nilssen (1870-1931), who was in love with Oda, was cast as the brooding figure in the foreground. The British Museum's impression of the second version of the woodcut formerly belonged to Nilssen, who left it to his sister, Mrs Thorolf Holmboe; it then passed to her daughter Erna, who eventually sold it to the Museum; an inscription on the backboard reads 'to Erna from Mama according to Jappe's wishes'.

Gerd Woll believes that Munch may have cut the second version of *Melancholy* in 1901 because he feared the loss of the original block in the confusion over a trunk missing from the shipment he requested of his materials from Norway to Berlin, where he was again living at the time (his fears were unjustified, for the blocks in question had merely been omitted). Munch used the opportunity to vary the woodcut image so that it more closely reflected the painting than did the first version; the 1901 print is in the same direction as the painting, whereas the earlier one was in reverse, and it includes the figures on the pier in the background. In 1914 further impressions were pulled from the blocks for the 1896 version, which were inked in such a way as to suppress the shoreline apparent in the earlier woodcuts.

53 *Delius at Wiesbaden*, 1920

Lithograph printed on white wove paper. Signed in pencil on verso and annotated 'No. 1 29/8 – 22'. 253 × 403 mm

Sch.498

1936-11-28-7. Presented by the artist

Munch first met the composer Frederick Delius (1862–1934) in Paris in the early 1890s and they remained friends until the latter's death. Though he was born in Yorkshire, Delius came from a German émigré background and spent his adult life almost entirely outside England. He developed a lifelong enthusiasm for the Norwegian landscape from his first visit in 1892 and became deeply involved with Scandinavian culture from the late 1880s onwards, when he met Grieg at the Leipzig Conservatory. In 1888 he settled permanently in France, living in or near Paris where he formed close links with many of the Scandinavian writers, musicians and artists who passed through. Among these were the writer and critic Jappe Nilssen and the painter Jelka Rosen, who introduced him to the artists' colony at Grèz-sur-Loing and whom he married in 1903. Delius and Rosen were important allies for Munch in Paris during the early 1900s, offering practical advice and assistance in arranging the exhibition of his work. It was also a period when both Munch and Delius were keenly interested in the writings of Nietzsche (1844–1900), with the latter composing *A Mass of Life* based on *Thus Spake Zarathustra* in 1904/5 and Munch executing a portrait of the philosopher in 1906 as a commission for his Swedish patron Ernst Thiel.

By the early 1920s Delius was suffering the consequences of a syphilitic infection contracted many years earlier, which was shortly to render him blind and paralysed for the rest of his life. In April 1922 Munch visited Wiesbaden where Delius was taking a cure, and executed the portrait catalogued here of the composer attending an open-air concert. Two other drawings in lithographic crayon related to this portrait are in the Munch Museum, where the stone also survives. *Delius at Wiesbaden* was one of four lithographs Munch submitted to the first exhibition of the Norske Grafikeres (Society of Norwegian Printmakers) at Blomqvist in Oslo in 1922. (For further information on Delius and his relations with Munch see Lionel Carley and Robert Threlfall, *Delius: A life in pictures* (Oxford, 1977) and *Frederick Delius og Edvard Munch* (Munch Museum, Oslo, 1979), with text in Norwegian and English.)

The British Museum's impression was one of two lithographs presented by the artist in 1936 at the time of his first one-man show at the London Gallery, with an introduction by Herbert Read; the other subject was *Farm girl*

(Sch. 508) and there were two publications, the catalogue of the exhibition itself and Johan Langaard's book on Munch of 1932 for the Nasjonalgalleriet in Oslo. Munch's work was far less well known in Britain than on the Continent, and it was not until the Tate Gallery exhibition of 1950 that it achieved a major public impact. Otherwise, apart from the 1936 exhibition, some of Munch's paintings were shown in London and Edinburgh in 1928 and 1932; the first example to be acquired by a British public collection was a version of *The sick girl* presented to the Tate Gallery in 1939 by the Norwegian shipowner Thomas Olsen. (On Munch's contacts with Britain, including evidence of a brief visit in 1913, see Carla Lathe, 'Edvard Munch and Great Britain', *Scandinavia*, XXXIV, 2 (November 1995), pp. 211–20.)

Gustav Vigeland (1869–1943)

Vigeland, Norway's most famous sculptor, is commemorated by a museum and adjacent park at Frogner in Oslo which bears his name and contains 192 of his sculptures. The death of his father, who had been a master-carpenter with a furniture workshop, when Vigeland was seventeen made it difficult for him to afford the training necessary to become a sculptor, but his talent was quickly recognised after he exhibited in Christiania in 1889. He received scholarships which enabled him to travel extensively in Europe during the 1890s, visiting Rodin, who was to be the single most important influence upon him, in Paris in 1893. The following year he was in Berlin where he encountered Munch and other members of his immediate circle, including Stanislaw Przybyszewski, who wrote the first monograph on Vigeland entitled *Auf den Wegen der Seele* (The Path of the Soul).

Vigeland returned to Norway to take on numerous public commissions, working with carved stone and in cast bronze. In 1906 he presented his proposal for the monumental fountain which eventually became one of the groups of statuary to be incorporated into the sculpture park at Frogner; it achieved support as an official project from the municipality of Oslo in 1924 at the same time that Vigeland moved into the studio built for him at the city's expense, according to his express stipulation that after his death it should become a museum (Munch was reputedly angry at the lavishness of municipal support for the sculptor when compared with that for himself). From 1924 to 1943 he was constantly engaged in modelling new sculptures, which were executed by studio assistants, for the elaborate scheme for the park symbolising the life-cycle of man. At his death in 1943 he left 1600 sculptures, 12,000 drawings and 420 woodcuts.

Vigeland was accustomed to wood-carving from his youth, but his first woodcut prints were not executed until 1914/15 when a number of factors helped to focus his mind on the medium. At the Blaue Reiter exhibition at

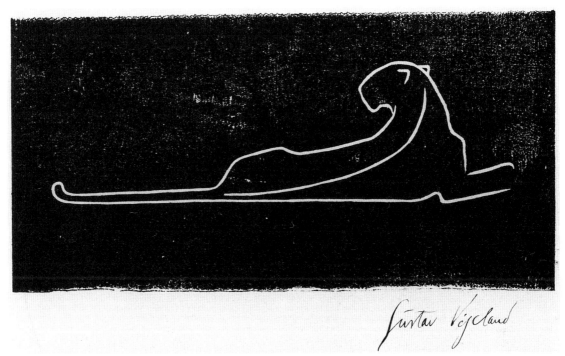

54

55

Blomqvist's gallery in Christiania and again at the Baltic exhibition in Malmö in 1914 he saw examples by the German Expressionist artists. Munch's woodcuts were shown at Tivoli in 1914 and clearly made an impact, although Vigeland later disparaged them, together with the woodcuts of Nolde, as 'amateurish' and cheating in their effects. In the same year the French periodical *L'Art et les Artistes* published an article on the woodcut illustrations for Virgil by the sculptor Maillol.

In April 1917 Vigeland exhibited his first group of fifty-seven woodcuts at the Kunstnerforbundet, where he made a substantial profit on their sale. The greater part of them were white-line compositions on a black background based on drawings of zoological motifs that Vigeland had made at the beginning of the century while travelling on the Continent. Others were compositions of figures wrestling or of motifs inspired by his work from 1897 to 1902 on the restoration of Trondheim Cathedral, where he worked on sculptures for the choir and gargoyles for the towers. Vigeland continued to find a successful outlet for his woodcuts, selling them directly from his studio, where 131 were last exhibited in 1932, as well as through dealers. The uniform shape of most of his woodcuts was determined by the traditional Scandinavian birch breadboards on which they were carved, now on display in the Vigeland Museum.

Twelve of the British Museum's group of thirteen woodcuts were the outcome of a personal visit paid by Laurence Binyon, then Deputy Keeper in charge of the Oriental subsection of the Department of Prints and Drawings at the British Museum and an authority on Japanese prints, to Vigeland's studio in 1924. He had seen the woodcuts at the home in Vettakollen, Oslo, of Andrea Butenschøn, who had introduced Vigeland to the Indian writer Rabindranath Tagore, winner of the Nobel Prize for Literature in 1913.

Bibliography

The principal monograph containing a full bibliography is that by the curator of the Vigeland Museum, Tone Wikborg: *Gustav Vigeland* (Oslo, 1983), followed by *Gustav Vigeland: His art and sculpture park* (Oslo, 1990). A more detailed account of his prints can be found in Gerd Hennum, *Gustav Vigeland i Svart og Hvitt* (Oslo, 1985) and in Tone Wikborg's most recent publication, *Gustav Vigeland: Woodcuts* (Oslo, 1996).

54 *Seated leopard*, 1915–17

Woodcut. Signed in ink. 100 × 201 mm

1924-5-28-17. Presented by Sir Karl Knudsen

The woodcut, based on a pen and ink drawing from life, was made either in Paris or in London in 1900/1, and was one of the subjects shown at the Kunstnerforbundet in 1917. Two of the other subjects from the British Museum's group, including one of a lion, are inscribed with dedications to Binyon. Karl Knudsen was a Norwegian banker living in London, a director of the British Bank of Northern Commerce which merged with Hambros in 1920.

55 *Bison*, 1915–17

Woodcut. Signed in ink. 144 × 204 mm

1924-9-8-3. Presented by Laurence Binyon

One contemporary who interviewed Vigeland in 1921 wrote: 'When Vigeland is abroad he first visits the art museums, then the zoological gardens in order to study the animals. He is more at home among animals, which are spontaneous, than among people' (Wikborg, *Gustav Vigeland: Woodcuts*, p. 39).

Roald Kristian (1893–*c*.1918)

Kristian was born Edgar de Bergen in Norway, but there are few verifiable facts about his life and no firm date for his death. In Paris he met the British artist Nina Hamnett (1890–1956), who brought him to England as her lover after the outbreak of war. They were married in October 1914, and de Bergen adopted the name Roald Kristian because it sounded less German. He immediately became involved in the Omega Workshops set up by Roger Fry in March 1913 at 33 Fitzroy Square in London, where in January 1915 Kristian staged a puppet performance of Debussy's *Boîte à Joujoux*. His woodcuts of animals and portrait heads of contemporary poets and writers were exhibited in June of the same year and included in the Omega publications, which were produced under the direction of a commercial printer, Richard Madley. These began with *Simpson's Choice* (1915), a poem by Arthur Clutton-Brock illustrated with three full-page woodcuts, followed by *Men of Europe* (also in 1915), Roger Fry's translation of a poem by Pierre-Jean Jouve; in 1917 *Lucretius on Death*, translated by Robert Trevelyan, appeared and finally *Original Woodcuts by Various Artists* (1918), containing fourteen individual woodcuts by the principal adherents of the Workshops led by Roger Fry – Vanessa Bell, Duncan Grant and Roald Kristian among others. By this stage Kristian had vanished from sight, having been deported to a detention camp in France three months after his arrest in April 1917 for being an unregistered alien. Sickert, who painted Hamnett and Kristian, talked of his 'acute and informed intelligence', but the marriage soon disintegrated under the pressure of poverty and she made no attempt to trace him after his letters petered out in 1918.

Bibliography

The little published information available can be found in Judith Collins, *The Omega Workshops* (London, 1983); Denise Hooker, *Nina Hamnett: Queen of Bohemia* (London, 1986) and Frances Carey and Antony Griffiths, *Avant-Garde British Printmaking 1914–1960* (London, 1990), pp. 48–9.

56 (I)

57 (I)

56 (II)

57 (II)

56 *Leaping deer* and *Stag*, 1916

Woodcuts. Signed in pencil. 76 × 115 mm and 76 × 122 mm
1916-9-15-1,2. Presented by the artist

57 *Cow* and *Horse grazing*, 1916

Woodcuts. Signed in pencil. 76 × 115 mm and 108 × 153 mm
1916-9-15-3,4. Presented by the artist

These two sheets, presented by the artist to the British
Museum in September 1916, are proofs printed on Japan
paper for woodcuts published in the first issue of *Form*, a
magazine that appeared only in 1916 and 1917. Three of the
blocks (not *Cow*) were used again for *A Bestiary by Roald
Kristian* printed by Jean Varda and John Rodker, with a
colophon by Edward Wadsworth, and published in 1920 by
the Ovid Press in an edition of 110; beneath the final woodcut in *The Bestiary* is printed the statement 'The Last of the
17 Blocks All Now Destroyed'. Kristian's artistic background is unknown, but his woodcuts evinced a very different sensibility from that of his Omega associates; they owe
more to the graphic style that emerged in Munich prior to
the First World War, represented by the work of Kandinsky
and the Blaue Reiter artists.

58

Harald Kihle (born 1905)

Kihle, who has worked as a painter and printmaker, studied at the School of Arts and Crafts in Oslo and at the Academy of Art under Axel Revold and Per Krohg in 1932/3, then under Marcel Gromaire in Paris in 1938. His prints were first shown in Oslo at the annual autumn exhibition in 1938. In his woodcuts (he also made lithographs from 1948 onwards) Kihle sought to create the effect of the texture and silvery-grey tone of a weather-beaten birch plank; the simple contours of his images often remained white against the grey background of the finished prints. Motifs of nude models and café and street scenes reflect his early Parisian experience but the great majority of his subjects are taken from the rural life of the Telemark region west of Oslo, and it is principally with a romanticised folk imagery that he has been associated.

Bibliography

The two books covering Kihle's prints contain full bibliographical details of other literature published on him prior to the early 1980s: *Harald Kihle Tresnitt* (Oslo, 1980) and *Harald Kihle: Litografier* (Oslo, 1982). Both were compiled by Grete Kobro and have brief summaries in English.

59

58 *Nude*, 1937

Woodcut. Signed and dated in pencil, inscribed with title and 'originaltresnitt. Nr 4 1/15'. 235 × 337 mm

1993-1-24-6. Purchased from the Rausing Fund

One of Kihle's earliest prints. Although the subject would appear to be indebted to his brief spell in Gromaire's studio in Paris in 1938, an inscription on the verso states that it was exhibited in Oslo in February of that year.

59 *Woman with a short scythe*, 1938

Woodcut. Signed and dated in pencil, inscribed with title and 'Tresnitt (handtrykk) nr.6 a.7'. 162 × 140 mm

1993-1-24-8. Purchased from the Rausing Fund

Kihle has sometimes printed impressions from the same block at different times; in this case, the one reproduced in Grete Kobro's book is dated 1940 and numbered '1 a 2'.

Jens Ferdinand Willumsen (1863–1958)

Willumsen was one of the most idiosyncratic of all Scandinavian artists. His early compositions in a realist vein give no hint of the vivid eclecticism that was to follow in his career as painter, printmaker, sculptor, architect, ceramicist, amateur photographer, artistic director of the main porcelain manufactory in Denmark, Bing & Grøndahl, from 1897 to 1900 and, latterly, a collector of work in all media from many different periods. In 1894 he articulated his position thus:

I think that within the natural limits of his field the artist is an inventor, a scientist, who invents new artistic means for the expression of his thought, and that like a philosophical scientist he busies himself with his thought, finds new sequences of ideas, wishes to say new truths that haven't been said before, wishes to find new combinations of form that have not been combined before, etc., etc. Like a public speaker the artist has an infinitude of means at his disposal, and each of the means he employs must be applied in such a way that they make his thought stronger. (quoted by Leila Krogh in *Fiction and Reality*, p. 25)

Although Willumsen's career spanned such a long period of time, the most creative part of it was concentrated between the late 1880s and the mid-1890s, when he played a central role in the relationship between Danish art and French post-Impressionism.

Willumsen was born the son of an innkeeper in Copenhagen, though he later believed his natural father to be the sculptor Jens Adolf Jerichau (1816–83), one of many instances in which he was to reinvent his past. From 1883 to 1885 he attended the Academy in Copenhagen, where he met Vilhelm Hammershøi (see p. 78). They became close friends and both studied under P. S. Krøyer at the indepen-dent Artists' Study School. The crucial period, as far as his contact with contemporary French art was concerned, was from November 1888 to the end of 1894 when he travelled back and forth between Copenhagen and Paris, where he maintained a studio from 1890 to 1894. In the same period he visited Brittany during the summer of 1890, the Jura and Haute-Savoie in 1891, Norway in 1892 and America in 1893 for the Chicago World's Fair. The impetus for his first visit to Paris came ostensibly from his admiration for the work of Raffaelli and Puvis de Chavannes, which he saw as part of an exhibition of French painting at the Kunstforening in Copenhagen; but the more important influence upon him was to be that of the Synthetists, which is immediately apparent in Willumsen's paintings, reliefs, prints and ceramics of 1890–3. Despite Willumsen's claims to the contrary, Gauguin must have had an impact upon him prior to their actual meeting in Brittany in the summer of 1890, through the latter's residence in Copenhagen in 1884/5 with his Danish wife, Mette Gad, and subsequently through the work that he both left behind and had exhibited there. More importantly, Willumsen would have been aware of the developments in Gauguin's style demonstrated by his first one-man show in Paris at the end of 1888 and again at the Café Volpini at the Exposition Universelle in Paris in 1889, which proclaimed the identity of a 'Groupe Impressioniste et Synthétiste'.

Willumsen hoped to cultivate his position as a professional artist in Paris as a means to gaining acceptance both there and in Denmark; in three successive years between 1891 and 1893 he exhibited paintings and ceramics at the Salon des Indépendants. One of the most striking examples of his eclecticism, the *Jotunheim relief* (J. F. Willumsen Museum), was shown at the Champs de Mars exhibition in 1893; executed after his visit in 1892 to the Norwegian mountain range associated with Norse mythology, the painted composition with an elaborate carved wooden frame represented a peculiarly Nordic interpretation of French Symbolism. At the same time in Copenhagen, Willumsen, together with Hammershøi, was one of the prime movers among the group of artists who set up Den Frie Udstilling (The Independent Exhibition) as a mark of protest against the official Academy exhibitions. Willumsen's etching *Fertility* (cat. 63) caused a sensation at the first exhibition held at Kleis's art gallery in 1891. He remained a constant and controversial participant until the end of his life, designing the permanent building – Copenhagen's counterpart to the Vienna Secession – into which the exhibition moved in 1898 from the temporary wooden structure it had occupied since 1893.

Willumsen returned to Copenhagen at the end of 1894 because the father of his first wife refused to subsidise his stay in Paris any longer, and he was based there until the First World War, when he settled in the south of France. His painting style underwent many changes in style and rendition, his startling colouristic effects reflecting a similarly exploratory interest in the glazes he used for his ceramic work. A new interest which he used to inform his painting and sculpture was photography, after he acquired a camera on his first visit to the United States in 1893. Although he spent the last forty years of his life in France, Willumsen did not participate in the mainstream of artistic activity there; he became increasingly preoccupied with the heroic status he felt he deserved, even casting himself as Titian in an astonishing triptych of 1936 called *The death of Titian*, and the perpetuation of this status through a museum devoted to the totality of his achievement. The latter finally materialised in 1957 at Frederikssund outside Copenhagen, housing, apart from examples of Willumsen's own work, an archive of documentary material and his collection of paintings, ceramics, textiles, sculpture, drawings and prints comprising almost two thousand items, including about two hundred Italian drawings acquired mainly in London between 1919 and 1928.

Willumsen's printmaking was done sporadically throughout his career, amounting to some ninety-seven etchings between 1886 and 1949, ninety-eight lithographs between 1910 and 1951, four lithographic posters of 1896–1902 and twenty-seven woodcuts between 1920 and 1946. By the end of 1891 his first and artistically most successful phase of printmaking was over: this consisted of ten

60

etchings of realist subjects done in 1886–8, then a further seven made in 1889–91 which were altogether more radical in their spatial composition and use of contemporary motifs. This latter group showed the same French influence apparent in his other work, but with one exception they were done in Copenhagen of local subjects. Willumsen did not return to etching until 1916, when he executed subjects prompted by wartime events such as *The martyrdom of Edith Cavell* and *Invasion*, working on a press he had installed in the south of France. His dramatic use of aquatint in many of the etchings of 1916–26, inspired by Goya's example, was one of several instances from 1910 onwards in which Spanish art – El Greco as well as Goya – influenced his painting and printmaking.

Bibliography

Willumsen's memoirs were published as J. F. Willumsen, *Mine Erindringer fortalt til Ernst Mentze* (Copenhagen, 1953). Shortly afterwards Merete Bodelson set the record straight about Willumsen's indebtedness to Gauguin in *Willumsen i halvfemsernes Paris* (Copenhagen, 1957, with a summary in English). Sigurd Schultz, who first wrote about Willumsen as a printmaker in 1943, published what remains the only *catalogue raisonné*, *Willumsens Grafik*, in Copenhagen in 1961 with a supplement in 1967. Most of the remaining bibliography can be found in the catalogue to the Willumsen Museum published in an English edition in 1996 by the present curator, Dr Leila Krogh, to whom I am indebted for reading a draft of my entries. Other publications of interest from the Museum include Chris Fischer's *Italian Drawings in the J. F. Willumsen Collection* (1984 and 1988) and Leila Krogh's *Fiction and Reality: J. F. Willumsen's photographs* (1995), both of which have been published in Danish and in English. Apart from the collection at Frederickssund, there is a private museum devoted to the preparatory studies of Willumsen belonging to Mr Victor Petersen at Odden in northern Jutland.

60 *Two women weaving*, 1887

Etching. Signed and dated within the plate. 168 × 125 mm
S.8
1989-5-13-61. Purchased

This is one of the small group of realist subjects showing the influence of the Danish artist Carl Bloch (1834–90), whose image of Christ adds to the dramatic effect of another of Willumsen's early prints entitled *Marriage* (1886). The women seated at the loom are the wife and daughter of Pastor Wied, the parish priest in Knebel at Mols, where Willumsen stayed in the summer of 1887 with the local schoolteacher. Four of Willumsen's realist etchings, including the plate for *Two women weaving*, were reprinted at the workshop of Carl Malthe and Bølling in Copenhagen and signed and dated in pencil 1895.

61 *Lady out walking*, 1889

Etching, drypoint, roulette and aquatint. Signed and dated within the plate. 355 × 275 mm

S.13; second and final state

Josefowitz Collection

The woman shown in the foreground is Juliette Meyer, who became Willumsen's first wife in 1890. His interest in depicting figures *en promenade* was very much apparent in his work of 1890, including the largest of his prints, of the newly laid Aborrepark in Copenhagen.

62 *Polling day in the fifth constituency of Copenhagen*, 1890

Etching and roulette. Signed and dated within the plate. 227 × 340 mm

S.16

Josefowitz Collection

Willumsen dated this subject 21 January 1890: it was his second attempt to create accents of colour using the etch-ing medium, the first being *Woman with an umbrella* (S.14), done at the end of 1889; the same principle was applied on a more ambitious scale in a painting from later in the same year, *Picture of life on the quays of Paris*. A note accompanying this etching when it was exhibited at Den Frie in 1892 explained the technique in the following terms with reference to Willumsen's painting as well: 'Throng of workers on a polling day. Etching 1890. Printed simultaneously in black and colours with the help of a copper-plate broken in pieces which is then reassembled. Through this means of producing the coloured areas, the etching provides the point of departure for the technique in all the following pictures' (quoted in Schultz's entry, p. 23). Willumsen varied the colours from one impression to another with further examples dated 1892, 1894 and 1895; his own copy, which according to his annotation he considered the best, was dated 1892.

Willumsen's particular use of colour for the election scene was prompted by what he had seen of French Synthetism, but an account he gave of the analogous painting, *Picture of life on the quays of Paris*, conveys that Willumsen saw his urban views essentially in monochrome:

As the street is whiteish-yellow like the houses, and the people

62

L'art ancien a son ancienne langue que le monde peu á peu a appris á comprendre Un art nouveau a formée que le monde doit apprendre avant de la comprendre

J.F.Willumssen jvier 1891

63

with a few exceptions are black, the picture has no colour and works through the contrast of light and black; it is remarkable how colourless a town can be in winter in grey weather, as it is in the picture, a colourist, no matter how talented, how hard he tried, would not be able to get a colourful picture out of it. (quoted in Krogh, *Fiction and Reality*, p. 105)

In the context of these remarks, his elements of colour appear less like an exercise in Synthetism and more akin to selective hand-tinting in contemporary photography.

63 *Fertility*, 1891

Etching, roulette and aquatint. Signed and dated within the plate 'Jvier 1891'. 247 × 342 mm

S.17

Josefowitz Collection

Willumsen's portrayal of his wife Juliette beside a symbolic

spray of wheat, shortly before the birth of their first child Jan on 20 January 1891, attracted more attention than any of the other submissions to Den Frie later that year. The print was executed in Paris and its declamatory text in French reads: 'Old art has its old language that the world has gradually learnt to understand. A new art has a newly created language that the world must learn before it can be understood.' The composition and statement reflect the influence of Gauguin more than any of Willumsen's other etchings, but *Fertility* proved to be an end rather than a beginning as far as his printmaking was concerned, for thereafter Willumsen made no further prints, with the exception of four exhibition posters, until 1910 when he embarked upon lithography. In the same year as *Fertility* Willumsen made a ceramic *Family vase*, with portraits of himself and his wife and the infant figure of his son moulded in relief, which made a similarly controversial appearance in 1892.

Peter Ilsted (1861–1933)

Born into a merchant's family on the island of Falster, south of Zealand, Ilsted entered the Copenhagen Academy in 1878. In the late 1880s he travelled as a private tutor through Europe, North Africa and Asia Minor, visiting Italy and Paris in 1891. From 1893 to 1905 he taught in the model school at the Academy, where he regularly exhibited his paintings until 1915.

The greatest influence on his work came from one of Denmark's most original painters, Vilhelm Hammershøi (1864–1916), who married Ilsted's sister Ida in 1891. The intense stillness of Hammershøi's figures and interior scenes, executed in varying tones of black, grey and opalescent white, owed much to the critical rediscovery in the second half of the nineteenth century of the paintings of Vermeer, which Hammershøi had the opportunity to study at first hand in Berlin, the Netherlands and Paris from 1885 to 1889. A similar debt was owed to the concomitant interest in Denmark in the intimacy of the art of the Danish 'Golden Age', whose leading representative, Christian Købke, was first shown comprehensively in 1884 at the Kunstforeningen in Copenhagen.

Hammershøi, however, was interested in interior views not for their accumulation of genre detail or allegorical meaning but as a way of using space as a metaphor for an inward state of mind. After the turn of the century he expanded his repertoire to include more urban architectural subjects.

Ilsted's own painting was heavily dependent on that of his brother-in-law, but his interest in printmaking was quite separate. His first prints were fifty-two etchings mostly done between 1882 and 1900 – portraits, landscapes and interiors – when he also began to collect the etchings of Rembrandt and other Dutch seventeenth-century artists; his portrait of 1900 of his father, for example, of which the British Museum has an impression, is closely based on Rembrandt's portrait of Jan Lutma of 1656. More directly allied to his painting, however, was Ilsted's use of mezzotint, which he first attempted in 1906. From 1910 onwards he concentrated on this form of printmaking, executing some seventy-six mezzotints before his death, many printed in colour as well as in monochrome. Ilsted's grandson, Peter Olufsen, related this development to the onset of severe asthma which inhibited his painting out of doors, but mezzotint was in any case an ideal medium for the transcription of the carefully modulated tones and structured spaces beloved by Ilsted and Hammershøi. There was a similar affinity to early photography which was noted at the time by an English photo-journal; in 1907 those interested in photography for its artistic possibilities were advised to study Hammershøi's paintings then on view at Van Wisselingh's Gallery in London: 'They are examples of the extreme value of quiet spaces free from detail to give emphasis to the rest' (Vad, *Vilhelm Hammershøi*, p. 372).

Ilsted came to London in 1913 to study the collections of mezzotints at the British Museum and elsewhere, as well as to visit his sister and brother-in-law who were lodging in Brunswick Square. The latter had paid several visits to London in 1904 and 1905/6 (when Hammershøi executed two views of the exterior of the British Museum) as well as in 1912/13, partly because of their friendship with the pianist Leonard Borwick, a pupil of Clara Schumann, to whom they had been introduced by Hammershøi's main patron, Alfred Bramsen. Ilsted was one of a small group of Scandinavian artists to display an interest in mezzotint at this time, coinciding with the boom in the market from the 1890s to the 1920s for eighteenth-century prints in this medium (for a discussion of this aspect of taste see Sheila O'Connell's essay 'William Second Baron Cheylesmore (1843–1902) and the Taste for Mezzotints', *Landmarks in Print Collecting*, pp. 134–58). Ilsted would no doubt have been aware of publications such as the special edition of *The Studio* in 1910 on 'Old English Mezzotints' and of the reputation of Frank Short, who as head of the engraving school at the Royal College of Art from 1891 to 1924 revived the use of mezzotint to interpret the work of other artists, most notably that of J. M. W. Turner, whose *Liber Studiorum* prints he recreated.

Ilsted's mezzotints were sometimes done after earlier artists including Jens Juel (1745–1802) but generally they were based on his own paintings, often executed many years before. Although he is best known for interior views of his Copenhagen apartment or the eighteenth-century pavilion at Liselund where he spent his summers from 1913 to 1917, Ilsted made a number of paintings and mezzotints of landscapes and still-lifes.

Bibliography

There has been very little literature specifically about Ilsted as opposed to the flood of recent publications on Hammershøi, which contain information relevant to Ilsted as well; the standard monograph in this case is by Poul Vad, *Vilhelm Hammershøi and Danish Art at the Turn of the Century*, translated by Kenneth Tindall (New Haven and London, 1992). For Ilsted alone there is Peter Olufsen and Clod Svensson, *Peter Ilsted: Maleren, grafikeren, mennesket*, with a checklist of his prints (Copenhagen, n.d.). Lady Abdy, whom I would like to thank for her assistance in connection with Ilsted, has a long-standing interest in Danish art of this period which she showed at her Bury Street Gallery in 1986 and 1988 accompanied by the catalogues *Danish Paintings 1880–1920* and *Peter Ilsted: Paintings and prints*.

64 *At the spinet,* 1911

Mezzotint printed in colours. Signed in pencil and numbered 150/110. 356 × 325 mm

O&S.10

1996-9-29-8. Purchased

One of Ilsted's early mezzotints, this subject, unlike many of the others, was printed only in a coloured version and not in monochrome. According to a checklist of his prints published in 1924 by the Copenhagen dealer Vilhelm Tryde (a copy is in the library of the Department of Prints and Drawings), the coloured mezzotints usually sold at 200 kroner each and the uncoloured ones at 100 kroner. The colouring, which Ilsted did himself, *à la poupée*, varied slightly from one impression to another.

The motif of a woman seen from behind playing a musical instrument was ultimately borrowed from Dutch seventeenth-century painting, but the more particular occasion for it arose because Ilsted's sister, Ida Hammershøi, was a dedicated pianist and appeared in a similar guise in many of her husband's compositions.

65 *A rainy day,* 1931

Mezzotint. Signed and inscribed in pencil 'Orig. Radering of Peter Ilsted'. 409 × 487 mm

O&S.71

1989-5-13-79. Purchased

This was printed in colours as well as in monochrome; it was one of Ilsted's last mezzotints, but the composition is based on a much earlier painting showing the artist's wife

65

Ingeborg and their four children, Kamma, Eva, Ellen and Jens, in their third-floor apartment in the heart of Copenhagen, which was often the subject of his work. His grandson's account of this apartment consciously evokes the muted tones and stillness of the prints themselves:

From the long dark entrance hall where English prints hung on the walls, you came into the corner room with the delicate English furniture with the green covers. … In all the windows green plants twisted themselves round … almost like a jungle. Nature was stirring within the home.

He describes the paintings by Hammershøi, Constantin Hansen and Zahrtmann, the distinct sound of the clock ticking and his grandfather's special room where Ilsted kept his coin cabinet and made his mezzotints, working from a mirror reflection of the original painting: 'For hours as a young boy I could stand there rocking away across the blank copperplate' (Olufsen and Svensson, *Peter Ilsted*, pp. 31–4). Ilsted was an avid collector of many types of material – antiquities, Greek coins, Dutch and English prints and English furniture – but these possessions were subject to a carefully disciplined aesthetic when it came to his domestic décor. The apparent simplicity of the Ilsted home reflected Hammershøi's admonition in an interview for the magazine *Hjemmet* in 1909 about 'Our Home's Arrangement': 'If only people would open their eyes to the fact that few good things in a room give it a far more beautiful and finer quality than many mediocre things' (Vad, *Vilhelm Hammershøi*, pp. 402–3).

Aksel Jørgensen (1883–1957)

Jørgensen came from a working-class background in Copenhagen with access to only a technical education. He emerged as a serious artist in 1909 when he contributed prints, drawings and paintings to an exhibition of a group of artists known as The Thirteen held at the premises of Den Frie; the following year he visited Germany, Holland and Paris. In 1911–13 Jørgensen received his first major commission as a painter, a series of subjects illustrating the life and work of the radical Danish writer and poet Holger Drachmann (1846–1908), for the decoration for an inn named in his honour at Fredericksberg in Copenhagen. Jørgensen's most important artistic contribution, however, was a pedagogic one in his capacity as a professor at the Copenhagen Academy from 1920 to 1953; through the Graphic School that he founded there he became a crucial figure for the development of printmaking in Denmark, exercising a particular influence on the generation of artists such as Palle Nielsen (p. 91) who came to maturity after the Second World War.

Printmaking was integral to Jørgensen's artistic expression; between 1908 and 1955 he executed 141 subjects, largely black and white woodcuts and etchings apart from a small group of lithographs produced in 1943/4 and then again in 1950–4. His use of the woodcut medium is the most interesting aspect of his printmaking, taking the work of Munch, Félix Vallotton and William Nicholson as its point of departure. The prints of Vallotton and Nicholson would have been known to Jørgensen largely through reproduction (Julius Meier-Graefe's monograph on Vallotton had been published in 1898), but Munch's work was exhibited on a number of occasions in Copenhagen, including a show of sixty of his prints which excited considerable interest in January 1905 at the commercial gallery of Winkel and Magnussen; some of his prints were again included in a general exhibition at the Kunstforeningen in November 1908, by which time Munch was a patient at Dr Jacobsen's clinic in Copenhagen.

In 1917/18 Jørgensen's woodcuts briefly evinced some Japanese influence until he established a distinctive style of his own, culminating, after a labour of thirteen years, in the series of fifty-six sheets with elaborate decorative borders illustrating 'Thor's Journey to Jotunheim' taken from *Nordens Guder* (Nordic Gods), a text by the Danish Romantic poet Adam Oehlenschläger (1779–1850), first published in its entirety in 1819. The series appeared in folio form in 1928 to mark the seventy-fifth anniversary of the Danish Etching Society (DDRF) and must have been inspired by the publications of the Kelmscott Press, in particular the lavish edition of Chaucer which had appeared in 1896 with illustrations designed by Burne-Jones and decorative devices by William Morris. After *Nordens Guder* Jørgensen returned to the woodcut only on three occasions towards the end of his life, when he used it for portraiture, including a self-portrait of 1953.

Jørgensen, who shared many of the political ideals of William Morris, was described in 1946 as uniting the air of a 'foreign type of anarchist or idealist' with that of a traditional Danish craftsman (see Olaf Rude's preface to the Aksel Jørgensen retrospective exhibition at Den Frie, Copenhagen, 1946). Printmaking was of importance within the context of the social democratic system Jørgensen sought to advance, and 1946 was also the year in which he became a founder member of the Workers' Art Association, whose main purpose was to 'arouse an interest in the visual arts and establish contact between the artists and the working-class population and hereby make art a part of the everyday life of the labour movement'.

Jørgensen carried out his own printing with the exception of the work published in book form or by the Danish Etching Society, which first issued one of his etchings in 1910. Almost all subsequent reprints were made within the artist's lifetime under his supervision, the principal reprinting occurring in 1935 for the benefit of the collection at the Statens Museum for Kunst. Jørgensen's own archive of his prints, plates and blocks was deposited in the early 1970s with the Silkeborg Kunstmuseum in Jutland, providing the basis for the catalogue cited below; in 1988 a set of

66

67

impressions was pulled for the museum by Anders Georg Jensen from those blocks and plates for which there were no known examples.

In addition to the three works catalogued here, the British Museum owns an impression dated 1910 of Jørgensen's illustration to Jens Pedersen's novel *Godhed* (M.18), a copy of *Nordens Guder* presented by Mr Erik Hansen (M.82), the woodcut self-portrait of 1953 presented by the Silkeborg Kunstmuseum (M.134), an etching of the artist's studio interior of 1944 (M.105), a group of early sketchbook drawings of Copenhagen and a portrait drawing of 1941.

Bibliography

The extent of Jørgensen's influence as a teacher can be gauged from a catalogue of an exhibition held at the Copenhagen Academy in 1946 to represent the work of his pupils over the preceding twenty-five years. A collection of articles by Jørgensen was issued as *Den Sort-hvide Kunst*, edited by Erik Clemmensen (Copenhagen, 1966). Clemmensen also wrote a short account of his work in the series *Danske Grafikere* (Copenhagen, 1960). The *catalogue raisonné* of his prints, *Aksel Jørgensen: Det grafiske værk*, with a checklist by Lars Møller, was published by the Silkeborg Kunstmuseum in 1989. The work done in connection with *Nordens Guder* was written up by the printer, Chr. Christiansen, as 'Axel Jørgensens Træsnit-Udgave af "Nordens Guder"', *Aarbog for Dansk Bogtryk* (Copenhagen, 1929), pp. 149–66. I would like to thank Mr Erik Hansen in particular for his unstinting generosity in sharing with me his personal knowledge and collection of material relating to Aksel Jørgensen. Troels Andersen of the Silkeborg Kunstmuseum was also kind enough to read my draft entries.

66 *The florists*, 1909

Woodcut printed on thin Japan paper. Signed and dated in pencil. 315 × 291 mm

M.12

1996-6-8-4. Purchased

Among the early influences on Aksel Jørgensen's graphic style was the work of William Nicholson (1872–1949), whose woodcut series of the late 1890s were widely known through their reproduction in lithographic editions and in contemporary periodicals. Nicholson was also one of the artists admired by the prominent collector Alfred Bramsen, who published an article on him in 1909. Jørgensen has not made a literal borrowing of any of Nicholson's subjects but in this composition he evokes the spirit of the characters portrayed by Nicholson in *London Types* (1898).

68

67 The narrator: illustration to a short story by V. Korolénko, 1912

Woodcut printed on thin Japan paper. Signed and dated in pencil. 224 × 164 mm

M.49

1996-6-13-11. Purchased

This impression belonged to Erling Frederiksen (1910–94), one of Jørgensen's many students at the Copenhagen Academy. It was originally reproduced in 1914 in a satirical weekly magazine known as *Fyrtøjet* (The Tinderbox) to accompany a Danish translation of a story entitled 'It is the Wood that is Whispering' by the Russian author Vladimir Korolénko (1853–1921). Korolénko was a populist writer and social activist from the Ukraine who based many of his stories on his period of exile in Siberia in the early 1880s; a standard device in these tales is his use of a narrator who is an exile himself of one kind or another.

A new edition of this subject was printed in 1935. On the back of the original woodblock is a study for another composition, *Suburb*, of 1910 (M.39).

68 Two actors/Drunken man/Man beating a woman, 1917

Woodcut printed on paper with blind stamp of DDRF, who published it in 1918. 395 × 292 mm

M.58

1989-7-22-36. Purchased

By 1917 Jørgensen had developed a more fluid, linear style of woodcutting which he used to impart greater dynamism to his compositions. In this instance the artist's choice and handling of his subject recalls the early eighteenth-century Japanese prints from the Edo period, of actors from Kabuki plays (I should like to thank Tim Clark of the British Museum for supplying me with an appropriate illustration). The block was retained by DDRF, who in November 1990 published a new edition at 700 kroner each.

Povl Christensen (1909–1977)

Christensen was one of Aksel Jørgensen's many protégés at the Graphic School of the Copenhagen Academy which he attended from 1930 to 1938, travelling to Berlin, Dresden, Munich and Norway during the same period. His early prints included drypoints, etchings (the British Museum has recently acquired one of 1935) and lithographs as well as woodcuts; it was with the latter medium that he made his name as an illustrator in the 1940s and 1950s after his début in 1933 with an edition of Steen Steensen Blicher's *Brudstykker af en Landsbydegns Dagbog* (Fragments of a Country Dean's Diary). Christensen's style was a consciously archaising one, echoing the scale and intensity of Thomas Bewick's wood-engraving, which was perfectly attuned to many of the texts Christensen illustrated by Danish writers of the eighteenth and nineteenth centuries. The mood of his woodcuts is, however, very different from the vernacular humour of Bewick, its austerity reflecting the deeply pietistic vein running through Danish literature of this period, including Hans Christian Andersen's fairy tales. In addition to the work of Blicher (1782–1848) discussed below, other examples in this manner represented in the collection of the British Museum are six proofs for the 1943 edition, containing twenty-two woodcuts, of *Salmer i Udvalg* (Selected Hymns) by Bishop Thomas Kingo (1634–1703), and nine out of the twenty-eight for a 1945 edition of the *Salmer* by another episcopal author, Hans Adolf Brorson (1694–1764).

Christensen moved away from his miniaturist style during the 1950s, when he taught at art schools in Bergen in Norway from 1955 to 1957 and produced engravings on zinc on a larger scale. He continued to work as an illustrator, and by his death in 1977 had been responsible for some sixty books containing original prints, both etchings and woodcuts.

Bibliography

Poul Holst, *Povl Christensen: En bibliografi* (Ringkjøbing 1968) is a complete bibliography both of illustrations by the artist and of publications on him. Erik Fischer wrote a booklet on Christensen published in the *Danske Grafikere* series (Copenhagen, 1961) and no. 9 in the *Lommebog* (pocketbook) series published by the Statens Museum for Kunst in 1979, entitled *Povl Christensen: Den blå fugl*.

69 *Illustration to 'Three Holy Eves'*, 1950

Woodcut printed on thin Japan paper. 235 × 359 mm

1992-10-3-114. Purchased from the Rausing Fund

Christensen's illustrations to *De Tre Helligaftener* by Steen Steensen Blicher (1841, translated into English 1945) were published by the Berlingske Bogtrykkeri in 1950 in an edition of 375 numbered and signed copies together with an edition of fifteen in folio form, containing twenty-one original woodcuts; six of these were included in the exhibition Danish Illustrators of Today arranged by the Arts Council of Great Britain in 1951.

Blicher had been a country pastor in Jutland. He translated Oliver Goldsmith's *The Vicar of Wakefield* among other works, and became one of Denmark's most popular short-story writers after the instant success in 1824 of his first published piece, *Fragments of a Country Dean's Diary* (see above). The author was himself keen to have his work illustrated because he saw the combination of words and pictures as a means of educating the rural populace from whom he drew his material. 'Three Holy Eves' is a short story set on Easter, Whitsun and Christmas Eve about the capture of a band of Jutland robbers who finally meet their just deserts in this illustration by Christensen.

Torsten Billman (1909–1989)

Billman's outlook and the tenor of his career as an artist were shaped by the circumstances of his home town of Gothenburg, Sweden's major port, and the radical political climate engendered by the labour unions associated with its commercial activities. He signed on as a ship hand himself in 1926, making several extended voyages over the next six years until he decided to concentrate on his work as a graphic artist, which began in 1929 with his first woodcut, of hands held aloft at a seamen's meeting. In 1931 he attended courses at the Arts and Crafts School in Gothenburg, including one directed towards book illustration, which involved lino and woodcutting; he went on in 1933/4 to spend a year at the main art school, Valand (formerly the Gothenburg Museum School), where he had the opportunity to draw from studio models; but the school's prevailing emphasis on colouristic painting was irrelevant to his natural inclinations towards narrative draughtsmanship and printmaking (in 1974/5 he was to return to Valand as a teacher himself). In this respect he was very much self-taught from reproductions of the work of Daumier, Käthe Kollwitz and Frans Masereel, whose urban social themes appealed to him as well as their graphic style. Billman's subject matter during the 1930s reflected his origins as a seaman (cat. 70), which he was able to exploit on a far larger scale for the frescoes he was commissioned to design for the new seamen's home in Gothenburg in 1944 and further north in Sweden for the Gävle Folkets Hus (Community House) in 1947. His socialist political sympathies were a persistent thread to his work, surfacing as outspoken anti-Fascism during the late 1930s and 1940s (in 1949 he travelled to Warsaw to record the devastation of the city and the concentration camps nearby), then again in relation to political events in the United States and Europe during the 1960s.

After the Second World War Billman became one of Sweden's leading practitioners of book illustration, for which the technique that he developed in 1940, of printing woodcuts in black and grisaille tones, was well suited. His first (unpublished) illustrations were linocuts for Upton Sinclair's novel *Jimmy Higgins* in 1931, but the main published series came from 1948 onwards, with *Crime and Punishment* (which he first read in 1936), *Cousin Pons* by Balzac in 1961 and Büchner's *Woyzeck* in 1967.

The British Museum's collection of seven woodcuts by Billman was purchased from the artist's widow in 1992.

Bibliography

A complete account of Billman's career, with a checklist of his graphic work and full bibliography, is given in the monograph by Küllicke Montgomery, *Torsten Billman* (Stockholm, 1985).

70

70 *Brothel scene Algiers, c.* 1937

Woodcut printed on thin Japan paper. Signed in pencil and numbered '6'. 181 × 225 mm

1992-12-12-19. Purchased from the Rausing Fund

71 *Nietzsche and his mother,* 1963

Woodcut printed on thin Japan paper. Signed in pencil and inscribed 'Original träsnitt'. 240 × 276 mm

1992-12-12-22. Purchased from the Rausing Fund

During the last years of Nietzsche's life, 1897–1900, when he suffered from increasing physical paralysis and mental illness, he was cared for by his mother and sister in Weimar.

71

Marcel Rasmussen (1913–1964)

Like Povl Christensen (p. 83), Rasmussen studied under Aksel Jørgensen at the Graphic School in Copenhagen, and his earliest prints – illustrations to R. L. Stevenson's *Dr Jekyll and Mr Hyde* in 1946 and to Bunyan's *Pilgrim's Progress* in 1951 (cat. 72) – showed an affinity to Christensen's style. By the mid-1950s he had developed his own imagery, producing a distinctive group of woodcuts depicting sinister marionettes and masked figures (cat. 73). At the same time he began to experiment with compositions of geometric landscapes (cat. 74), which became a dominant theme in his work from 1957 until his death. These were no doubt informed by the exercises in perspective he taught in his capacity as a drawing instructor to surveying students from 1949 to 1964, and in 1960 he published a book on the subject. He would have known C. W. Eckersberg's series of etchings, published in 1841 under the title *Linear perspective useful to painters*, with their reductivist treatment of cast shadows within an urban landscape. Rasmussen, however, worked within an entirely modern idiom, marrying solid geometry to an interpretation of space that was indebted to the metaphysical landscapes of the Surrealists. On two of

his sketches he inscribed the title of T. S. Eliot's poem *The Waste Land*, in English, while on a third he wrote 'There is nothing so sad / as a cone / that's frustrated and / stands all alone'.

Bibliography

The main publication is by an artist who was a contemporary of Rasmussen: Helle Thorborg, *Marcel Rasmussen* (Den Danske Radeerforening, 1967). This includes a list of all his prints. Erik Dal published an account of his book illustrations, 'Marcel Rasmussens bogillustrationer', in *Bogvennen* (Copenhagen, 1977), pp. 207–17. I am grateful to the artist's daughter, Lene Steenbuch, for reading this text.

72 *Illustration to 'Pilgrim's Progress'*, 1951

Wood-engraving printed on thin Japan paper. 163 × 241 mm
1992-10-3-93. Purchased from the Rausing Fund

The *Pilgrim's Progress* illustrations, of which there were approximately twenty-five, were Rasmussen's first major work. Although Helle Thorborg described the technique in terms of relief metal-engraving, the evidence of a surviving

72

73

74

block for one of the other illustrations leaves no reason to doubt that they were all executed as wood-engravings. (I am indebted to Lis Clausen, Ole Sporring and the artist's daughter for their advice on this matter.)

73 *Masks*, 1956

Woodcut printed on thin Japan paper. Signed and inscribed in pencil 'Eget tryck'. 252 × 349 mm

1992-10-3-95. Purchased from the Rausing Fund

This image exists both as a separate print and as the lower left-hand section of a four-part composition, *Masks II*. It was reproduced in 1957 in *Hvedekorn*, III (p. 71), to accompany a poem by Rasmussen entitled 'Hell', but there is no reason to believe that the woodcut was originally conceived with the poem in mind.

74 *Morning*, 1963

Woodcut printed on thin Japan paper. Numbered '5' in pencil. 327 × 564 mm

1992-10-3-97. Purchased from the Rausing Fund

A preparatory drawing connected with this composition describing the path of the sun bears these words in English by the artist: 'It burns in the void / Nothing upholds it. / Still it travels'. (I am indebted to Lene Steenbuch for informing me of this sketch and of the two inscribed *The Waste Land*.)

Morning was one of the subjects included in Rasmussen's final exhibition at the Maison du Danemark in Paris in 1964, which he shared with two other notable Danish printmakers and illustrators, Palle Nielsen (p. 91) and Mogens Zieler. The British Museum's other example of a geometric landscape by Rasmussen is *By the sea* (1957).

Erik Wessel-Fougstedt (1915–1990)

Wessel-Fougstedt was born in Paris, the son of the artist Arvid Fougstedt (1888-1949), a student of Matisse, who spent much of his time there until 1922 when the family returned to Stockholm. Erik studied at a private painting school in Stockholm, then briefly with Aksel Jørgensen in Copenhagen at the beginning of 1940 and at the Graphic School attached to the Academy in Stockholm, where he was a pupil of Harald Sallberg (p. 49). He felt a strong affinity to Denmark, adding the Danish name Wessel to his surname after his father's death; Palle Nielsen's work (p. 91) was to be an important influence upon his own when he decided around 1950 to concentrate on linocut printing and wood-engraving.

Wessel-Fougstedt's output as a printmaker focused entirely on city life, principally that of Stockholm where he had his studio but occasionally incorporating views of some

76

of the other cities he visited, such as London and Barcelona (cat. 75). The early prints consisted on the one hand of schematically composed episodes of urban street life that owed an obvious debt to techniques of graphic design and to the work of Frans Masereel; on the other, there were more descriptive wood-engravings of specific locations reminiscent of late nineteenth-century reproductive illustration, whose appropriation by Max Ernst within a Surrealist context was admired by Wessel-Fougstedt. From the 1960s onwards the tenor of his work again changed as well as his handling of the medium, which became far more adventurous in the variety of marks made with the engraving tools. Within the compass of the small scale of his prints he developed a more impersonal and monumental architecture, conjuring up the totalitarian world of an imaginary dystopian metropolis such as those compellingly evoked in the writings of Aldous Huxley and George Orwell. The images share with many of Palle Nielsen's urban narratives a marked cinematic quality that has been linked to Italian Neo-realism.

The British Museum acquired eight wood-engravings from the artist's estate in 1992.

75

Bibliography

An anthology of the Stockholm subjects was published by Hans Eklund in *Erik Wessel-Fougstedts Stockholmsbilder* (Stockholm, 1981). Kim Nicklasson has included Wessel-Fougstedt as number twelve of his extended series of monographic booklets, *Ur Vår Tids Grafik Fredem* (1990), and the Nationalmuseum in Stockholm published a short catalogue to accompany a joint exhibition, *Erik Wessel-Fougstedt – Arvid Fougstedt*, in 1991.

75 *Paralelo, Barcelona*, 1956

Colour wood-engraving printed on thin yellow Japan paper in violet and black ink. Signed in pencil and inscribed 'arkivel'.
223 × 356 mm

1992-4-4-82. Purchased from the Rausing Fund

The artist visited Barcelona in 1955 as part of a trip which included Berlin and Madrid.

76 *The great monument*, 1963

Wood-engraving. Signed in pencil and numbered 21/40.
201 × 160 mm

1992-4-4-81. Purchased from the Rausing Fund

Palle Nielsen (born 1920)

Since the mid twentieth century Nielsen has been one of the most important graphic artists in Scandinavia. His engagement with varying modes of graphic expression, encompassing drawing, wood-engraving, woodcut, linocut, etching and, to a lesser extent, lithography and engraving on stone, has been unwavering, the product of his training under Aksel Jørgensen. This gave him the necessary technical and analytical vocabulary for his distinctive series of existential urban narratives, constructed within a carefully defined pictorial space; they constitute a commentary sometimes direct, at other times oblique, on the anxiety and dislocation of the modern world in the wake of the Second World War.

Born into the family of a wholesaler who lived near Copenhagen's harbour district, Nielsen worked in the early 1940s as a commercial draughtsman at an advertising agency, until he decided on Aksel Jørgensen's recommendation to attend the painting school run by Erik Clemmensen (1905–84) in 1943/4. It was Clemmensen who introduced him to the work of the Belgian printmaker Frans Masereel (1889–1972), whose *Book of Hours* (*Mein Stundenbuch*), published in Munich in 1920, was an immediate influence on the content and structure of Nielsen's own pictorial narratives. Another source of inspiration was Hogarth's engraving *Gin Lane* (1750), which first captured Nielsen's attention in a slide lecture given by Aksel Jørgensen with reference to pictorial structure; Hogarth's 'modern moral subject' revealed to Nielsen the possibilities of creating through purely graphic means an imaginary world which could use an apparently 'realistic' pictorial space and narrative content to induce a suspension of disbelief. Years later, when Nielsen was himself the professor in charge of the Graphic School from 1967 to 1973, the Hogarth print was the basis for one of his series of drawings known as *Examinations of exemplary art*, in which he superimposed on his own copies after other artists' work various annotations and diagrammatic lines analysing the structure and rhythm of the composition. In this respect he was influenced not only by Aksel Jørgensen but also by the methods associated with the Bauhaus basic course of instruction as expounded by Klee and Kandinsky.

While he was at the Academy from 1944 to 1949, Nielsen was already engaged in the first of the narrative cycles that became the hallmark of his work, *Picture history I*, 153

drawings in pen and wash done between 1944 and 1946. Although the drawings preceded his work as a printmaker, the two activities have operated in tandem throughout his career, covering similar themes. His first visit abroad to Paris in 1947 expanded his range of intellectual and visual ideas, as well as providing him with motifs for some of his prints which he began in 1948/9. Nielsen's foreign travel in the immediate postwar period, to Hamburg, Kiel, Rome and Florence, and his experience of the ruins of the ancient and modern worlds, contributed to the architectural vocabulary of his 'histories', just as other elements were appropriated from cinematic, literary, biblical and philosophical contexts. Certain architectural forms such as the rotunda became archetypal structures within his compositions, imbued with a particular mystery. The psychological and physical devastation of war is embedded in almost every one of his narratives from the thirty-six wood-engravings of 1949 called *Passion* (Nielsen's counterpart to Masereel, whose first 'story without words' had been *25 images de la passion d'un homme* in 1918), through the fourteen *Anti-war pictures* of 1950 to the woodcuts about Vietnam, *Sacrifice*,

78

made in 1967 and the linocuts he did in 1970 and 1975–7 designated as *Series without a name*. An apocalyptic foreboding pervades even the images in a series such as *The enchanted city (Den fortryllede by)* – one of his most persistent themes, running to about ninety etchings between 1961 and 1984 – which do not always dwell specifically on destruction.

Palle Nielsen has proved adept at exploiting the properties of different graphic techniques to vary the mood of his compositions, using etching from 1961 onwards for the dream-like vistas of *The enchanted city*, for example; with linocut he created a deliberately cinematic effect, most notably conveyed by his *Orpheus and Eurydice* series of 1955–9 (cat. 77, 78), for which he was awarded a prize at the 1958 Venice Biennale. The latter theme emerged in his work in 1951, the same year as he first used the title of *The enchanted city*; both were to be recurrent vehicles for his ideas and marked a move away from the social realism of his earliest pictorial narratives towards a more fantastical train of thought. The first group of *Orpheus and Eurydice* prints were five wood-engravings triggered by a dream Nielsen had of the death of his wife Elsa, enacted in the railway

station at Kiel. When he returned to the subject, the more appropriate medium seemed linocut, to which he adhered throughout the first series of fifty-seven prints of 1955–9 and for the two sequels, *Isola* of 1961–9 (forty-two) and *Orpheus and Eurydice III* of 1971–84 (twenty-seven). His original prints were often reproduced in book form, as were the first and second *Orpheus and Eurydice* cycles in 1959 and 1970; in the preface to *Isola an interlude*, Nielsen explained the essential dynamic common to all his series:

In more than one respect this series of pictures is set in a borderland, for not only does it consist of pictures and endeavour to express itself in pictorial language, but, because the pictures appear in series, present a sequence of events and illustrate a narrative, it also closely approaches literary form. This narrative is to some degree planned and intentional, but also to a large extent controlled and guided by the happenings which belong exclusively to the pictures themselves; the message to be found in each individual is largely determined by whatever happened in that instant to manifest itself in pictorial form. Not until the very last moment these snap-shot pictures or pages from a diary themselves invoked the final sequence of events.

(An English translation of the Danish text is provided in the 1970 edition.)

The British Museum's collection holds several examples of Nielsen's drawing from different periods: nine of the twelve pen and ink studies comprising the series *Morning* of 1950, three of the *Examinations of exemplary art* from 1968–73 (they are based on works by three Danish artists, Nicolai Abildgaard, Ejler Bille and Egil Jacobsen), a watercolour of 1983 whose title was changed from *The enchanted city* to *Pandemonium* in 1988, and a figurative study in bodycolour dedicated *To Camille Flammarion* of 1988. The only prints belonging to the Museum are the linocuts catalogued below and an etching of 1976.

Bibliography

There is no *catalogue raisonné* of Palle Nielsen's approximately 1,100 prints, or of his drawings. The first checklist of the prints appeared in the magazine *Hvedekorn*, v–vi (October to December 1963), compiled by his fellow artist Richard Winther, and a concise list of the series to 1989, both prints and drawings, is among the information provided in the most substantial publication on Nielsen, by Kristian Romare: *Den Fortryllede By: En bog om Palle Nielsen* (Copenhagen, 1990). This contains a detailed chronology and a bibliography of writings on, by and of relevance to the artist. The only texts in English on him are the brief introductions to Nielsen's series *Orpheus and Eurydice* (Copenhagen, 1959), *Isola* (Copenhagen, 1970), and to *Katalog*, published in English as *Scenario: Visions from the end of time* (New York, 1983), as well as an anthology of his prints by Erik Fischer, entitled *The Enchanted City: Graphics by Palle Nielsen* (New York, 1987).

77 *Flight* from *Orpheus and Eurydice*, Opus 337, 1956

Linocut printed on thin Japan paper. Initialled and dated in pencil and inscibed 'ET'. 141 × 204 mm

1989-12-9-2. Purchased

In the book publication of part I of the series (Hans Reitzel Forlag, Copenhagen, 1959), the sequence of the two subjects catalogued here is in reverse order, with *The self-confident* appearing as number 25 and *Flight* as 29, but the sequential narrative did not assume its final shape until Nielsen decided to bring it to a halt:

With some hesitation a postscript, intended as a key to the action, was added to the 1st part of Orpheus and Eurydice – I say with hesitation, because it is a dangerous matter to add to what has already been said; to separate the pictorial from the literary is to disrupt the continuity which is the characteristic mode of expression in this genre. . . . Part one describes departure, a hurried passage through a coastal region which has been traversed or touched fleetingly by a host of incidents; the drama presents itself as omens. The foreland – the banks of the

Styx, must be forgotten and the pictures still present there, left behind. On the opposite bank – imminent and fully unfolded – the events are waiting. (Preface to 1970 edition of *Isola*)

Retrospectively Nielsen justified his return to the theme during the following decade on these grounds:

The postscript to Isola, then, must be this: It has not been possible to forget the pictures from the foreland, neither has it been possible to see the events fully unfolded. The island is an intermediary station, the environment remains unchanged and Orpheus continues on his travels immured within his own loss. ... But Orpheus's attitude has been changed by certain experiences; the personal retreats into the background and the Rotunda, which is at the same time Orpheus's old house – his one-sided endeavour – cannot withstand the new situation that now points towards that self-abnegation which should be the power of song – and Eurydice seems nearer than before.

78 *The self-confident* from *Orpheus and Eurydice*, Opus 347, 1958

Linocut printed on thin Japan paper. Initialled and dated in pencil and inscribed '347 Eget tryk'. 174 × 247 mm

1989-12-9-3. Purchased

Seppo Mattinen (born 1930)

Born in Helsinki, Mattinen studied at schools for the applied arts there and in Gothenburg in 1949–51 and 1952–4 respectively, before going on to the Graphic School of the Academy in Copenhagen from 1955 to 1960. Mattinen's first woodcuts were made from 1952 onwards, achieving a genuine assurance by 1957/8; in 1962 he started to make etchings but continued with the woodcut medium, often in colour and on a more substantial scale than his etchings; the checklist of his prints published in 1964 (see below) describes 96 woodcuts from 1952 to 1964 and fifty etchings from 1962 to 1964. He settled in Denmark for thirty years, then tried unsuccessfully to live again in his home country, which he left in 1985 for Rome, where he has remained ever since.

Mattinen made his reputation as a printmaker and illustrator, often drawing upon his own experiences in a mixture of memories and fantasy expressed in a stark, deliberately stiff figurative style, reminiscent of the Russian icons he would have seen during his childhood in Karelia on the border with Russia. The isolation of many of his figures and the pervasive atmosphere of sorrow also reflect the loneliness of his own upbringing in a family from which his father was absent and his mother absorbed by a doom-laden religious fanaticism. One of his most recent publications is an illustrated edition in Danish of the Norwegian author Knut Hamsun's short stories, *Liusfragmenter: Noveller* (1994; first published 1907), in which Mattinen blends his own imagery

80

with a quotation from Munch's *Scream* to provide a visual counterpart to the introspection of Hamsun's writing.

Bibliography
Hvedekorn (The Ear of Wheat), the journal for literature and graphic art, published a short autobiographical sketch (1961, V, pp. 154–7) and a checklist of his graphic work from 1952 to 1964 (1964, IV, pp. 118–21).

79 Accident, 1957

Woodcut printed on thin Japan paper. Signed and dated in pencil and numbered 2/13. 385 × 452 mm

1992-10-3-70. Purchased from the Rausing Fund

The artist has supplied the following commentary to accompany this image:

At night-time you cross the Knippelsbro (a bridge connecting the City of Copenhagen and Christianshavn) on a bicycle, heading towards the City.
You pass a group of silent figures gathered around a cyclist lying still on the tarmac.
Immediately you start thinking about yourself – it could be me lying there!
The ambulance should be here soon.

80 Guard of honour, 1959

Woodcut printed on thin Japan paper in black and brown. Signed and dated in pencil and inscribed 'E.T.' 325 × 301 mm

1992-10-3-72. Purchased from the Rausing Fund

The British Museum owns another impression of this subject printed in black only. The artist again has a narrative basis for the composition, which was executed like the one above while he was still a student at the Copenhagen Academy:

For an illustration: The Guard of Honour.
How to find models for the characters surrounding the coffin? Will the professors of the Danish Academy of Fine Arts do? They have a suitable age and weight for the task.
Consequently, it will be our teachers at the academy: Holger J. Jensen, Hjort Nielsen, Sterup-Hansen, and Leergaard (a few characters I've found on the tram). Not that it has to be portraits of the professors as such: rather it ought to look like the characters in the short story.

(I am grateful to the artist for supplying the texts quoted in both of the entries here to Lis Clausen in Copenhagen for my benefit.)

Rolf Nesch (1893–1975)

Nesch, a naturalised Norwegian citizen, first went to Oslo in 1933 because of his desire to leave Germany upon the advent of National Socialism and his admiration for the work of Munch. Although the two artists met on only one occasion, their artistic lives had many points in common through their contacts and sources of patronage in Berlin and in Hamburg. Nesch's move to Norway introduced another link with Expressionism, on which Munch had been such a powerful original influence.

Born at Oberesslingen in Württemberg, Nesch entered the Dresden Academy in 1913 but volunteered for the German army on the outbreak of the First World War; he was captured by the British at Ypres in 1917 and sent to a prisoner of war camp near Derby. After his release Nesch returned in 1920 to Dresden, where two years later he was visited by one of his wartime acquaintances, Carl Vincent Krogmann. Krogmann, a Hamburg merchant, together with his brother-in-law, the pediatrician Reinhard des Arts, was to be Nesch's most important patron and supporter until the mid-1930s. From 1922 Krogmann's hospitality and his range of contacts ensured a vital source of income for Nesch, leading eventually to his decision to settle in Hamburg in 1929. Until he left for Norway in 1933 Nesch was actively engaged in painting as well as printmaking, but the latter increasingly predominated after his move to Hamburg.

Nesch's interest in printmaking had first been manifested around 1919, his earliest documented prints being the series of eight drypoints, *The Swabian Three Magi* (1921); his letters of the following years to Krogmann are full of references to prints, to lithography as well as to etching, and it is evident that Krogmann was already helping him with the cost of materials. A six-week visit to Kirchner in Davos in 1924 galvanised Nesch's imagination; his printmaking became more daring in 1925/6 while he was living in Berlin, after he had accidentally discovered the effects of etching right through his plates: this was to become a characteristic of his work. Nesch wrote to Krogmann:

I have been truly successful with the etchings. But they are very heavily printed. I come increasingly to the point of view that a painter actually sees things quite differently from other mortals. One cannot exactly define this distinction but it is definitely there. ... Deep etching, which I have already described to you, worked well at the first attempt. All the lines were etched deeply into the plate, the ink lightly applied with a roller then printed. The actual drawing stands out against the black ground. In this fashion I will probably make my next sheets. It is something completely new and a technique that I am probably developing quite independently. (*Rolf Nesch: Zeugnisse*, pp. 38, 43)

Such an unorthodox method made it essential that Nesch should have sole charge of the actual printing, and in December 1927, when he had left Berlin for Esslingen, he enquired of Krogmann the cost of a copper-plate printing

97

press after complaining about the expense of having to send plates to Felsing in Berlin, then wait fourteen days for the prints only to discover that they were totally unsatisfactory. Nesch did not find any significant commercial outlet for his work in Berlin, where his poverty was such that the critic Julius Meier-Graefe (see p. 62), who had befriended him, organised a group of art-lovers, in conjunction with Krogmann in Hamburg, to form a 'Nesch relief committee'. This provided the artist with a monthly stipend in exchange for his prints. At the beginning of 1927 Nesch poured out his gratitude to Krogmann, expressing the hope that one day when the latter had a grand enough house, he would turn it into a museum for displaying his collection in the way that Hudtwalcker had done with Munch's work. Hudtwalcker, another prosperous Hamburg businessman, also became a serious patron of Nesch, who refers to his purchase of seven etchings in September 1927.

Nesch's move to Hamburg in 1929 gave him direct access to a lively cultural milieu which included the avant-garde artists of the Hamburg Secession, the commercial Galerie Commeter, collectors such as Hudtwalcker, the shipowner Hugo Stinnes, Munch's cataloguer the judge Gustav Schiefler, the art historian Rosa Schapire and the directors of the Hamburg Kunsthalle and the Kunst- und Gewerbemuseum, Gustav Pauli and Max Sauerlandt. It was the latter who commissioned Nesch's most remarkable graphic undertaking to date, twenty-four etchings to mark the seventieth birthday in 1931 of Karl Muck, conductor of the Hamburg Orchestra. The frenzied portrayal of Muck reflected the intense nervous effort expended by Nesch on this series. He further extended his range of expression and technical innovation with the *St Pauli* series of the same year: twelve etchings focusing on Hamburg's red-light district for which he used colour, double-inking some of the plates. The culmination of his experimentation came with the twenty plates comprising the *Hamburg bridges* of 1932; this marked the emergence of Nesch's distinctive 'metal print', using tools such as the drill, fretsaw and soldering iron to create an articulated printing surface whose sculptural qualities were conveyed in the finished prints through their variety of texture and high relief.

The excitement engendered by the *Hamburg bridges* prompted another series related to the Hamburg Zoo at Hagenbeck, but this was cut short by the political events of 1933. In March the twelfth exhibition of the Hamburg Secession, which included Nesch's work, was closed on the grounds of 'cultural Bolshevism', followed in May by the members' decision to dissolve the Secession rather than obey Nazi orders to expel their Jewish colleagues. Nesch's patron Krogmann was a powerful ally in so far as he was appointed Mayor of Hamburg in March 1933 by the Nazi leadership in Berlin, but the deteriorating climate for any freedom of expression persuaded Nesch to leave Germany altogether and move to Oslo, equipped with letters of introduction from Schiefler to Munch and from Hudtwalcker,

who owned a fish oil factory there. Some of Nesch's support in Hamburg vanished over the next few years – Sauerlandt resigned his position and died at the beginning of 1934, Schiefler died the following year and Rosa Schapire was gravely compromised by her Jewish background – but his relationship with other patrons remained very close. He was largely dependent on financial assistance from Hudtwalcker and Reinhard des Arts throughout the 1930s when he had little or no income in Norway, while Krogmann strove to achieve a formula which would make Nesch's work acceptable to the cultural dictates of National Socialism. He succeeded in averting its proscription by emphasising Nesch's preoccupation with the 'Nordic' landscape, always less contentious than any depiction of the human figure, but Krogmann's official position rendered the former relationship between the two men impossible.

Once in Norway, Nesch had to build his life again from scratch, deprived of the environment in Hamburg which had proved so conducive to his career. Despite the introductions he had been given and an early acquaintance with the influential critic Pola Gauguin, son of the French artist, there was nothing to compare with the audience for modern art in Hamburg. Renewed financial hardship did not, however, lead to any diminution in his creativity; as soon as he arrived Nesch asked des Arts to arrange for his printing equipment to be sent to Norway, specifying his printing press and above all his soldering iron. Four months later he was completing his *Snow* series, twenty prints evoking the impressions made by the winter landscape around Oslo (cat. 81, 82). Other print cycles inspired by new subject matter that presented itself to Nesch in Norway for the first time were *Lofoten* of 1936 and *Herring catch* of 1938 (cat. 83). A related development was the execution from 1934 onwards of his first 'material pictures' (see cat. 83), a logical progression from his increasingly sculptural treatment of his printmaking plates, which were sometimes exhibited alongside the prints. Although these pictures were produced in a variety of forms, some incorporating found objects like the work of Kurt Schwitters, who took refuge in Norway from 1937 to 1940, the predominant type was that of a mosaic of glass and other materials applied within a reticulated framework on a metal surface. They were to be a major influence on the work of other Norwegian artists such as Sigurd Winge (p. 105) and later Jørleif Uthaug (p. 135), once they began to be known in 1937/8 after their first publication and exhibition. Nesch's circumstances remained precarious, reaching a point in 1938 when he thought he would be compelled to return to Germany in the wake of his wife Irma. The situation was retrieved only at the eleventh hour, after he had bought his ticket to Hamburg, through the purchase of one of his material pictures by the collector Rolf Stenersen, Munch's friend and adviser. Stenersen furthermore guaranteed Nesch a monthly income of 200 kroner for one year in return for certain acquisitions, the first being the six-part printed composition *Herring catch* (cat. 83).

81

Stenersen's support gave Nesch a temporary reprieve, but the war years brought a further set of problems: his German nationality isolated him from the Norwegian community as well as exposing him to harassment from the occupying forces after April 1940. His work of 1941/2, the *St Sebastian* triptych (cat. 84) and the four-part print *God the Father*, reflected his anguish until self-inflicted injury in 1943, to avoid conscription into the German army, curtailed his artistic production for two or three years. After the war Nesch was enraged to discover that the material pictures he had sent to England in 1938, for the exhibition of German artists in exile organised by Herbert Read at the New Burlington Galleries, had subsequently been impounded and then destroyed as the work of an 'enemy alien'.

In December 1946 Nesch became a Norwegian citizen, marrying the well-known actress Ragnhild Hald in 1950. Touring with her company to Finnmark in 1947 gave rise to his first bout of printmaking since the early 1940s, a series of approximately thirty-five plates of theatrical, landscape and local subjects executed in lithography, etching or a

combination of the two. They heralded a change in the mood and content of his pictures, both prints and reliefs: apart from theatrical motifs, there was a new element of fantasy and humour; the decorative effect of the work became more pronounced, with an increasing variety of materials and an ever more striking use of colour. Nesch abandoned his former method of soldering pieces of metal on to the plates in favour of applying colour to individual pieces arranged loosely on the surface, so that several colours could be printed simultaneously. His technical innovations came to the attention of S. W. Hayter, who had encouraged a similarly radical approach among those artists who frequented Atelier 17 in Paris and in New York, and Hayter included a reproduction of a Nesch print of 1955 in his 1962 book *About Prints*.

In 1951 Nesch acquired a farm, Ål in Hallingdal, where in 1963 he built a studio capable of accommodating his print-making and the large material picture that developed out of *Herring catch*, on which Nesch worked for nearly twenty-five years in all before it was installed in 1965 in Oslo's new headquarters for Industry and Export. He achieved widespread recognition in Norway and abroad from the late 1940s. His work was exhibited in the United States for the first time at the Kleemann Gallery in New York in 1949, with essays by Pola Gauguin and Rolf Stenersen, and the Museum of Modern Art purchased eight of the seventy-one prints included. Nesch's friends in Hamburg, with whom he had never severed his contacts, were more disposed than ever to honour his achievement, culminating in a major retrospective in 1958 where he received the Alfred Lichtwark prize for his graphic work; his acceptance speech for this prize remains the standard autobiographical source. In 1960, with some amusement, he felt he had received the ultimate accolade when he discovered there was a Rolf Nesch Road in his home town of Esslingen.

The British Museum's collection of fifteen compositions by Nesch is the only significant holding of his work in Britain. It ranges in date from a self-portrait of 1922 to the trumpet-blowing angel of 1955 (cat. 86) and includes a representation of his work in Germany and in Norway. All have been acquired since 1980, some in Germany, for example the famous portrait of Max Sauerlandt in 1930 with a wood sculpture by Kirchner, which formerly belonged to Reinhard des Arts, and the *St Sebastian* triptych (cat. 84); the greater part, however, came in 1983 and in 1993-5 from the artist's estate, which is kept on deposit at the Nasjonalgalleriet in Oslo.

Bibliography

Pola Gauguin published an article on Nesch in 1948, 'Rolf Nesch' in *Kunsten Idag*, 11, 2, pp. 2-22. The standard monograph remains that by Alfred Hentzen published in Stuttgart in 1960 and translated into English in 1964; the 1958 acceptance speech referred to above was reprinted in the 1966 exhibition catalogue of the Akademie der Künste in West Berlin. All aspects of Nesch's work are covered in the catalogue for the exhibition of 1993 to mark the centenary of his birth, held in Schleswig-Holstein, Esslingen and Heidenheim; this lists at the back the main exhibition catalogues from 1958 onwards. Nesch's relationship to his Hamburg patrons is discussed in the same catalogue in an essay by Maike Bruhns, who has also edited his letters to Krogmann and des Arts in *Rolf Nesch: Zeugnisse eines ungewöhnlichen Künstlerlebens in turbulenter Zeit* (Gifkendorf, 1993). A *catalogue raisonné* of his prints is being compiled by Sidsel Helliesen of the Nasjonalgalleriet in Oslo, but until its publication the main guide and one of the few sources in English is *The Graphic Art of Rolf Nesch* (The Detroit Institute of Arts, 1969); this contains an account of his technique by Jan Askeland who, like Sidsel Helliesen, his successor at the Nasjonalgalleriet, produced a number of short books on specific themes in Nesch's work. Some of the British Museum's prints from the German period of his career were included in Frances Carey and Antony Griffiths, *The Print in Germany 1880–1933* (London, reprinted 1993).

I am grateful to Sidsel Helliesen for her help with Nesch since I first visited the collection at the Nasjonalgalleriet in 1982 and for commenting on a draft of my entries. Nesch's son-in-law, Mr Eivind Otto Hjelle, has been equally generous over the years in making the prints and information available to me, as well as alerting me to the vital differences between cod and herring fishing!

81 *Skaugum*, 1933–4

Metal print. Signed in pencil, inscribed with title and 'Probedruck'. 431 × 580 mm

1994-5-15-40. Purchased from the Rausing Fund

82 *Holmenkollen*, 1933–4

Metal print. Signed in pencil and inscribed 'Selbstdruck'. 430 × 578 mm

1995-12-10-2. Purchased from the Rausing Fund

These are two of the twenty plates from *Snow*, the series Nesch completed by the end of March 1934, within a few months of his arrival in Norway. He was deeply affected by his first experience of the Norwegian landscape in winter, its stillness and solitude, the individual character of the trees, the rhythm of their lines and the contours of the snowy landscape around the fjord. Skaugum is the name of a farm (the official residence of the Crown Prince) situated south-west of Oslo, while Holmenkollen is a famous ski-jump on another side of the city. Although the jump has been altered several times to render it more dramatic, it has been a feature of the resort since Holmenkollen was first developed at the end of the nineteenth century, when in 1895 Monet, for example, made a point of visiting it; in 1912 Gustav Schiefler, while on a visit to Munch, was another admiring tourist.

Snow, like all of Nesch's more complex plates, could be executed only in very small editions of between six and ten impressions apiece. In a letter to Schiefler of 25 January 1934 he refers to having completed work on the printing of one plate at one o'clock in the morning:

I am very happy that it is over because it was a huge effort. First came the five drawings from nature, followed by about twenty transfers, then one plate and another as I discarded the first and created a makeshift plate. And the whole thing looks so simple and easy that everyone can say, 'This is what he has bashed out once again'! (*Rolf Nesch: Zeugnisse*, p. 198)

Three weeks later, again discussing the progress of his *Snow* series, Nesch explained to Leni des Arts how the plates gave rise to the notion of 'metal pictures': 'The metal plates are so extraordinary that I have a plan, as soon as the prints are ready, to make *metal pictures*. Instead of canvas, something robust for the wall! A new art form! It has unsuspected possibilities which I perceive more from day to day' (*ibid.*,

82

p. 203). The original zinc plate for *Skaugum*, which is on deposit at the Nasjonalgalleriet in Oslo, demonstrates the sculptural quality of Nesch's approach; copper wire threaded through holes in the plates was used to create not just contours but also a sense of energy in the landscape; in *Holmenkollen* the drama of the subject is derived from the blank space of much of the paper, representing the immensity of sky and snow-covered landscape surrounding the bird-like figure of the ski-jumper.

On 16 April 1934 the series went on exhibition at the Galerie Commeter in Hamburg, only to be threatened with closure two days later by order of the authorities in Munich. Krogmann, in his capacity as the Mayor of Hamburg, obtained a stay of execution and arranged for a discussion of the issues involved in the City Hall on 30 April. The transcript or protocol of the ensuing debate is a key document of cultural attitudes under the impact of National Socialism in Germany (it is published in full in the 1993 exhibition cata-

logue). Krogmann sought to demonstrate that Nesch's apparent tendencies to abstraction were part of a process of experimentation with technique and colour rather than an end in themselves, leading up to a new art form in his *Snow* series in which Nesch wanted to capture the essential spirit of the landscape that lay behind its merely superficial appearance. To refute the claim that Nesch's mode of expression could not be understood by the general public, Krogmann resorted to the distasteful justification that even relatively unsophisticated people had bought Nesch's work, never Jews. With arguments such as these and the support of a number of senators and local artists including Eduard Bargheer, Krogmann was able to secure the continuation of Nesch's exhibition.

  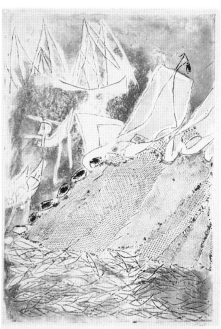

83 (I)   83 (II)   83 (III)

83 *Herring catch*, 1938

Colour metal print in six parts, each plate signed in pencil,
measuring 598 × 420 mm

1983-6-25-51 (1–6). Purchased

Nesch's observation of the herring catch off the west coast
of Norway near Ålesund early in 1938 was to be one of the
most important experiences of his life, strengthening his
sense of identification with Norway. Previously he had executed a series of twenty-one prints inspired by his visit to
the cod-fishing grounds off the Lofoten Islands near the
Arctic Circle in April 1936, undertaken at the invitation of
the son of his Hamburg patron, Heinrich Hudtwalcker. (For
a detailed account of the Lofoten expedition see Jan Askeland, *Rolf Nesch: Lofoten* (Oslo, 1976). The only known complete set, which was dedicated to Hudtwalcker, belongs to
the Städtischegalerie in Stuttgart.)

   In February 1938 Nesch wrote to Leni des Arts in Hamburg: 'I am still alive and on the herring catch. I have invited Strømme and Winge along on the journey. Crazy? Yes,
probably, but it is marvellous. Lofoten is far outdone, it is
fantastic, new prints will follow' (*Nesch: Zeugnisse*, p. 270).
Then again in April: 'The herring catch was an immense
experience that I shall never forget. I have made a series of
prints, six coloured sheets that go together, which will soon
be seen at Gurlitt [Fritz Gurlitt's gallery in Berlin] in three
passepartouts. It is my best graphic work so far. Under no
circumstances whatsoever would I leave this country without having seen the herring catch. My depression is helped
by the knowledge that I gave my utmost' (*ibid.*, p. 271).

   The drama of the scene to which Nesch responded so
readily was a vivid element in part of Knut Hamsun's narrative in his novel *The Wayfarers* (1927):

Joakim, very much the seine owner, very much in charge, wait-
ed for the decisive second. He wanted to cut through the shoal
in a great arc and run the net from shore to shore. The birds
were already overhead; they were surrounded on all sides by
herring.

   'Row!' Joakim ordered, and every man lay on his oar.
They were literally rowing in herring. (English edition (1994),
p. 149)

The seine net with its vast shoal of fish was the central feature of Nesch's six-part print which differed markedly from
his previous series because it was intended to be seen as a
single composition; its effect was compared by one critic
with that of a Japanese screen: 'a tour de force as impressive
as a six-panel painted screen of the Korin school, of which
he had long been an admirer' (Robert Simmons, 'With Eye
and Heart: The Art of Rolf Nesch', *Artist's Proof*, I, 1 (1962),
pp. 2–11). Out of his work on the prints came Nesch's most
ambitious material picture (see above) and a new approach
to his printmaking; the multipartite compositions were a
more public form of expression than the conventional 'portfolio' series of the past.

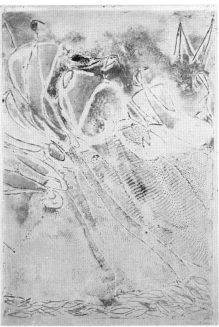

83 (IV)　　　　　　　　　　　　　　　83 (V)　　　　　　　　　　　　　　　83 (VI)

84 *St Sebastian*, 1941

Colour metal print in three parts. Signed in pencil and inscribed 'II Zustand' on the first panel, 'III Zustand' on the second and third. Each panel 600 × 431 mm

1985-5-4-2 (1–3). Purchased

Illustrated in colour on plates 2 and 3

The *St Sebastian* is often referred to as Nesch's *Guernica*, of which he had seen the original at the Kunstnernes Hus in Oslo in 1938. After reading a false report in the Oslo newspaper that Picasso had been sent to a concentration camp, Nesch added a dedication to Picasso to the scroll held by the creature on the far right of the material version of this composition, which he worked on between 1941 and 1943. (This was at one time installed in the Hotel Astoria in Oslo and now belongs to the Städtischegalerie in Stuttgart.) There can be little doubt about the artist's own identification with St Sebastian at a time of intense political and personal anxiety. The large number of preparatory drawings for the prints show that the composition was originally conceived in five parts and included a photographer and a film cameraman among the figures in the background (see Detroit exhibition catalogue, no. 96). The Nasjonalgalleriet in Oslo has black and white impressions from the key plates for the final version of the subject, before the colour was applied. Nesch reprinted the plates later in the 1940s with very different colouring, but the British Museum's version, made up of the second state of the first part of the composition and the third state of the other two panels, belongs to the first printing.

85 *Sleepwalker I*, 1953

Colour metal print. Signed in pencil and inscribed '1 état'. 593 × 425 mm

1994-1-22-9. Purchased from the Rausing Fund

Other versions of this subject, which is sometimes known as *Arab woman*, differ not only in colouring but also in the composition of the figure and its direction. With the print catalogued below, it demonstrates very well the increasing eclecticism of Nesch's later work, executed almost as though each print were a monotype:

Nowadays, Nesch makes few sketches before going on to work on a plate, preferring to work out his ideas directly as he cuts the copper pieces and twists the wire into outlines. When this step is at last finished, he places the plate in the press, applies various colours to the various parts of the configuration, using the finest of dry pigments in an oil vehicle, places over it a prepared sheet of heavy Van Gelder Zonen, sets the blankets, turns the press, and removes his first impression, all colours printed at once. In some variations one or more underplates are used to build up even more complicated colour strata. Nesch usually takes five or six impressions from one plate, rarely more, each with a different harmony of colours. Thus each print is unique, as an oil painting is unique. (Robert Simmons, *The Artist's Proof*, 1 (1961), p. 3)

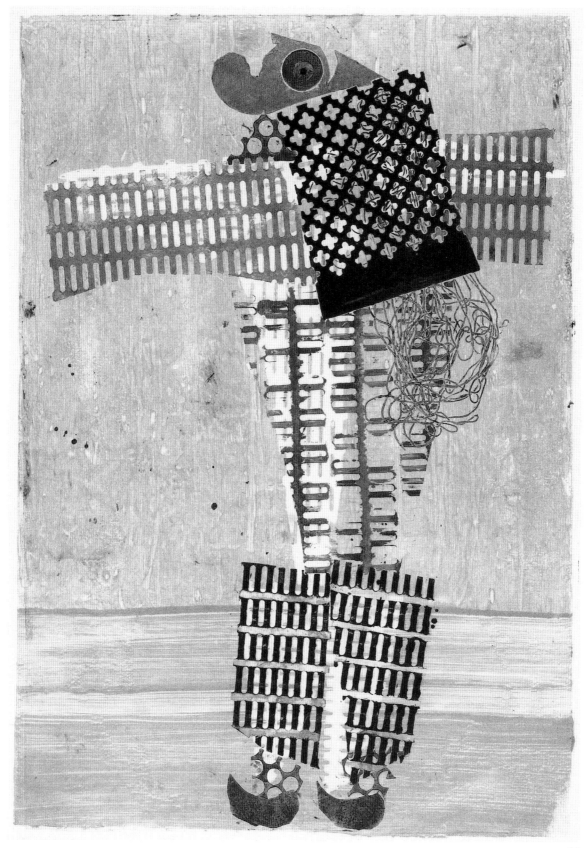

86

86 *Angel blowing trumpet, c.*1955

Colour metal print. Signed in pencil, inscribed with title and 'Et trykk'. 418 × 594 mm

1994-1-22-10. Purchased from the Rausing Fund

In this case the British Museum's impression appears to be unique, as no other is recorded on the database for the *catalogue raisonné* currently in progress at the Nasjonalgalleriet in Oslo.

Sigurd Winge (1909–1970)

Winge was born in Hamburg of Norwegian family who returned in 1917 to Norway, where he later studied at the Academy in Oslo under Axel Revold from 1929 to 1932. His early work was influenced by German Expressionism, which he encountered in 1932 at an exhibition at the Kunstnernes Hus, followed by a visit to Germany in April to June 1933 with his fellow students Erling Enger and Gert Jynge. There in Hamburg he met Max Sauerlandt (just before his resignation from the Kunst- und Gewerbemuseum), Schmidt-Rottluff, Heckel and Nolde and first became acquainted with the work of Rolf Nesch (p. 97). Further trips abroad were made to Paris and Germany in 1937 and to New York in 1939. Winge's first prints in 1933/4 were three linocuts and one woodcut, his self-portrait linocut of 1933 showing a similarity to the work of Schmidt-Rottluff and Pechstein. This, however, was short-lived, for it was the

Ortype 8/10 «Mesias 1944» Sigurd Winge febr. 45

87

88

89

influence of Nesch that predominantly affected his career from Winge's first exposure to the artist's work in Hamburg followed by their personal contact from the autumn of 1933 onwards. Winge's 1934 picture *Street*, for example, took as its point of departure one of the plates from Nesch's *Hamburg bridges* (p. 98) of 1932 (*Woman on the bridge*). He made no more prints until 1942, but in the interim gravitated towards material pictures, making his first glass mosaic in 1937. In 1938 Winge and Olaf Strømme (1909–78) accompanied Nesch on his memorable journey to observe the herring catch off the west coast of Norway (see cat. 83), the same year in which they received their first decorative commission, for the Casino Restaurant in Oslo. Winge's subsequent frieze of fishing boats for the Norwegian pavilion at the 1939 World's Fair in New York was clearly related to Nesch's treatment of the same subject matter.

The link with Nesch remained of considerable importance throughout the rest of Winge's career, both in his printmaking, to which he returned in 1942, and in his reliefs. Although he worked on colour lithographs and screenprints between 1953 and 1969, his etchings were his most distinctive contribution to Norwegian printmaking. Many were related to his mural commissions – for example, the *Expulsion from Paradise* for the auditorium of the Oslo Commercial Gymnasium (1945–56) – and were often done in the same elongated horizontal format. Virtually all his plates belong to the archive of the University Library in Oslo.

Bibliography

Reidar Revold, 'Efterkrigskunst: Fem Malere', *Kunst og Kultur*, XXXII (1949), pp. 151–74, puts Winge in the context of other artists in Norway whose work responded vigorously to the circumstances of the Second World War. Jan Askeland in *Sigurd Winge og hans Dekorsjon i Oslo Handelsgymnasium* (Oslo, 1956) discusses Winge's most important decorative commission, while a more recent source is Steinar Gjessing, *Sigurd Winge og hans Samtid*, an exhibition catalogue from the Nasjonalgalleriet, Oslo (1978). The only publication specifically on his prints is a catalogue and checklist from the Galleri KB in Oslo, *Sigurd Winges Grafikk* (1978), to which the KB numbers given below refer.

87 *Messiah I*, February 1945

Drypoint. Signed and dated in pencil, inscribed with title and 'Eg. trykk 8/10'. 197 × 179 mm

KB.14

1993-1-24-4. Purchased from the Rausing Fund

A second state of this composition, *Messiah II* (KB.63), was executed by Winge in 1964, showing further working on the hat and graveyard beyond. The first state was one of two related prints, the other being called *Secrets*, executed in April 1945; both were caricatures of Nazi militarism.

107

88 *Anguish (Air-raid)*, 1945

Etching, drypoint and aquatint. Signed and dated in pencil and inscribed 'Eget trykk'. 195 × 181 mm

KB.15

1993-1-24-3. Purchased from the Rausing Fund

Winge printed impressions of this subject in black and white as well as in the terracotta colour of this example owned by the British Museum. It showed in reverse a motif he had already executed as a mosaic in glass and copper called *Air-raid*, and may have been influenced by Nesch's bronze sculpture of 1943/4 of the same title, which consists of an upturned head with a face expressive of fear. Two earlier reliefs similarly related to the terrors of war were *Terror* and *Adam and Eve fleeing from Telemark*, both of 1942, while a later etching of 1948 called *Fighter plane* showed the destruction after an air-raid.

89 *'Jesus, Jesus'*, 1945

Stencil print. Signed and dated in pencil. 204 × 194 mm

1993-1-24-5. Purchased from the Rausing Fund

Winge made a number of satirical images for the Norwegian underground press during the German Occupation, which lasted until June 1945. 'Jøss og Jøss' is Norwegian slang for 'My, My' or, more accurately, 'Jesus, Jesus', and the image relates to the Allied advance on Berlin, with the cigar-smoking American offering '5000 dollars for the soldier in the Red Army who is first to Berlin'. It does not appear in the main checklist of Winge's prints produced by Galleri KB but is illustrated at the back of that catalogue.

Asger Jorn (1914–1973)

One of the most original and prolific minds of twentieth-century art, Jorn was important as a theoretician, polemicist, writer, painter, ceramicist, printmaker and sculptor. His insatiable intellectual and visual curiosity coupled with a naturally subversive temperament made him central to the Cobra movement composed of artists from Copenhagen, Brussels and Amsterdam who coalesced briefly from 1948 to 1951; through their collective activity they sought to express what Jorn termed 'a concept of artistic polyvalence', in which a diverse range of texts and imagery were closely interwoven. Jorn remained a tireless proponent of the principles of the movement long after it had disintegrated, transferring some of his energy to later collectives such as the Mouvement International pour un Bauhaus Imaginiste (1953–7) and the Situationist Movement (1957–61). The internationalism of these different alliances was of crucial importance to Jorn, who maintained a consistently ambivalent attitude towards Denmark, his country of origin, while insisting upon its importance in creating the preconditions essential to Cobra, which 'was made exactly to break through the nationalistic isolation of the northern countries' (quoted from a letter to Gordon Bailey Washburn, Director of the Carnegie Institute of Art, Pittsburgh, 15 January 1964, in the Jorn archive at the Silkeborg Kunstmuseum).

Jorn grew up in Jutland, where he was born Asger Jørgensen, moving with his family to the town of Silkeborg in 1929; the first exhibitions he saw of contemporary art were at Århus and Odense. From 1930 to 1935 he was enrolled in a teacher training course, becoming politically radicalised under the influence of the Syndicalist leader Christian Christensen. He also began painting and made contact with Linien, a group of abstract and Surrealist artists in Copenhagen. After completing his training Jorn left for Paris, where he attended Léger's Académie Contemporaine in 1936/7 and worked for Le Corbusier. Later he acknowledged the importance of the structural discipline he received in drawing everyday objects and in handling the picture plane, but at the time he felt stifled and it was his exposure to Surrealism in Paris, where he returned briefly in the summer of 1939, that determined his subsequent development.

In April 1940 the Germans occupied Denmark, effectively cutting off contact with the rest of Europe, but a lively artistic scene none the less managed to flourish in Copenhagen, as shown by an exhibition held at the Ålborg Museum in 1941, *Surrealisme – Abstrakt Kunst*. This included Henry Heerup (p. 118), Ejler Bille, Egill Jacobsen, Richard Mortensen, Carl-Henning Pedersen, Wilhelm Freddie, Vilhelm Bjerke-Petersen and Jorn, still under the surname of Jørgensen. Artistic activity was fuelled by anti-Nazi resistance, and a principal focus of cultural subversion was *Helhesten* (The Horse from Hell) magazine, produced from 1941 to 1944. It prefigured the ideals of the Cobra movement in its determinedly pluralistic approach to all art and culture, refusing to defer to conventional hierarchies and emphasising instead the importance of spontaneity of expression as epitomised by folk and primitive art. The artists involved, such as Ejler Bille (born 1910, to whom Jorn had worked in close proximity in Copenhagen since 1937), Egill Jacobsen, Carl-Henning Pedersen and Jorn, were striving to unite the forms and ideas of European modernism with Danish traditions to create a new type of expressionism. It was a crucial period for Jorn's formulation of a comprehensive theory of art and culture based on Marxist philosophy, and for the evolution of his idiosyncratic mythology of mask-like faces, fabulous zoomorphic beasts and cosmic landscapes. One of the major influences he acknowledged was a book on symbols in abstract art published by his fellow Dane Bjerke-Petersen in 1933; Jorn's experiments with his own automatic drawings in 1946 convinced him there could never be an objective analysis of the symbolical content of a work of art.

In 1945 he changed his name from Jørgensen to Jorn; he returned to Paris the following year, alternating between Paris, Brussels and Denmark until 1951. His encounter in Brussels in 1947 with the writer Christian Dotremont (1922–79), a member of the Belgian Revolutionary Surrealist group, was the catalyst for the formation of Cobra at a meeting in Paris at the end of 1948. Exhibitions associated with the movement were held in Brussels, Liège, Paris and Amsterdam, the one that received most attention being that organised by the Director of the Stedelijk in Amsterdam, Willem Sandberg, in November 1949. Jorn later caustically remarked: 'There has never in the whole development been one Cobra-exhibition in Denmark, and even the other Danish Cobra-artists didn't care any god-damned bit, and were forced in it by me' (from the letter to Gordon Washburn, quoted above). Denmark, however, not only contributed to the language of Cobra, it was where the first issue of the magazine of the same title was printed in 1949 and where some of the liveliest encounters took place, typified by this account in December 1949 by one of the Dutch members, Corneille (born 1922): 'I am just back from a 20-day stay in Denmark and a 50-hour interlude in Sweden. We did some good work out there, we painted a house in Jutland, we did the walls / every single wall there was + objects – cupboards – mirrors, bottles – glasses and so forth. We did a combined lithograph in Malmö, a true Indian party round a stone' (*Cobra: 40 years after*, exhibition catalogue for the J. Karel van Stuijvenberg Collection (Amsterdam, 1988), p. 29).

The real stimulus of the Cobra years for Jorn came from the constant bustle of activity and climate of experimentation which Dotremont in particular encouraged, collaborating with Jorn on 'word pictures'. After 1949 the inherent divisions between many of the artists came to the fore and the temporary cohesion of the Cobra group crumbled in 1951. By this stage the two main protagonists, Dotremont and Jorn, were suffering from tuberculosis, which led in both cases to a lengthy period of hospitalisation at the sanatorium in Jorn's home town of Silkeborg. Jorn's interludes in Silkeborg were usually associated with bouts of extreme poverty and illness, and his characteristic ambivalence was expressed on this occasion in a painting on hardboard entitled *Return to the detested town*. Notwithstanding his debilitation, the seventeen months he spent undergoing treatment and convalescence were very productive; out of this time came his treatise on aesthetics, *Held og Hasard* (Risk and Chance), a vivid group of linocuts (cat. 95) and colour lithographs, two cycles of paintings and his first involvement with ceramics, drawing upon the regional traditions that he learnt from a local potter. Another outcome was the idea of building a collection to be kept as part of the Silkeborg Museum, which would represent his work and that of the artists who had inspired him. The first donation of his own work was made in 1953, followed during the 1950s by examples by other artists acquired by Jorn for this purpose. Over the years until his death this led to a remark-

able concentration of mainly graphic material by artists as varied as Redon, Ensor, Kubin, Nolde, Beckmann, Max Ernst and Arp, with substantial holdings of the drawings of Henri Michaux, the prints of Wilfredo Lam, Matta and above all Dubuffet, as well as material by Jorn's Cobra associates and related artists.

In October 1953 Jorn left Silkeborg to convalesce in Switzerland, where he executed a suite of twenty-three etchings. Then in the spring of 1954 he moved to Albisola near Genoa where he concentrated on ceramics, working with Appel, Corneille, Matta and the Italian artists Enrico Baj and Lucio Fontana. Albisola and Paris became his principal centres of operation from the mid-1950s (he added a third base ten years later at Læso, an island off the northeast coast of Jutland). Thereafter his reputation rapidly gained ground; Børge Birch had represented Jorn in Copenhagen since 1948 but during the 1950s Carlo Cardazzo at the Galleria del Naviglio in Milan, Otto van de Loo in Munich and the Galerie Rive Gauche in Paris regularly handled his work abroad. In Britain Peter Cochrane of Tooth's Gallery featured his work in group and one-man shows from 1958 onwards, and the ICA gave exhibitions of his graphics in 1957 and paintings the following year; Herbert Read, Lord Croft, Ted Power and Guy Atkins (see bibliography) all acquired examples of his work ahead of some of the European collections. His first major retrospective was in Basle in 1964.

Among Jorn's multifarious interests was a scheme to build an archive and publish material on ancient Scandinavian art, an idea originally formed in 1949 with the archaeologist P. V. Glob, who had contributed an article to the first issue of *Cobra* (cat. 94). Jorn financed a photographic record from 1961 to 1965, calling his operation, which he directed from Paris, the 'Institut Scandinave de Vandalism Comparatif' (Scandinavian Institute for Comparative Vandalism), 'vandalism' being the ironical name that Jorn applied to the architecture and ornament of the Viking period. Although the study centre did not materialise, he was responsible for publishing a number of books on early graffiti in Normandy churches, prehistoric and Viking carving and early medieval sculpture. This hectic spate of intellectual and artistic activity continued unabated until his death from lung cancer on 1 May 1973 in Århus.

Drawing and printmaking were an integral part of Jorn's constant quest for new forms of expression throughout his career. He produced more than four hundred prints in linocut, etching, lithography and woodcut, many of them assembled in series. His earliest prints were linocuts for his *Blasphemous Christmas carols* that appeared in *Frem*, a Marxist monthly magazine. These were followed by a linocut reminiscent of Arp made in 1937 and a small number of etchings of female figures done in 1933 and 1937. Between his three visits to Paris, Jorn sporadically attended Aksel Jørgensen's classes at the Copenhagen Academy in 1937/8 (see Jorn's article on Jørgensen in *Kunst*, VIII

(April 1964), pp. 202–4). The Graphic School gave him access to printing equipment, which artists were entitled to use without being formally registered as students, and it was here that he made a number of drypoint etchings from 1939 to 1945; twenty-three of these were eventually to be published in 1960 under the title of *Occupations* (cat. 90, 91). Many of these early plates were left lying around with no thought for any proper edition because Jorn lost interest in the process once he had finished experimenting with motifs. A more systematic approach to his printmaking was later enjoined upon him when the Munich dealer Otto van de Loo became his publisher in the late 1950s, and Jorn himself began to organise his material with a view to the collection for Silkeborg. In the 1950s he continued with drypoint etching, using S. W. Hayter's Atelier 17 in Paris for *Mask composition* in four states in 1958 (vdL. 202a–d). In the same year he branched out into colour etching, assisted in the printing process by the young Munich artists Heimrad Premm and H. P. Zimmer (cat. 96), producing compositions whose greater degree of abstraction indicated the impact of the work of Wols (1913–51), which Jorn acquired for the collection at Silkeborg. Despite his successful mastery of a range of etching techniques, Jorn made no further prints in this medium until 1966.

Jorn's early lithographs were less haphazardly executed than the etchings because he tended to need the assistance of a professional printer. After his first work, a series of twenty-one calligraphic compositions executed at the Graphic School in 1940 to accompany his Danish version of a French translation of some Chinese love poems entitled *The Jade Flute*, he used the workshop in Copenhagen of J. Christian Sørensen, who printed some of the *Cobra* publications (cat. 93, 94) and his portfolio of eight untitled lithographs published in 1949 (cat. 92). Sørensen visited Jorn in 1952 in the Silkeborg Sanatorium, where the latter made a group of seven coloured drawings on transparent paper for translation into lithographs; the original drawings were re-used in 1970 and formally published under the title *Silkeborg suite* (vdL. 110–16). Jorn pursued the transfer technique further with his contribution to the portfolio issued by the artists' group The Spirals in 1951, using the services of another workshop in the Copenhagen area, Permild and Rosengreen, who were to become his regular printers. The third lithographic specialist with whom he established a close relationship was Peter Bramsen, the Danish printer and eventual partner in the Clot workshop in Paris where Jorn increasingly worked from 1966 onwards.

Relief printmaking was a more sporadic feature of Jorn's work than lithography, but it was responsible for some of his most expressive images, especially during the period in Silkeborg in 1952/3. There he printed linocut motifs on a small proofing press for use as marginal illustrations or vignettes to accompany his treatise *Held og Hasard*, and a group of more ambitious compositions (cat. 95), some of

which combined lino and woodcut. Several of the images were related to a theme he was working out in painting and lithography as well, *On the silent myth*, whose *raison d'être* was that 'the relation between visual art and the narration of myths must be silent, not illustrative' (quoted by Atkins, *Jorn in Scandinavia 1930–1953*, p. 89). Among Jorn's last prints were two series of colour woodcuts published in 1970 by the Galerie van de Loo and in 1971 by the Atelier Clot, where they had been printed on a lithographic press by Peter Bramsen.

The marketing of Jorn's prints was transformed by his association with the Galerie van de Loo, which he joined in 1958 shortly after it opened. Prior to that there was no systematic record of what he had printed, although when he was in Silkeborg in the early 1950s Jorn did begin an inventory of his prints which he failed to maintain after 1953. Neither was he interested in selling his prints on anything other than an *ad hoc* basis through the occasional exhibition or by touting them round himself with a portfolio simply to pay his way when abroad. Other artist friends were sometimes used for this purpose, including the architect Robert Dahlmann Olsen, who amassed a substantial collection of the prints for himself, or Enrico Baj in Milan, to whom he sent prints for sale in the early 1950s (see *Baj Jorn: Lettres 1953–1961*, Musée d'Art Moderne, St Etienne, 1989). He did make a number of sales in the United States, principally through the Biennials of Color Lithography held during the 1950s in Cincinnati, the Pittsburgh Internationals at the Carnegie Institute and the Philadelphia Print Club. In Britain the Redfern Gallery included some of his prints, under the School of Paris in their exhibitions in the late 1950s and early 1960s, priced between 12 and 25 guineas, and at a later date they were handled by the London Arts Group. In Denmark there were a few committed collectors, the collection of Jorn's friend Robert Dahlmann Olsen being the earliest and most comprehensive, but a full retrospective exhibition of his printmaking did not take place in Copenhagen until after Jorn's death in 1976 (Statens Museum for Kunst). The *catalogue raisonné* of his prints likewise did not appear until 1976, although Jorn had proposed such a publication to the Galerie Rive Gauche in 1955.

The main repository and archive for Jorn's work is to be found at the Silkeborg Kunstmuseum, which was built in 1982 to house the collection that had outgrown its original home in the Silkeborg Museum. Recently Otto van de Loo has made a substantial gift from his personal holding of prints to the Kupferstich-Kabinett in Dresden, as recorded in an exhibition catalogue for October 1994.

Bibliography

There is a voluminous literature in several different languages on the Cobra movement as a whole. The references here are specific to Jorn, who is well served in English and Danish thanks to the publications of the Silkeborg Kunstmuseum, presided over by Troels Andersen, and to the work of Guy Atkins. Atkins (1912–88) was a remarkable linguist who began as a German specialist, taking his doctorate at Prague in 1937. His wartime service turned him into an Africanist and lecturer in Bantu languages at the School of Oriental and African Studies at London University from 1946 to 1979. The work of Jorn, whom he first met in London in 1956, was a corollary to his interest in African art and became his great passion from then onwards. By 1961 he had been authorised by the artist to prepare the *catalogue raisonné* of his paintings, which appeared in three volumes with a supplement as *Jorn in Scandinavia 1930–1953* (London, 1968); *Asger Jorn: The crucial years 1954–64* (London, 1977, including a separate chapter on his graphics by Ursula Lehmann-Brockhaus); *Asger Jorn: The final years 1965–1973* (London, 1980) and *Asger Jorn: Supplement to the oeuvre catalogue of his paintings from 1930 to 1973* (London, 1986). (I should like to thank John Picton of SOAS for drawing my attention to his obituary of Atkins in *African News*, IX (October 1988).) Otto van de Loo produced the *catalogue raisonné* of Jorn's prints, *Asger Jorn: Werkverzeichnis* (Munich, 1976), while a catalogue of the Silkeborg Kunstmuseum's holdings of the drawings was published in 1983.

Troels Andersen has been working on a biography of Jorn, the first part of which appeared in 1994 as *Asger Jorn: En biograf. Årene 1914–53* (Borgen). Jorn's early writings have been addressed by Graham Birtwistle in *Living Art: Asger Jorn's comprehensive theory of art between Helhesten and Cobra (1946–1949)* (Utrecht, 1986), and Per Hofman Hansen has published the complete *Bibliography of Asger Jorn's Writings* (Silkeborg, 1988, text in Danish and English).

Of the many exhibition catalogues, *Asger Jorn 1914–73* (Stedelijk Museum, Amsterdam, 1994; paintings and drawings only) includes a full chronology by Troels Andersen with text in Dutch and English. I should like to thank Mr Andersen for his comments on a draft of this text.

90 *Beat generation*, 1942

Etching printed on off-white wove paper. Signed in pencil.
168 × 122 mm

vdL.50

1993-12-12-45. Purchased from the Rausing Fund

Beat generation and the following subject are early proofs of two of the plates chosen by Jorn for the series of twenty-three etchings from 1939–45 that he had reprinted by R. Tamburro in Paris in 1960 under the title *Occupations*, published in an edition of fifty by the Galerie Rive Gauche (vdL.45–67); the venture was part of Jorn's increasing desire to preserve a record of his early work in connection with the archival holding he was creating for Silkeborg. By the time the full edition was executed there had been a noticeable deterioration in the surface of this particular plate, which had become densely pitted; but the chance effect evidently did not deter Jorn from its inclusion.

90

Although the prints were executed only in a casual manner in the first instance, without forming part of a predetermined series, they are an invaluable guide to the evolution of Jorn's pictorial vocabulary in which the influence of Klee is very much apparent. The titles for the individual plates as well as the series as a whole were not applied until the date of their proper publication in 1960, when *Beat generation* was the only one given in English, the others being in French.

91 *Masked game*, 1942

Etching printed on buff-coloured wove paper. Signed in pencil.
169 × 122 mm

vdL.51

1993-12-12-46. Purchased from the Rausing Fund

The mask motif became one of Jorn's principal motifs from 1940/1 onwards. On this impression Jorn has placed his signature as though the composition were meant to be read horizontally, but in the 1960 edition it is clear that it should be seen as a vertical image.

91

92 ARS-portfolio, 1945

Eight lithographs with a lithographic design on the cover,
printed in colour and black and white. Signed and dated in
pencil. Sheet size 495 × 309 mm

vdL.83–91

1993-12-12-47 (1–8). Purchased from the Rausing Fund
Illustrated (VIII) in colour on plate 5

Like the etchings referred to above, this portfolio displays
the range of invention Jorn could already achieve despite
being a novice to the medium; his early lithographs were
deliberately calligraphic in execution, but by the late 1950s
his use of the medium had become more painterly.

   The portfolio was printed in Copenhagen and published
for an exhibition in 1949 in an edition of 160 by Ars-Verlag
in Stockholm, the creation of the writer Arne Häggqvist,
who translated Salvador Dali into Swedish. The Ars
Konstserie was a series of print editions commissioned
from different artists *c.*1944–6 that included the work of
the Danish Surrealist Wilhelm Freddie (1906–95) and the
émigré artists Endre Nemes (p. 119) and the Latvian Adja
Yunkers (1900–83), who was in Stockholm from 1938 to
1947 and participated in the Surrealist exhibition of

the Minotaur group in Malmö in 1943 (see p. 119). (I would
like to thank Ragnar von Holten for this information on
Ars-Verlag.)

93 Cover for 'Abstract Art in Denmark', 1947

Colour lithograph printed on coarse beige-coloured paper.
Signed and dated within the composition. 243 × 352 mm

vdL.96

1991-4-6-29. Purchased from the Rausing Fund

Early in 1947 Jorn organised an exhibition of Danish avant-
garde painting and sculpture which was meant to travel to
a number of venues in Scandinavia but for financial rea-
sons was shown only in Oslo and Gothenburg. The image
reproduced here was the second design made by Jorn for the
catalogue cover, which was printed by Sørensen and published in an edition of 500 by the Tokanten Gallery in
Copenhagen.

94 Cover for 'Cobra no. 1', 1949

Colour lithograph on white wove paper. Signed by Jorn, Egill
Jacobsen and Carl-Henning Pedersen within the composition.
310 × 487 mm

vdL.101

1991-4-6-31 (1). Purchased from the Rausing Fund

Cobra was one of several experimental journals produced
during the 1940s and early 1950s, including the Danish
Helhesten, the Dutch *Braak* and *Reflex*, the German *Meta*
and *Blok* from Czechoslovakia. The composition of *Cobra*
throughout its ten issues from 1949 to 1951 (no. 8/9 existed
only in proof form because there was insufficient money for
its publication) exemplified the collaborative spirit that was
an essential tenet of the movement as a whole. Much of the
activity took place within the transient community of
artists and writers who congregated at the Ateliers du
Marais in Brussels, where Pierre Alechinsky (born 1927)
installed a lithographic press on which the Belgian numbers of *Cobra* were printed. The editor-in-chief was Christian Dotremont, with a changing cast of guest editors.
Among them was the Danish architect Robert Dahlmann
Olsen, guest editor for the first issue, which was produced in
Copenhagen at the Sørensen workshop in an edition of
1000 copies. The design for the cover was a joint effort by
Jorn, Egill Jacobsen (born 1910) and Carl-Henning Pedersen
(born 1913), and within the magazine were four other original lithographs by Jorn, Jacobsen, Ejler Bille and Pedersen.
Other publications associated with *Cobra* were *Le Petit
Cobra*, also edited by Dotremont, the first number of which
was printed in Brussels in 1949, and *Bibliothèque de Cobra*,
which produced fifteen volumes in 1950 under the editor-
ship of Jorn in Copenhagen. (All the issues of *Cobra* are
reproduced in *Cobra 1948–1951* (Paris, 1980).)

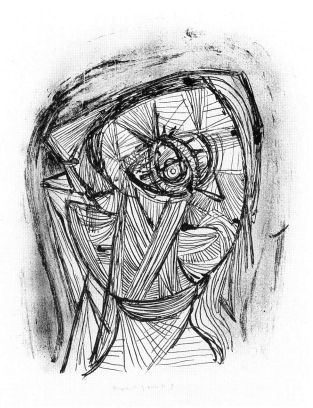

92 (I)

92 (II)

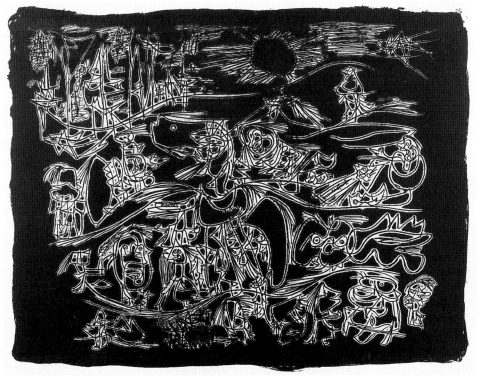

92 (III)

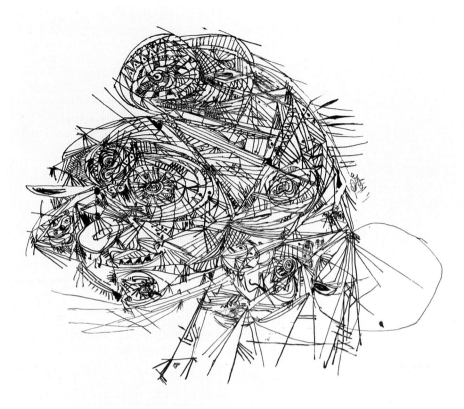

92 (IV)

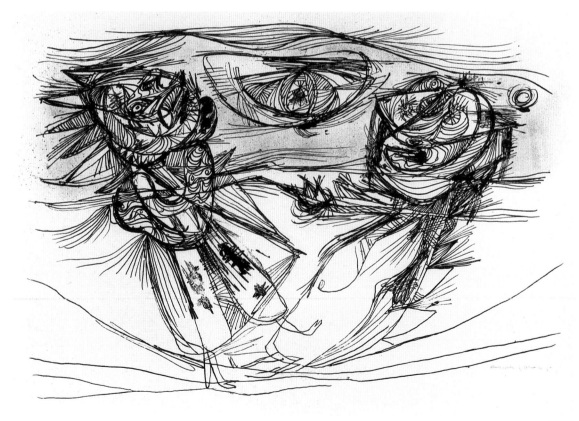

92 (V)

92 (VI)

92 (VII)

93

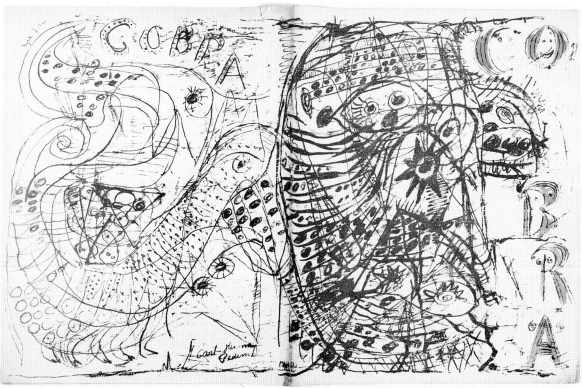

94

95 *Council for the Propagation of Danish Beauty in Foreign Lands*, 1952

Colour woodcut and linocut printed on thin off-white paper. Signed and dated in pencil, inscribed 'La Comité' and numbered 20/25. 350 × 427 mm

vdL.124

1995-11-5-7. Purchased

Illustrated in colour on plate 4

Council for the Propagation of Danish Beauty in Foreign Lands distilled Jorn's seething vocabulary of forms into his most ambitious print so far, redolent in its title and content of the ironies he perceived in his situation. From the autumn of 1950 to the early spring of 1951, Jorn and his family lived in conditions of abject poverty at Suresnes, a suburb of Paris, in a hostel known as La Maison des Artistes Danois which was administered by a committee in Copenhagen. When tuberculosis and malnutrition forced Jorn to return to Silkeborg, he construed it as a personal defeat; nevertheless, the respite his medical care and convalescence afforded from incessant hardship, together with the studio facilities provided by the town, enabled Jorn to turn this period to excellent artistic account. Out of these circumstances Jorn achieved a new understanding of his relationship with Denmark and Silkeborg in particular; this was demonstrated by his decision to endow the latter with a museum collection of his choice, and by his comments in a letter of 1952 to his fellow artist Mogens Balle (born 1921) that even though an artist may spend most of his life away from his native background, he must recognise the strength and identity he derives from his 'provincialism': 'Picasso was always a Spaniard even though he lived his whole life in Paris' (quoted by Andersen, *Jorn: En biograf*, p. 233).

Council for the Propagation of Danish Beauty in Foreign Lands was printed in a black and white version, of which only one or two proofs are known, and in the colour edition from two large sheets of lino sent to Jorn in June 1952 by Dahlmann Olsen. (There was also a related painting that has been lost since 1954; see Atkins, *Jorn: Crucial years*, Appendix no. 19.) An underlying colour (blue in the case of the British Museum's impression) was usually applied, printed from a woodblock, then the lino was cut up and reassembled like a jigsaw to permit the simultaneous printing of other colours for different parts of the composition. It was a method consciously indebted to that associated with Munch's colour woodcuts, which had greatly impressed Jorn when he saw them exhibited in Copenhagen in 1946. There is a noticeable variation in the colouring and sometimes the paper between each impression; the British Museum's example, which came from the collection of Otto van de Loo, is the one illustrated in the *catalogue raisonné* of 1976.

96

96 *Untitled. 'D'*, 1958/9

Colour etching printed in blue, black and brown on off-white wove paper that is pale blue on the printed side. Signed and dated in pencil and numbered 4/50. 244 × 169 mm

vdL.205

1991-12-14-38. Purchased from the Rausing Fund

Five compositions were printed by Jorn as colour etchings in different variants in 1958/9, assisted by Heimrad Premm and H. P. Zimmer, and were among the first of his prints to be published by the Galerie van de Loo (vdL.205–7, 209, 211).

Henry Heerup (born 1907)

Heerup was loosely involved with all the main avant-garde groups in Denmark from the 1930s to the 1950s – Linien, Høst, Helhesten and Cobra – but they served more as a vehicle for the exhibition of his work than as a definition of any particular theoretical standpoint on his part. A vigorously independent figure who created a picturesque idiom of deliberate wit and naivety in his sculpture, painting and printmaking, Heerup's most remarkable achievement has been a series of sculpture gardens, created as adjuncts to his homes in 1934 and 1946 and as part of the Louisiana Museum in 1972.

From 1922 to 1927 he served various apprenticeships with a lithographer, a bronze foundry and a stonemason, studying for the next five years at the Academy in Copenhagen, where Aksel Jørgensen (p. 81) was one of his teachers. He has always been primarily a sculptor, whose stone carvings of the 1930s attracted the attention of his fellow Danish artists because of their resemblance to pre-Christian traditions. In the 1940s he began to paint the surfaces of his carvings and to make assemblages of wood, often incorporating found objects in a way that is both visually appealing and humorous, producing a species of contemporary folk art that has ensured his long-term popularity.

Heerup's printmaking began with a number of small woodcuts in 1930 but did not develop in earnest until 1941/2, when he contributed several prints to the magazine *Helhesten* (see p. 108). Lithography and linocut were to dominate his total production of 282 prints up to 1980, his work being characterised by a strong narrative content combined with heavily outlined decorative forms that were often based on Viking ornament.

Bibliography

The two main sources consulted have been Poul Vad, *Henry Heerup*, Danske Grafikere 9 (Copenhagen, 1971) and the *catalogue raisonné* by Hans Moestrup, *Henry Heerup: Det grafiske vaerk 1930–80* (Charlottenlund, 1980; the entries are in English as well as Danish).

97 *Dustman finding a heart*, 1950

Lithograph. Signed and dated in pencil and inscribed with title. 455 × 362 mm

M.57

1992 10 3 91. Purchased from the Rausing Fund

This example is one of approximately ten copies from the original printing; further impressions were printed in the 1970s together with those from two other lithographs of the same date. The year 1950 was a productive one in terms of Heerup's printmaking: he made more than twenty lithographs and thirty prints altogether. The lithographs were drawn on irregular stones discarded from a printing

97

workshop and Heerup adapted his pictures to the shape of the stones.

The image of the dustman emerged as one of Heerup's *leitmotifs* in the 1940s, representing a figure with whom he identified in his role as an artist concerned with random discovery and the recycling of material discarded by others. Its first appearance was in 1943, when he included a dustcart in a colour lithograph for a portfolio with Jorn (p. 108), Mortensen, Jacobsen and Egon Mathiesen; another representation came in a crayon design of 1948 around a song of Heerup's composition called 'The Dustman'. If the dustman represents the artist, the heart, which was also a recurring feature, tends to stand for a sense of worth and integrity as well as affection. The narrative style developed by Heerup during the 1940s is encapsulated in a series of coloured crayon drawings dating from 1948–53 that were all done as illustrations to songs he composed himself to be played on the recorder (see the catalogue of twenty-two of them belonging to Holstebro Kunstmuseum, 1991). The artist variously shows himself playing a recorder while his wife looks at a book with a large heart wedged between them; or on his familiar bicycle with another view of him to one side, carving a granite block; in the composition called *The stonecarver* he is at work in his garden with his muse, a naked woman holding a heart, rising up before him.

Endre Nemes (1909–1984)

As a refugee from the German occupation of Czechoslo-vakia, Nemes was a cosmopolitan influence on artistic life in Sweden during the comparative isolation of the 1940s and played a major role in the dissemination of Surrealist forms and ideas. He was born in Hungary with the family name of Nágel, changing this to Nemes in 1928, by which time he was active as a writer and cartoonist in Prague. The Surrealist content of his work did not mature until the late 1930s, after he had completed five years as a student at the Academy of Fine Arts in Prague under Willy Novak (1886–1977) and visited Paris in 1933 with his close associate Jacob Bauernfreund (1904–76), who later emigrated to England and anglicised his name to Bornfriend. By 1938, the date of Nemes's departure from Prague, initially for Finland, his paintings, pastels and etchings showed a close affinity to de Chirico's *pitture metafisice*, to which he returned when he was able to resume painting in Sweden in the early 1940s. (For a survey of the artistic background in Prague from which Nemes emerged, see *Tschechische Kunst der 20er & 30er Jahre: Avantgarde und Tradition*, Mathilden-höhe Darmstadt, 1988.)

Nemes taught briefly at the Free Painting School in Helsinki and was given a one-man show of his graphic art at the Kunstnerforbundet in Oslo in 1939, but was soon forced into further exile to Norway and then to Sweden fol-lowing the German invasion of April 1940. After intern-ment he was able to establish residence in Sweden (becoming a citizen in 1948) and return to painting. One-man shows in Stockholm and Malmö in 1941 brought him to the attention of an important collector, Hermann Gott-hardt of Simrishamn in southern Sweden, who purchased some fifteen of his works, including two of his most impor-tant paintings after the manner of de Chirico, *The baroque chair* and *The baroque architect* of 1941. Nemes rapidly estab-lished himself as a catalyst for change within Swedish artis-tic life in Stockholm and in southern Sweden; in the former he first made his impact through the exhibition Artists in Exile on the Nybro Quay in 1944, and four years later with the sculptor Eric Grate (1896–1983) was a founder-member of the excellent but short-lived arts magazine *Prisma*. The Halmstad group of painters had already in the 1930s estab-lished a Surrealist idiom, but Nemes reinforced its position, exhibiting at Malmö Town Hall in 1943 as part of the Minotaur group whose affiliates included Adja Yunkers and two local artists, Max-Walter Svanberg (1912–94) and C. O. Hultén (p. 121). In 1947 Nemes took up the position of director of the Valand Art School in Gothenburg, where he transformed the relative provincialism of the teaching pro-gramme by his breadth of artistic and intellectual back-ground, remaining there until 1955 when he moved back to Stockholm to resume painting full-time.

After the mid-1940s Nemes departed from the pro-nounced influence of de Chirico, experimenting with glazes

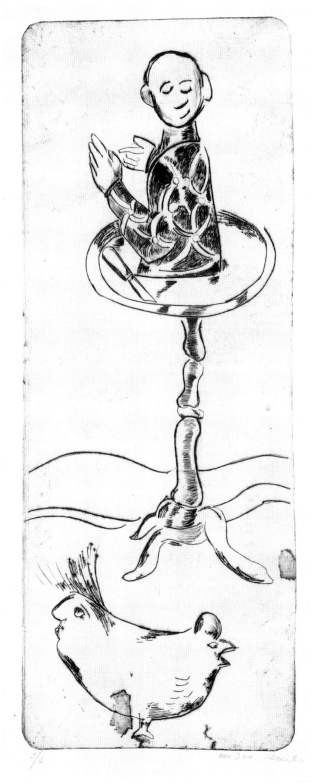

98

that gave a jewel-like quality to the colours and texture of his painting and incorporating motifs that were closer to the more whimsical imagery of Chagall. During the 1950s his compositions became more abstract but returned to overtly Surrealist invention from the 1960s onwards in collages and paintings which synthesised aspects of the work of Max Ernst and de Chirico. His prints were always closely allied to his work in other media, starting with a group of twelve etchings, predominantly drypoint, executed in 1936 and 1938 before he left Prague. Nemes returned to print-making in 1943, his work in this sphere gaining momentum once he was established at Valand, where he promoted the development of a thriving graphic school and encouraged the students to produce annual portfolios of prints from 1947 onwards, partly as a means of financing their study trips abroad. He experimented with aquatint in the late 1940s, recalling the work of Rouault, which provided an equivalent to the intense mosaic of colour he achieved in his painting. During the 1950s he displayed more interest in colour lithography, and the figurative element in his compositions diminished to be replaced by insect and vegetal forms, then by a more structured abstraction until the latter part of the following decade. Thereafter the fifty-four aquatints, lithographs and colour etchings he made, one-third of his entire production of prints, reflected the *collagiste* approach that dominated the rest of his work.

In addition to the two drypoints catalogued below, Nemes is represented in the British Museum by two 'metaphysical' pastels of 1938 and 1943, a drypoint of 1943, one aquatint of 1947–50 and two states of a lithograph of 1952, all of which were purchased from the artist's widow, Britt-Louise Sundell Nemes, in 1993.

Bibliography

Since the artist's death there have been several publications on his work, starting with the monograph by Thomas Millroth, *Endre Nemes* (Stockholm, 1985; the chronology is given in English as well as Swedish). The first part of a *catalogue raisonné* of the paintings and collages from A to K for the period 1965–85, arranged alphabetically according to the titles of the works, has been brought out by Jan-Gunnar Sjölin (Malmö, 1989). Ragnar von Holten of the Nationalmuseum Stockholm has published *Endre Nemes: Teckning – collage – måleri* (Moderna Museet, 1990) and the catalogue of his prints, *Endre Nemes: Grafik – oeuvrekatalog* (Nationalmuseum, 1990).

Outside Sweden the major holding of Nemes's work is to be found at the museum opened in his honour in 1984 in his home town at Pécs in Hungary and at the museum in Bochum, Germany which has developed a particular strength in the representation of artists from Central Europe.

99

98 *The two-headed chicken*, 1947–50

Drypoint. Signed in pencil and numbered 3/6. 294 × 114 mm
vH.38
1993-1-24-35. Purchased from the Rausing Fund

99 *Self-portrait*, 1947–50

Drypoint. Signed in pencil and numbered 2/50. 387 × 237 mm
vH.41
1993-1-25-36. Purchased from the Rausing Fund

C. O. Hultén (born 1916)

As an artist, writer, publisher and gallery organiser C. O. Hultén was a prime mover in the expression of a Surrealist aesthetic in southern Sweden during the 1940s and 1950s, and the main point of contact with the Cobra movement. Together with his two principal collaborators, Max-Walter Svanberg (1912–94) and Anders Österlin (born 1926), Hultén grew up in the Malmö area of Sweden without receiving any formal art education, taking employment in 1938 in the printing division of a packaging firm in Lund, Åkerlund & Rausing, where he later met Österlin. Although he was aware of the Surrealist paintings by the Halmstad artists, Hultén was less interested in what he perceived as their rather academic interpretations than in the work of Picasso, which he saw in the original at an exhibition of Spanish painting in Malmö in 1937, then again in Copenhagen in 1939 where *Guernica* was displayed. The other major influence was that of Max Ernst, particularly his frottages, which Hultén knew only in reproduction until he was able to make his first visit to Paris in 1947. Hultén was already producing his own Surrealist compilations in the late 1930s, in the form of a fur-coated file with loose-leaf illustrations and poetry of 1937–40 called *Tide*. In 1941 he encountered the work of Svanberg, Nemes (p. 119) and Adja Junkers, with whom he exhibited as part of Minotaur in Malmö in March 1943. The group promptly disbanded, but Hultén, Svanberg and Österlin established themselves in 1945 under the heading of Imaginism. This name was preserved as a separate identity for exhibition purposes until 1957 and was derived from Imagism, Ezra Pound's self-proclaimed form of poetic expression, appealing to the Swedish artists because of its literary and visual associations. The group invited other participants to their exhibitions, which were held at several different venues in Sweden and in 1953 in Paris and Florence, although Svanberg had left before the latter event.

The end of the Second World War prompted a burst of artistic activity and renewed contacts with the rest of Europe. In 1947 Hultén travelled to Paris with Österlin to see the international Surrealist exhibition at Galerie Maeght, and met Brauner, Riopelle, Léger and Breton. Hultén's experiments with automatism date from 1947–9, the period of his earliest frottages. These were immediately inspired by work such as Max Ernst's *L'Histoire naturelle* of 1926; prompted by the failure to sell his work at exhibition, Hultén had ten of the frottages reproduced in 1947 as the first publication of *Image*, the imprint of the Imaginist group, with the title *Drömmars ur Bladens Händer* (Dreams out of the Hands of Leaves). The book was a critical success, helping to establish the credentials of the Imaginists in Sweden and Denmark, where it attracted the attention of the artists associated with Cobra. Among other events this led at the end of 1949 to the 'Indian party round a stone' (see p. 109) in Malmö when Appel, Constant, Corneille,

Hultén, Österlin and Max-Walter Svanberg combined to produce the lithograph *One of these days*. Hultén's desire to establish a regular venue for bringing the European avant-garde to Sweden was the motive behind the Galerie Colibri, opened in Malmö in 1955, where Alechinsky, Matta, Michaux, Corneille, Lam and K. O. Götz were some of the principal foreign exhibitors. In his own work Hultén diversified to produce sculpture and enamel compositions during the 1960s, concentrating on public commissions. The most significant developments in his style and imagery were associated with his growing interest in African culture after his marriage in 1961 to his second wife Birgitta, who had close links with West Africa and the Senegalese poet Senghor. Hultén's involvement was in many ways a logical extension to the preoccupations of his main Surrealist phase; it was reflected in his personal collection of African art and in the new symbolic content of his work, which provided visual metaphors for the tension between a rampant natural world and the rigid forms of imposed European structures.

Hultén's printmaking has spanned his career from 1946 onwards, with the emphasis on lithography and, more recently, on colour etching and aquatint. Graphic art was another medium of experimentation and reproduction for the Imaginists, of whom Hultén produced the most interesting results. In addition to the early frottages for *Dreams out of the Hands of Leaves*, he was making drypoints and

100

101

inventing a technique of his own which he termed *Imprimage*, a form of stencil printing using collaged elements (cat. 102) which he says occurred to him when observing the accidental traces left on spare sheets of paper used for cleaning the rotary presses at Åkerlund & Rausing. A series of ten drypoints from 1946–50 (cat. 100, 101) adumbrated the development of his own form of Surrealism: 'This series illustrates the shifting from surrealism to an imagery which became characteristic of what I was to make as an "imaginist"' (letter from the artist to Birgit Rausing, November–December 1990). Each of the main proponents of Imaginism differed in his style but the common factor was their belief, like the Cobra artists, that they should allow new forms to emerge through experimention rather than seeking to reproduce the unconscious as a landscape of the mind.

The combined lithograph made in November 1949 was printed for the Image press in an edition of nine examples with the assistance of a commercial lithographer in Malmö, Birger Hammerstedt, with whom Hultén continued to work in the 1950s, producing a magazine and a print portfolio called *Salamander*. S. W. Hayter was favourably impressed by what Hultén and his associates were achieving in the context of offset lithography, which he observed at first hand in 1956:

But the most interesting use of this method of printing for creative purposes I discovered when visiting Malmö in Sweden in the spring of 1956. There I found a very original and active group of artists, noncomformists with regard to the well-organized if conventional artists' groups in the country and consequently entirely dependent upon themselves. As many of them were engaged in the field of publicity and printing and furthermore had access to an off-set press, they were producing with their own hands a magazine, *Salamander*, containing illustrations in full colour which were in effect originals. The print by C. O. Hultén is taken from this magazine, and is printed from what are called in the trade 'separations', but which I prefer to consider rather as components, the usual phrase suggesting that one has separated that which was once together for it to be put together again in the final result. (*About Prints* (1962), pp. 70–1)

The British Museum acquired six prints and two drawings directly from the artist in 1992; six of the works date from 1946–50 and the remaining two, a colour lithograph and an etching and aquatint, are from 1962 and 1973.

Bibliography
C. O. Hultén: Arbeten 1937–1982 (Malmö Konsthall, 1982) contains a detailed chronology and full bibliography.

100 *Paranoid interior*, 1946

Drypoint. Signed in pencil, numbered 1/10 and inscribed 'EA'.
207 × 145 mm
1992-7-25-64. Purchased from the Rausing Fund

102

101 *Come to me*, 1950

Drypoint. Signed in pencil and inscribed 'EA'.
299 × 247 mm
1992-7-25-66. Purchased from the Rausing Fund

The drypoints from the series of ten of 1946–50 were all published in small numbers with a maximum of fifteen, as in the case of this composition: 'There was no market for prints. What was interesting was to see the result of what was made in the plate' (letter to Birgit Rausing).

102 *Irrational things and moon on the wane,* 1948

Screenprint (*Imprimage*). Signed in pencil within the image.
566 × 368 mm
1992-7-25-63. Purchased from the Rausing Fund

Bertil Lundberg (born 1922)

Lundberg has been a pivotal figure in the development of printmaking as a freely expressive modernist idiom in southern Sweden, concentrating like S. W. Hayter, one of his principal mentors, on the effects that can be achieved through copper-plate printing. His only technical education came via his apprenticeship to a commercial photo-engraving firm in Malmö. From 1938 to 1940 he attended classes at the local painting school, but his artistic inclinations were really fostered by the influence of Surrealism mediated by the Imaginists after 1945 and by his visits to Copenhagen and Paris in 1949/50. Lundberg's own work in this vein began in 1952 with a charcoal drawing, followed by experiments with woodcut printing; then in the following year he acquired a copper-plate press from Copenhagen. His first etchings were produced in 1954 (cat. 103), inspired by the imagery and frottage techniques of Max Ernst and C. O. Hultén (p. 121) which he emulated by impressing organic shapes into the soft ground on his plates. Hultén's Galerie Colibri in the mid to late 1950s was an important vehicle for the exhibition of Lundberg's work, which in 1956 was described in the following terms by the poet Göran Printz-Påhlsson as part of his commentary for *New Generation II*:

There is a 'double plot' in Lundberg's etchings which gives them their calm, ironic, pastoral tone. The visionary and decorative elements follow each other like the two pairs of lovers in a light opera; the actual beauty in the shapes and subtleties of the vision is a superior commentary on the vision responding with its half-hidden, enigmatic smile.

The gallery also brought Lundberg into contact with an international avant-garde, including Hayter, with whom he formed an immediate friendship when the latter visited the Imaginists in 1956 (see p. 123).

The general tenor of Hayter's approach had a liberating effect on Lundberg at a time when the dominant printmaking traditions to which Lundberg had access were those laid down by Harald Sallberg (p. 49) in Stockholm and Aksel Jørgensen (p. 81) in Copenhagen. Lundberg never made prints himself at Atelier 17 in Paris, but he freely acknowledged the debt he incurred from observing the principles on which the Atelier was run when he came to set up an equivalent 'studio' in 1964 in Malmö, the Forum Graphic School, where he was the sole teacher until his retirement in 1991, encouraging the growth of a whole community of artists practising intaglio printmaking in southern Sweden (see, for example, p. 158).

His own work increasingly evinced the sculptural approach to etching that Hayter considered to be a distinguishing feature of Atelier 17, and one that characterised the printmaking of Rolf Nesch (p. 97), which Lundberg saw exhibited in Malmö from the 1950s. One of the prints to make a great impact on Lundberg when he saw it exhibited at the Galerie Colibri in the mid-1950s was *Glacial sun*

104

(1949) by Enrico Zañartu (born 1921), Hayter's deputy at Atelier 17 in Paris after the war. Lundberg, like Jürgen von Konow (p. 131), admired the Chilean artist's manipulation of the surface of the plate through his depth of biting, which Lundberg emulated in a number of compositions of landscape format from the period 1956–63: these departed from the Surrealist imagery and frottage effects of his other early prints. Like Hayter, Lundberg soon learned how much discipline was required in order to achieve apparently casual effects:

You learn more and more to control 'chance'. As Klee once put it: Chance is your best ally when you've learnt to curb it ... It's easy to fall for beautiful effects and have too much 'rubbish' left in a picture ... You avoid that by having a large share of self-criticism which makes you weed out what will only be a beautiful surface ... It's a question of making a picture. If for instance you're sitting looking at a wall you suddenly notice cracks and holes that 'look like' something. Not necessarily something we recognise, maybe just a nice shape. It may be very vague but so good or expressive that if you mark the spot then other people can also discover it. (von Holten, *Bertil Lundberg*, pp. 62–3)

In 1962 a one-man show of his prints at Galerie du Dragon in Paris, which also showed Lam and Matta, helped Lundberg's work to become more widely known abroad. He

105

often exhibited in group exhibitions with the Atelier 17 artists and on occasion with Hayter himself, who always kept a selection of Lundberg's prints in Paris. Lundberg's first colour prints were made in 1960/1 using open-bite and aquatint. From the mid-1960s he used these techniques with increasing subtlety for the depiction of enigmatic floating shapes, suspended in fields of saturated colour or darkness, sometimes in conjunction with contemporary poetry, such as that of Paul Celan in 1975.

Bibliography

The Swedish poet Lasse Söderberg has published *Bertil Lundberg* (Malmö, 1984), but a more comprehensive account can be found in *Bertil Lundberg* (Malmö Konsthall, 1992; text in English and Swedish), with an illustrated checklist of the prints at the back and an essay by Ragnar von Holten, 'Bertil Lundberg, Etcher', pp. 51–63.

103 *Dawn*, 1954

Etching and aquatint. Signed and dated in pencil, inscribed with title and 'original etsning 4/10'. 310 × 230 mm

1991-1-26-25. Purchased from the Rausing Fund

104 *Pastoral*, 1955

Etching and aquatint. Signed and dated in pencil and inscribed 'original etsning 3/5'. 328 × 252 mm

1991-1-26-26. Purchased from the Rausing Fund

105 *Gabriel*, 1955

Etching and aquatint. Signed and dated in pencil and inscribed with title and 'original etsning 1/5'. 310 × 256 mm

106 *Out of the surface*, 1956

Etching and aquatint. Signed and dated in pencil, inscribed with title and 'originaletsning p.t.'. 327 × 244 mm

1991-1-26-22. Purchased from the Rausing Fund

The 1992 catalogue cites figures of five, six and sometimes ten for the number of impressions printed of Lundberg's earliest prints from 1954–6.

107 *Sorrow*, 1982

Etching and aquatint. Signed and dated in pencil, inscribed with title and 'originaletsning' and numbered 2/60. 276 × 258 mm

1991-1-26-94. Purchased from the Rausing Fund

108 *Relic*, 1985

Colour etching on paper with blind-stamp 'KARSTEN'. Signed and dated in pencil, inscribed with title and 'originaletsning 12/60'. 440 × 423 mm

1991-1-26-28. Purchased from the Rausing Fund

The blind-stamp is that of Lundberg's son, who works as a printer in Malmö.

106

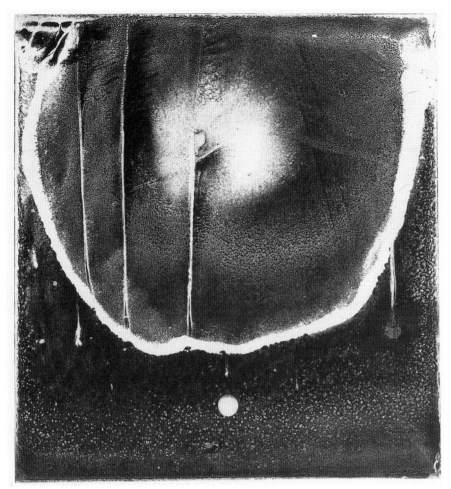

107

108

Siri Rathsman (1895–1974)

Siri Rathsman was a painter and printmaker who spent most of her adult life in Paris, where in addition to her artistic activity she was a correspondent for the *Gothenburg Business and Shipping News* (*Göteborgs Handels- och Sjöfarts-Tidning*) writing under the pseudonym of Contessa Belloni. During the Second World War she was involved with the Resistance together with her friend Greta Knutson, who was married to the Surrealist poet Tristan Tzara. Rathsman published a book attacking the Vichy regime in 1943; this resulted in her expulsion from Paris but she resumed her residence there as soon as the war was over.

Her early training was in Stockholm at Carl Wilhelmson's painting school, then at the Valand Art School in Gothenburg, before spending three years in Copenhagen from 1916 to 1919. She lived from 1919 onwards in Paris, where she studied at the Académie Moderne with Othon Friesz and Raoul Dufy in 1920, and with Diego Rivera in 1921. By 1933 Rathsman was already a visitor to Hayter's Atelier 17 but her main association came after the Second World War when she concentrated more on her work as a printmaker.

109

110

Bibliography

During the 1940s and early 1950s Siri Rathsman showed at the Svensk-Franska Konstgalleriet in Stockholm, with a catalogue and introduction by the painter Otte Sköld produced in 1951. The only other exhibition catalogue in Sweden was that from the Göteborgs Konstförening, Konsthallen Göteborg in 1957, which covered her paintings and prints from 1919 to 1956, but none of the latter was illustrated.

109 *Flight*, 1937

Engraving and soft-ground etching. Signed and dated in pencil, inscribed with title and numbered 1/30. 105 × 304 mm

1992-5-16-104. Purchased from the Rausing Fund

Both of the prints catalogued here attest to the dominant personality of S. W. Hayter, to whom this particular impres-

sion belonged, along with cat. 111–115, by Jürgen von Konow, Sam Kaner, Inger Sitter and Nikolai Astrup (pp. 131–3). From 1933 onwards Hayter extended his range of printmaking to include aquatint and the impression of textures into a soft ground, which he and his protégés explored to a much greater extent in New York where Atelier 17 operated for the duration of the 1940s. The print below is the result of this type of experimentation, which Hayter fostered in Paris once the Atelier had been re-established there in 1950.

110 *Composition II*, c.1950

Engraving with soft-ground etching printed on pale blue laid paper. Signed in pencil and numbered 2/30. 221 × 294 mm

1989-3-4-24. Purchased

111

112

Jürgen von Konow (1915–1959)

Von Konow was one of many Scandinavian artists for whom the experimental approach of S. W. Hayter's Atelier 17 in Paris and his influential publication of 1949, *A New Way of Gravure*, were of supreme importance in determining their own direction as printmakers. Von Konow had studied in Paris at Marcel Gromaire's studio in the late 1930s, like Harald Kihle (p. 72) from Norway. His work as a printmaker, however, was a development of the postwar period when his contact with Hayter and Joseph Hecht inspired him to try to change the climate of printmaking at the Graphic School in Stockholm, where he first studied under Harald Sallberg from 1946 to 1953 and then became a teacher until his death in 1959.

Von Konow's handbook on techniques, *Om Grafik* (1955), was heavily indebted to *A New Way of Gravure*, and Hayter in his turn acknowledged von Konow's book in his next publication, *About Prints* (London, 1962). *Om Grafik* illustrated a number of von Konow's own prints as well as the work of many other artists, particularly those associated with Atelier 17 in Paris and New York, introducing to a Swedish audience the concept of printmaking as a vehicle for innovation in technique and composition.

Bibliography

Om Grafik (Stockholm, 1955) is the best source for von Konow's attitudes towards printmaking, together with an article published in 1958, 'Fantasins Verkstad' (An Imaginary Workshop), in *Grafisk Konst i Vår Tid* (Folket i Bilds Konstklubb), pp. 39–49.

111 *Woman hanging out laundry*, 1954

Colour lithograph. 380 × 478 mm
1992-6-20-31. Purchased from the Rausing Fund

112 *Finisterre*, 1957

Etching and aquatint. Signed and dated in ink, inscribed with title, 'Epreuve d'artiste I' and the dedication 'To Bill Hayter with all the best Nov 1957'. 345 × 493 mm
1992-5-16-102. Purchased from the Rausing Fund

Sam Kaner (1924–1987)

Kaner had many interests as an artist, film-maker and gallery owner, which he pursued in New York, Paris, London and Copenhagen. Born in Brooklyn, New York, he studied with Philip Guston among others from 1946 to 1948 before working with Léger and the printer Roger Lacourière in Paris in 1949/50. The next year he moved to England, where he wrote, designed and edited *Between Two Worlds*, the UK's experimental film entry for the 1952 Venice Film Festival. He was back in America in 1954 working as an instructor at Atelier 17 in New York followed by two fellowships in California and in Italy before he finally settled in Denmark in 1959. There he gave up being an artist to concentrate on experimental film-making and to run a commercial gallery in Copenhagen called the Court Gallery, which specialised in the work of American artists.

Bibliography
There is nothing of real substance published on Kaner apart from brief biographical details in a plethora of small exhibition catalogues from the late 1940s to the early 1960s; the most recent of these are from the Galerie Moderne, Silkeborg and the Galerie Gammel Strand in Copenhagen in 1963. I am grateful to Jan Würtz Frandsen of the Kongelige Kobberstiksamling at the Statens Museum for Kunst in Copenhagen for kindly supplying the relevant information.

113 *Abstract composition*, 1952
Colour etching and aquatint. Signed and dated in pencil and numbered 2/75. 273 × 199 mm

1992-5-16-106. Purchased from the Rausing Fund

This is another of the prints that formerly belonged to S. W. Hayter.

Inger Sitter (born 1929)

Inger Sitter's main career has been as a painter, but for a brief period in the 1950s she focused on printmaking under the influence of S. W. Hayter's Atelier 17, whose subsequent impact on other Norwegian artists led to the establishment in 1965 of Atelier Nord in Oslo, conducted along similar lines (see p. 17).

Sitter was born in Trondheim but spent her early childhood in Antwerp because her father was in the merchant navy. In 1939 the family had to return to Norway, where she studied at the Academy in Oslo, 1945/6. When her family moved back to Antwerp she attended the Institut Supérieur des Beaux-Arts for three years to 1949, with a brief period in Paris in 1948 under André Lhote. From 1950 onwards she worked in Paris, Norway and Spain, visiting for the first time in the winter of 1954/5 Hayter's Atelier 17 in Paris, where she continued to work intermittently from 1956 to 1958. From 1957 to 1967 Sitter exhibited her prints in Paris at the Salon des Réalités Nouvelles. Thereafter she was principally based in Norway until returning to live in Paris in 1984.

Bibliography
Peter Anker and Ole Henrik Moe, *Inger Sitter* (Oslo, 1987).

114 *Granite II*, 1955
Etching and aquatint. Signed and dated in pencil, numbered 7/25 and inscribed 'aquatinta'. 300 × 396 mm

1992-5-16-100. Purchased from the Rausing Fund
Illustrated in colour on plate 6

The British Museum's impression is another of the small group of prints by Scandinavian artists which came from the estate of S. W. Hayter.

Sitter's keenest activity in printmaking coincided with her work on sandblasting a wall for a relief composition on one of the Oslo government buildings (1957/8). This was in many ways analogous to her treatment of her etching plates such as *Granite* and *Paris*, both of 1955.

Nikolai Astrup (1931–1990)

Nephew of the important Norwegian painter and printmaker of the same name (1880-1928), Astrup practised a form of colour printing, often incorporating collaged elements, that was indebted to the work of Rolf Nesch (p. 97) and to his own experience at Atelier 17 in Paris, where Astrup studied from 1954 to 1958. His first exhibition was in Paris at Galerie Mary in 1955, his second in Oslo at Galleri KB in January 1961, when twenty-seven of his prints and forty-one of his gouaches were shown; a further exhibition at the same gallery in November 1963 was devoted exclusively to his prints, including a number of colour woodcuts. After 1975 he divided his time between Oslo and Hyen in Nordfjord, where he had a graphic workshop.

115 *The wood*, 1957
Colour etching and aquatint. Signed and dated in pencil and inscribed 'Epreuve d'Artiste'. 300 × 396 mm

1992-5-16-99. Purchased from the Rausing Fund
Illustrated in colour on plate 6

This impression formerly belonged to S. W. Hayter.

"EVE"   original litografi nr. 24/30   Jørleif Uthaug 1951

118

Jørleif Uthaug (1911–1990)

Uthaug's use of welded metal construction from 1960 onwards transformed sculptural expression in Norway; prior to this he had trained as a draughtsman and painter, turning in the early 1950s to mosaic reliefs which were closely related to the work of Sigurd Winge (p. 105) and above all Rolf Nesch (p. 97).

Born near Trondheim, Uthaug studied drawing there before moving to Oslo in 1936. His artistic education was continued during the war at the School of Arts and Crafts from 1941 to 1943 and at the underground academy run during the German Occupation by Per Krohg and Axel Revold, finishing from 1945 to 1947 at the Academy itself, where he was taught by Jean Heiberg, one of the main conduits for French modernism to Norway. Uthaug's first exhibitions in 1948/9 in Trondheim and Oslo revealed the influence of Picasso and Braque, which during the 1950s gave way to a more expressive style particularly evident in his mosaic reliefs. These were executed for a variety of public commissions, Norwegian pavilions at trade fairs in Milan in 1951 and in Leipzig in 1953, for the vestibule of the Stefan Hotel in Oslo in 1952, and the vast wall decoration for the Municipal Building in Tromsø, which was completed in 1960. Uthaug's interest in sculpture, which to some degree was a natural extension of the work he had previously done on creating the armatures for his mosaics, prompted him to study metallurgy and welding at the State Institute for Technology in 1961/2, with a further period of instruction in 1974. Apart from his exhibitions in Norway, Uthaug's work was shown in Newcastle, his wife's home town, in the 1960s, in Copenhagen and in Chicago.

Of the eighteen prints Uthaug made between 1947 and 1973 (one drypoint, thirteen lithographs, two woodcuts, one screenprint and one monotype), almost all date from 1947–58 and were printed by the artist himself in the basement of his apartment building in Oslo. The British Museum owns four of Uthaug's lithographs, acquired as a group from the artist's widow.

Bibliography

A monograph on Uthaug, which includes a list of his work at the back and a summary in English, was published by his close associate Øistein Parmann in Oslo in 1981.

135

117

116 *Eve*, 1951

Lithograph on off-white wove paper. Signed and dated in pencil, inscribed with title and 'original litografi' and numbered 29/30. 555 × 382 mm

1993-12-12-48. Purchased from the Rausing Fund

The influence of Picasso is evident in this portrait, whose title refers to the artist's wife Eve Chris, whom he married in 1949. Uthaug would have seen the exhibition of *Guernica* and Picasso's prints at the Kunstnernes Hus in Oslo in 1938 as well as having access to the work in reproduction.

117 *Arab woman*, 1951

Lithograph on off-white wove paper. Signed and dated in pencil, inscribed with title and 'orig lito' and numbered 24/30. 557 × 382 mm

1993-12-12-49. Purchased from the Rausing Fund

118 *Fishing fleet*, 1951

Lithograph on off-white wove paper. Signed and dated in pencil, inscribed with title and 'origin. lito' and numbered 2/30. 296 × 449 mm

1993-12-12-50. Purchased from the Rausing Fund

The subject relates to Uthaug's mosaic relief of the Lofoten fishing boats of the same date, executed for the trade pavilion in Milan in 1951.

Ludvig Eikaas (born 1920)

Eikaas has produced reliefs in granite, painted aluminium and brass for public and commercial buildings, paintings, sculpture and prints, working with woodcut, lithography and etching. He comes from the same part of western Norway (Jølster) as Nikolai Astrup (the elder; see p. 133), who was a friend of his father. From 1942 to 1946 he studied at the School of Arts and Crafts in Oslo, where he was taught by Chrix Dahl (born 1906), one of Norway's most influential etchers throughout his long tenure at the School from 1945 to 1974. Eikaas's first work as a printmaker was, however, with woodcut, which he exhibited at the Autumn Art Exhibition in 1946 in Oslo. He encountered Rolf Nesch (p. 97) in the course of using the printing facilities in the basement of the Kunstnernes Hus, and Nesch encouraged him by saying that after he had seen the woodcuts in the 1946 exhibition by Eikaas and by Knut Rumohr (born 1916), he realised there could be good printmaking in Norway. After the School of Arts and Crafts, Eikaas spent two years at the Academy in Oslo followed by a period in 1948 at the Copenhagen Academy, where he came into contact with Aksel Jørgensen (p. 81). Copenhagen provided a more cosmopolitan milieu than existed in Norway; he was exposed to abstract art by artists such as Richard Mortensen, Robert Jacobsen, Hans Hartung and Serge Poliakoff, and was given his first one-man show there at the Galerie Birch in 1951. Since the 1950s his work has been shown regularly in Oslo at the galleries Horst Halvorsen and Haaken, among others, and at the Nasjonalgalleriet in 1959, 1965 and 1967; recently a museum dedicated to him has been opened near his original home in Jølster.

Eikaas's early woodcuts were executed in an Expressionist figurative style, printed in colour as well as black and white. As a printmaker he has tended to emphasise the sculptural quality of his medium, literally transforming it into sculpture in 1957 when he showed at the Galleri Per in Oslo some of his woodblocks that had been cast in bronze and then treated with acid to create a patina on the surface. The analogy was again borne out in his use of intaglio techniques, in which Eikaas, influenced by Nesch, has gouged out his plates to dramatise the final printed surface.

The British Museum's representation of his work consists

6 — 15   Eikaas

120

of two woodcuts and an abstract colour etching in addition to the prints catalogued below.

Bibliography

The published sources consulted have been Jan Askeland, 'Ludvig Eikaas', *Kunsten Idag*, XXXVII (1957), pp. 33–45; Peter Anker, 'Ludvig Eikaas' Portretter', *Kunsten Idag*, IV (1967), pp. 22–41 (both with English translation); and Jahn Otto Johansen, *Ludvig Eikaas* (Oslo, 1981).

119 *Autostrada*, 1967

Etching and aquatint. Signed in pencil and numbered 7–20. 749 × 495 mm

1993-1-24-51. Purchased from the Rausing Fund

This is one of a number of urban subjects by Eikaas from the 1960s, in which he captured the effect of the light from oncoming traffic along a motorway approach, printing the work himself on his own press. The subject exists in two other versions with the rays in white and in blue against a black background. In December 1968 an exhibition of forty-four of Eikaas's prints was held at the Galleri Haaken, starting with his woodcuts from 1958 and including the more recent etchings, *Autostrada* and *Airport*.

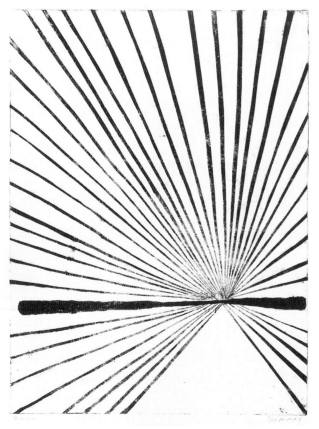

119

120 *City lights, c.* 1968

Etching and aquatint. Signed in pencil and numbered 6–15. 494 × 493 mm

1993-1-24-53. Purchased from the Rausing Fund

Lennart Rodhe (born 1916)

One of the leading exponents of postwar abstraction in Sweden, Rodhe was part of a group known as the Concretists, who emerged at an important exhibition in 1947 held at the Färg och Form (Colour and Form) Gallery in Stockholm; the other main figures were Lage Lindell (1920–80), Karl Axel Pehrson (born 1921), Pierre Olofsson (born 1921) and Olle Bonniér (born 1925). They were counterparts to the artists whose focus was the Galerie Denise René in Paris at the same period; the latter group included the Danes Robert Jacobsen (1912–93) and Richard Mortensen (1910–93), who encouraged commercial galleries in Copenhagen to show the work of their colleagues in Paris and were among the organisers and contributors to the exhibition Klar form (Clear form) which toured Copenhagen, Stockholm and Oslo in 1951 showing the work of Arp, Vasarely, Herbin and Léger as well. The Scandinavian Concretists shared a belief in the democratic nature of abstraction and a desire to create an art of the environment that would integrate art with architecture, 'to create a richer existence for the individual in an industrialised society' (Ib Geertsen, *K. E. -kataloget*, 1954, quoted in *From the Golden Age to the Present Day*, City Art Gallery Edinburgh, 1995, p. 65); it was an outlook similarly espoused in Britain in the early 1950s by Kenneth Martin and Victor Pasmore.

Rodhe was born in Stockholm but from 1925 to 1934 his family lived in Hamburg. His artistic education was divided between Copenhagen and Stockholm from 1936 to 1941. By the mid-1940s his compositions were becoming increasingly schematic and abstract, although they began with naturalistic motifs, as demonstrated, for example, by the series of preparatory studies (now in the Nationalmuseum) for the two subjects catalogued below; those for the *Sawmill* include precise studies of machinery and very free drawings evoking the movement of the men as well as a detailed compositional study for the lithograph as a whole. His use of rhythmic contrapuntal patterns to impart dynamism to his form of abstraction was even more evident in the next group of black and white lithographs of 1947/8, including one called *Space* (which is represented in the British Museum). By the end of the 1950s Rodhe's work was almost totally abstract, changing during the next decade to become organic rather than geometric in form, influenced by Rodhe's interest in micro-organisms and Rorschach ink blots; one of his major commissions from this period was an enamel decoration for the Limnological Institute at Uppsala University. In his subsequent work Rodhe has attempted a synthesis of the two approaches to abstraction, retaining the shifting optical effects that have distinguished his work from the beginning.

According to the *catalogue raisonné*, Rodhe has produced some 316 prints. The earliest were etchings of 1941/2 followed by colour lithographs of the mid-1940s, black and white lithographs from the late 1940s, linocuts in 1949 and 1955/6, lithographs again from the late 1950s to mid-1960s, and thereafter mainly screenprints. The British Museum's collection comprises four of his lithographs.

Bibliography
Rodhe has been well served by recent literature in the form of exhibition catalogues, an artistic biography and *catalogue raisonné* of his prints. The main publications are *Lennart Rodhe: Teckningar* (Nationalmuseum, Stockholm, 1988); Thomas Millroth, *Lennart Rodhe: En verkbiografi* (Stockholm, 1990) and *Lennart Rodhe som Grafiker* (Stockholm, 1993).

121 *Greenhouse*, 1945

Colour lithograph. 550 × 685 mm
M.6
1993-4-4-3. Purchased from the Rausing Fund
Illustrated in colour on plate 1

This ambitious composition evolved from studies in crayon and watercolour of the Victoria-Regia Conservatory in Uppsala. Much later, in 1971, the artist recalled the subject in terms of a metaphor for his own situation and that of his Swedish contemporaries, cut off from the grim reality of what was happening elsewhere in Europe: 'Our little world was the greenhouse and the churchyard [another motif of his at the time] was Buchenwald and all that represented' (Millroth, *Rodhe som Grafiker*, p. 75). It was printed on an offset press at the firm of Esselte in Stockholm, using six plates to print the different colours, for the 1945 exhibition at the Nationalmuseum in Stockholm on God kunst i hem och samlingslokaler (Good Art in the Home and Public Places), one of a long line of initiatives in the Scandinavian countries to educate popular taste through the sponsorship of 'democratic' art forms. The immediate postwar period witnessed an upsurge of enthusiasm for the promotion of improved standards of taste in the fine and applied arts among the population as whole, and colour lithographs in large editions were deemed the most appropriate vehicle for fine-art appreciation; accordingly, thirteen prints by ten different artists were produced in editions of two hundred for the purposes of the exhibition. In the same issue of the Norwegian periodical *Kunst og Kultur* in 1947 in which the lithographs were reviewed by the Swedish critic Carlo Derkert, there was an article by J. P. Hodin on the democratisation of art in England, referring to the activities of the

newly created Arts Council. (For a discussion of the prints see Carlo Derkert, 'Farglitografien – Ett Led i Konstpropagandan', *Kunst og Kultur*, XXX (1947), pp. 105–14. Working proofs for *Greenhouse* are reproduced in *Från Graafikerns Verkstad: Provtryck genom fyra århundraden* (Gothenburg Museum, 1984), pp. 40–1.) *Greenhouse* was Rodhe's first lithograph; he found the offset process difficult to control because of the speed with which the colours were applied, to the extent that he did not return to the same printers for his subsequent lithographs.

122 *Sawmill*, 1947

Colour lithograph. Signed and dated in pencil and inscribed 'provtryck'. 384 × 604 mm
M.9
1992-12-12-16. Purchased from the Rausing Fund
Illustrated in colour on plate 4

For this work Rodhe based his lithograph on studies made from direct observation of a sawmill at Strömsberg in the winter of 1946/7. The composition also exists as a tempera on masonite of the same date and colouring.

After *Greenhouse* the rest of Rodhe's lithographs until the end of the 1950s were printed by Rolf Jansson, usually in editions of between twenty and thirty, but in this case the edition was 250 because it was published by another of the ventures to increase public awareness of art, the Folkrörelsernas Konstfrämjandet (Society for the Public Encouragement of Art). The Society, founded in 1947, operated through circulating exhibitions to a wide variety of venues and publishing original prints at low prices. The first secretary of the organisation, Bror Ejves, was particularly adventurous in his choice of artists from whom the prints were commissioned, and the policy continued to flourish throughout the 1950s; its high point came in 1957 with an exhibition and ancillary programme of films and demonstrations on the subject of how prints are made, which led to the sale of 15,713 prints by the end of the year. None the less, the large-scale production of original prints in this context faced many of the same ideological and financial problems that beset similar schemes in Britain from the 1930s onwards – issues concerning the subject matter and style appropriate to material aimed at a 'popular' audience and the status of offset lithography, which some critics felt reduced the finished product to little more than a reproduction. (For a discussion of comparable British schemes see Frances Carey and Antony Griffiths, *Avant-Garde British Printmaking 1914–1960* (London, 1990) and Antony Griffiths, 'The Print Publications of the Artists' International Association: Attitudes to Lithography in Britain, 1938–1951', *The Tamarind Papers*, XIV (1993), pp. 57–69.) By 1962, the date of Ejves's death, the society was facing an economic crisis and the impetus behind the first phase of the print scheme had faltered. Lennart Rodhe, however, remained one of the most constant supporters of the Konst-främjandet, and for its twenty-fifth anniversary exhibition in 1972 at the Nationalmuseum he executed an edition of forty-six different screenprints.

Frans Widerberg (born 1934)

For the past twenty-five years Frans Widerberg's reputation in painting and lithography has been as a vivid and experimental colourist whose etiolated human and equine figures inhabit a psychedelic extra-terrestrial space. His genesis as an artist was within an expressive tradition of black and white printmaking established in Norway in the 1950s that dominated Widerberg's own approach for nearly fifteen years. From 1953 to 1955 he studied book design in Oslo at the School of Arts and Crafts, which placed particular emphasis on graphic techniques, and he also spent four months in 1955 at Goldsmiths' College, London; he furthered his interest in woodcut and wood-engraving during a six-month period in 1956 at the Bergen College of Arts and Crafts, where he was a pupil of the Danish illustrator Povl Christensen (p. 83), and finally studied painting at the Academy in Oslo from 1957 to 1960. His professional debut was made in 1963 at the annual Autumn Exhibition in Oslo with a painting and a large panoramic woodcut, *Landscape, horses and dogs* (P. 49), his most ambitious print to date, which used one of his favourite motifs, the horse and rider, as part of a complex narrative scene influenced by the visionary watercolours of Lars Hertering (1830–1902); from 1965 to 1985 Widerberg worked in Munch's old studio at Ekely, a western suburb of Oslo. Widerberg's woodcuts predominated over his painting for much of the 1960s, showing some similarity in technique to the work of his compatriot Ludvig Eikaas (p. 136) and the Dane Palle Nielsen (p. 91), whom he admired. At a later date some of his early woodcuts were reworked and issued in proper editions, including colour variations with different colours printed simultaneously. His relationship to Italian art and landscape, which he first experienced in 1957, intensified from the early 1970s when he began to make regular visits to Villa Faraldi, on the Ligurian coast in northern Italy.

The emphasis within Widerberg's work shifted decisively towards painting in the late 1960s, accompanied by a concomitant change from relief printing to lithography. Until 1970 he had printed virtually all his work himself, but thereafter he collaborated with a number of professional printers, pulling proper editions for the first time. The decisive moment in his use of colour printing came in 1973 in conjunction with Eystein Hanche Olsen, who worked in the lithographic workshop at the School of Arts and Crafts:

It was then the technique of using one and the same stone for all the colours began – litho became printmaking. I tried with overprint of complementary colours to bring out deeper and better grey tones, went amok in etching technique and all degrees of spraying to the finest of the fine tone spraying. Began with pale colours and ended with dark ones, or the other way round: first with dark and last with light colours. Reproduced and improvised. Experimented with techniques: iris print, inversion to bring out the next colour, grounding with gum Arabic, and so on. (quoted by H.-J. Brun in Pedersen, *Frans Widerberg*, p. 239)

Colour printing extended to Widerberg's etching as well in the period from 1979 to 1983 and among his recent work, but overall his most startling effects have been achieved through lithography, which bears the closest relationship to his painting.

The *catalogue raisonné* of Widerberg's prints lists 540 separate images executed between 1954 and 1990, of which the British Museum owns ten representing his work in woodcut, lithography and etching from 1964 onwards, including two of the etchings and aquatints from a series of eight *Tarot* sheets produced in 1985 and one work printed since the catalogue's publication.

Bibliography

The main publications from Norway have been Hans-Jakob Brun, *Frans Widerberg* (Oslo, 1978) and *Nicolaus Frans Thomas Widerberg* (Lillehammer Kunstmuseum, 1995). In Britain there was a catalogue to accompany the exhibition *Frans Widerberg* in 1986/7 (Brighton Polytechnic Gallery and Polytechnic Gallery, Newcastle upon Tyne) with an essay by Michael Tucker, 'Dreamer in a Landscape'. Øivind Pedersen, *Frans Widerberg: Grafikk 1954–1990* (Oslo, 1990) includes an essay by H.-J. Brun, 'Frans Widerberg – the Printmaker', in English. A display of Widerberg's recent prints was held at the Barbican Art Gallery in London to coincide with the Scandinavian exhibition Border Crossings in 1992.

123 *The dancer (Salome series)*, 1964

Woodcut on thin Japan paper. Signed and dated in pencil and inscribed 'Salome'. Second of three states. 620 × 458 mm
P.56

1993-1-24-11. Purchased from the Rausing Fund

The figure of *The dancer* was the central subject in Widerberg's *Salome* series, the result of a collaboration with the Norwegian author André Bjerke for his translation of Oscar Wilde's play of the same name. Widerberg's first *Salome* subject was a woodcut entitled *Night landscape (Salome)* of 1961 (P.39), followed in 1962 by another woodcut entitled *Johannes, landscape*, but the series as such consisted of thirteen woodcuts of varying size and format, including one in colour, all executed in 1964; twelve were eventually used in the book, published in a limited edition in 1975. In 1965 the theme surfaced again in the form of three etchings on zinc (P.73–5), including *The dancer*. There were three variant

123

forms of this figure in the woodcut version, which became progressively more elaborate in its execution and more dynamic in its expression (P.55–7). All three are virtually identical in size except that the second, catalogued here, lacks a fraction of the full height of the printed area shown by the other two. The following print is a proof impression from the same series and bears a dedication to his wife Aasa (a fellow student at the Academy whom he married in 1960).

124 *Angel of Fate (Salome series)*, 1964

Woodcut on thin Japan paper. Signed, dated and inscribed with dedication in pencil. 662 × 464 mm

P.62

1993-1-24-10. Purchased from the Rausing Fund

125

124

Niclas Gulbrandsen (born 1930)

Gulbrandsen followed the same educational path as his friend Frans Widerberg (p. 140), whom he slightly preceded at the School of Arts and Crafts in Oslo from 1951 to 1954 and at the Academy from 1954 to 1957. He first exhibited his paintings as part of a mixed show at the Galleri Horst Halvorsen in Oslo in 1963 which included work by Widerberg, and his prints in 1965.

Since 1965 Gulbrandsen has concentrated wholly on figurative woodcuts in black and white, often working in series either directly related to specific literary texts or inspired by them in a more general way, with occasional pictorial narratives entirely of his own invention. His method of working is a laborious one, starting from pencil sketches in which he establishes the 'situations' which constitute his narratives and the relative positions of his figures; these are followed by the cutting of the blocks themselves, a particularly complex process in Gulbrandsen's case because he reverses the normal role of the negative and positive values in the finished prints, using the empty spaces to articulate his subjects rather than the areas inked in relief. This

"Søndag eftermiddag kl. 13⁰⁰" Tresnitt ¹⁹/₂₅ Niclas '94.

127

125 *Sunday afternoon 12.45*, 1974

Woodcut. Signed and dated in pencil, inscribed with title and medium and numbered 22/25. 300 × 216 mm

1993-1-24-31. Purchased from the Rausing Fund

126 *Sunday afternoon 13.00*, 1974

Woodcut. Signed and dated in pencil, inscribed with title and medium and numbered 19/25. 300 × 216 mm

1993-1-24-30. Purchased from the Rausing Fund

Both prints are from the series of twenty-three woodcuts entitled *A Sunday walk to the bridge and home again*, which the artist devised as a narrative covering the period of time from 10.45 to 14.00 with five *Dreams* as an interlude between 11.25 and 12.05.

127 *The boaster*, 1990

Woodcut. Signed and dated in pencil, inscribed with title and medium and numbered 18/30. 300 × 210 mm

1993-1-24-32. Purchased from the Rausing Fund

The third of Gulbrandsen's woodcuts catalogued here is one of two purchased by the British Museum from the fifteen he executed as illustrations to *Hâvamâl*, which were printed in Paris for the published edition by François Da Rose. *Hâvamâl* is the part of the Icelandic saga, *The Edda*, which has been of greatest significance in relation to Norwegian heritage, because of its descriptions of Norwegian scenery and the rule of kings. The title (The High One) refers to Odin, whose sayings are declaimed in the poem. The theatricality of Gulbrandsen's figures in these compositions, who, like Daumier's characters, appear to be actors performing an ironical mime, was repeated in his next series, *Theatre* (1992), based on his observations of the National Theatre in Oslo.

method of working was first brought to fruition in his illustrations to Hans Henrik Holm's *Sòga um Kapergastane og Deira Vâde-rum*, one of four long epic poems, first published in 1933, that were all written in archaic local dialect and blended folklore with the author's invention; according to an interview with Aasa and Frans Widerberg in 1969 (see Trygve Nergaard's introduction to the Norske Grafikere exhibition (1995), p. 12), Gulbrandsen used nearly 150 woodblocks to create the twenty-seven prints associated with this commission.

Bibliography

A summary of Gulbrandsen's printmaking, with a bibliography and an introduction by Trygve Nergaard, is given in the catalogue *Niclas Gulbrandsen: Tresnitt*, published to accompany a retrospective at the Galleri Norske Grafikere (Oslo, 1995). I am indebted to Sidsel Helliesen for information in connection with these entries.

Ove Stokstad (born 1939)

Stokstad, who is professor and head of the printmaking department at the Academy of Fine Art in his home town of Trondheim, has combined the careers of graphic artist and serious jazz musician with a commitment to human rights issues. He studied in Trondheim before attending the College of Arts and Crafts in Bergen, with its tradition of expertise in woodcut and wood-engraving, from 1961 to 1965. Bergen's links with Danish printmaking through the illustrator Povl Christensen (p. 83) were important for Stokstad, who in 1973 studied in Denmark, where the work of Palle Nielsen (p. 91) and Svend Wiig Hansen (p. 161) was an example to those who wished to focus on graphic art as a primary means of expression.

Stokstad has worked with all the different printmaking

Lino 17/50 Tir. p. IIA. Tykk landskap I OVE STOKSTAD 88

128 (I)

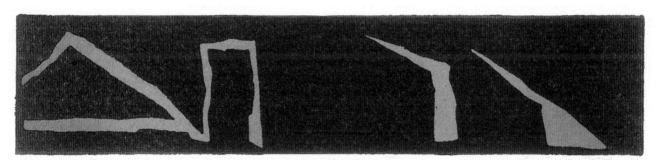

128 (IV)

Lino 3/50 Tir. p. IIA. Tykk landskap VII OVE STOKSTAD 89

128 (VII)

128 (VIII)

media starting with linocut, a technique he found appropriate for his black and white series from the 1970s, *A statesman's art*, which dealt with torture and directly reflected his concern for human rights. Another aspect of his political engagement, this time with environmental issues, prompted a series of landscapes at the end of the 1980s beginning with eight small linocuts known as *German landscape* (cat. 128). They refer to the artist's reflections upon the sheer magnitude of industrial pollution witnessed during a long and frustrating night journey through the region of the Ruhr in Germany; Stokstad's choice of red as the contrast with black for these compositions was influenced by the dramatic resonance of the title of Edgar Allan Poe's novel *The Mask of the Red Death*. He continued the theme in 1991–3 with a larger format series called *European landscapes*, executed as drawings in charcoal and pastel and as lithographs on zinc, also printed in black and red. Recently the *European landscapes* have become more complex in their technique and composition:

At the moment I am working with large plates of acrylic glass, on which I screenprint X-rays combined with acrylic painting. These acrylic plates are mounted on thick, white-painted wood plates, possibly reminding of coffin lids, at a distance of about 5 cms between the acrylic and wood plates. Then you also get the effect of shadows as the daylight changes . . . using the X-rays of skulls, bones and brains, and calling them 'European landscapes', they are more dealing with the human rights and the terrible war situation in parts of Europe the last years. (Letter to the author, 20 June 1996)

Bibliography

Information on Stokstad's work is scattered among various leaflets, the most recent being that accompanying the exhibition in 1993 at Galleri Norske Grafikere, Oslo, of his works entitled *Pripjat*, *The red wood* and *European landscape*.

128 *German landscape*, 1988–9

Eight linocuts on white Japan paper. Signed and dated in pencil, inscribed with title, medium and 'Tir. p. 1'A' and numbered.

I: 1988, 17/50; 72 × 192 mm
II: 1989, 7/50; 110 × 490 mm
III: 1989, 3/50; 129 × 216 mm
IV: 1989, 5/50; 81 × 369 mm
V: 1989, 3/50; 70 × 212 mm
VI: 1989, 2/50; 90 × 178 mm
VII: 1989, 3/50; 80 × 255 mm
VIII: 1989, 5/50; 93 × 215 mm

1992-12-13-32 (−39). Purchased from the Rausing Fund

129

Gösta Gierow (born 1931)

Together with Philip von Schantz (p. 148) and Nils Stenqvist (p. 151), who have both been professors at the Academy, Gierow was a member of Group IX, formed in April 1964 by artists who had studied at the Academy in Stockholm in the 1950s followed by periods abroad in Paris, London and Copenhagen. The other members were Karl Erik Häggblad (born 1924), Alf Olsson (born 1925), Lars Lindeberg (born 1925), Göran Nilsson (born 1930) and Bengt Landin (born 1933); the youngest of the group, Per Gunnar Thelander (born 1936), studied at the Academy in the early 1960s as a pupil of Philip von Schantz. The nine artists were painters and sculptors whose styles and subject matter varied considerably; the intention of the group, which functioned as

an identity for exhibition purposes, was to establish a new *modus vivendi* for printmaking in Sweden, inspired by the example of Jürgen von Konow (p. 131), who was appointed as an assistant to Harald Sallberg (p. 49) at the Graphic School in 1953, and by the work of Hayter, Hecht and Friedlænder (see p. 17) in Paris. Group IX was formed at the same time as the Forum Graphic School was started by Bertil Lundberg (p. 125) in Malmö, and both initiatives represented a desire to move away from the craft-orientated 'cabinet prints' of Harald Sallberg to a more adventurous approach which challenged the traditional limits of printmaking. (See *IX-Gruppen 25 År*, Nationalmuseum, Stockholm, 1989.)

Gierow joined the Academy in 1947 together with Lennart Iverus (p. 152), who came from the same part of

Sweden. They were both drawn to architectural fantasy, with collapsing structures whose disintegration was rendered by Gierow as an organic process of decay. (For a survey of printmakers interested in architectural fantasy see *1900-talets Utopia*, Nationalmuseum, Stockholm, 1989.) From the late 1960s his subjects became increasingly surreal, with a group of colour etchings executed between 1967 and 1969 of insects attacking the Louvre; subsequently he has worked more with colour lithography, turning his attention to decay as a form of diseased corruption in connection with Venice. In the 1980s there were surreal interpretations of natural phenomena, sometimes in the form of marine life, and fantasies reminiscent of Bosch, such as his print of 1988, *Baroque fish*, in which ruinous buildings tumble forth from inside the rotting carcass of the fish (an impression of this subject belongs to the British Museum). Most recently his images have been concerned with enigmatic texts in different scripts.

129 *Roots of life*, 1960

Etching and aquatint. Signed and dated in pencil and numbered 18/30. 567 × 774 mm

1990-11-9-158. Purchased

Philip von Schantz (born 1928)

Philip von Schantz has had a distinguished career as a painter, printmaker, teacher and museum director. He broke off his initial training as a cavalry officer to study first at Otte Sköld's painting school in Stockholm in 1949/50, then with André Lhote in Paris in 1951 and from 1952 to 1957 at the Academy's art school, where he became assistant professor of printmaking in 1959. In 1962 he was made director of the printmaking department and a full professor in 1963, which marked the first time printmaking had achieved equal status with the painting and sculpture departments. From 1969 to 1972 von Schantz served as Director of the Academy as a whole followed by four years as Director of the Moderna Museet in Stockholm; he was elected President of the Academy in 1987.

Although he came to printmaking by chance, since it formed no part of his actual training as an artist, von Schantz has had a substantial output in etching and lithography, producing 240 works between 1952 and 1987, the date of Per Bjürstrom's *catalogue raisonné*. His early work in etching and aquatint began with still-lifes delicately arranged within interior settings, sometimes with steeply tilted picture planes. In formal terms the compositions were clearly influenced by his experience of French art, including the prints of Jacques Villon, and the still-lifes of Braque and Morandi, as well as resembling some of the etchings by his compatriot Louis Bastin (born 1912), who had studied

with Marcel Gromaire in Paris in 1934. Von Schantz's particular interest lay in the play of light, often showing his objects *contre-jour*. A more schematic use of the same compositional device recurs in some of the still-life paintings and watercolours of 1990, in which a shallow frieze of curved vessels in the foreground becomes part of the water and sky of the landscape of the Swedish archipelago beyond. (An example of this is the British Museum's watercolour *Towards Arholma* (1990), which is closely related to a painting of the same date.)

An exhibition of graphic art at Liljevalchs in Stockholm in 1959 marked a change in von Schantz's style, with a series of abstract linocuts of spiral patterns related to those formed in nature, with titles such as *Thunderwhirl* and *Rainlines*, and one published by the F.f.G.K., *Homage to Claude Monet* (an impression belongs to the British Museum). His interest in natural phenomena persisted, leading him into his next major series, *Pilot* (1960/1), eight etchings and aquatints concerned with aerial themes (cat. 130, 131). Von Schantz was one of many artists to respond to the excitement of early space travel and satellite photography, but a more literary source of inspiration was the life and work of Antoine de Saint-Exupéry, the French aviator and author of *Le Petit Prince*, to whom von Schantz dedicated the series. Several of the *Pilot* prints were concerned with areas of the earth's surface brought into close focus. Von Schantz proceeded to do this again with two linocuts of 1961 called *Landscape torsos* and *Part of the whole I, II, III*, followed in 1963/4 by human torsos treated as landscapes in linocut and aquatint, partly inspired by contemporary newspaper photographs of athletes.

His next change in subject matter and style occurred in 1966, with a suite of five aquatints and etchings based on a fifteenth-century Milanese war helmet that the artist had seen in the Metropolitan Museum of Art in New York. The same motif seen from a different angle recurred in a linocut and two etchings of 1967, followed by an aquatint of 1973. This marked a transition to a hard-edged and hyper-real precision in the treatment of the subject matter which von Schantz increasingly refined to achieve the startling *trompe-l'oeil* effects of his later prints. From the mid-1970s he used colour lithography to a much greater extent than etching, prompted by practical circumstances as well as his artistic intentions. He had developed an allergy to acid, and when he finished teaching at the Academy in 1973 he no longer had a workshop so readily at his disposal, leading him to rely on the services of a professional printer; when he did use etching he would have the plates grounded by a technician, etch the composition himself and then take them back to the studio for biting and editioning once he had checked the proofs.

The British Museum owns twenty-six prints by von Schantz. With the exception of one presented by the artist, all are from the period 1954–61 and were purchased from the Saga Gallery in London in 1989, together with the

130

Pilot VIII 6/28   Schantz 61

watercolour referred to above, which was acquired directly from the artist in 1992.

Bibliography

Von Schantz published his own handbook on printmaking, *Vad är Grafik? En handbok i grafisk konst* (Stockholm, 1966). The following literature exists in English: Brian Sewell, *Introduction to Philip von Schantz 21 Watercolours* (London, 1983); Per Bjürstrom, *Philip von Schantz och hans Grafik 1952–1987* (Trelleborg, 1988, with text in English and Swedish) and Allan Ellenius, *Philip von Schantz: Still lifes* (Trelleborg, 1991, with text in English and Swedish).

130 *Pilot VII*, 1961

Aquatint. Signed and dated in pencil, inscribed with title and numbered 4/28. 495 × 300 mm

B.92

1989-9-30-210. Purchased

131 *Pilot VIII*, 1961

Etching and aquatint. Signed and dated in pencil, inscribed with title and numbered 6/28. 495 × 356 mm

B.93

1989-9-30-211. Purchased

The British Museum owns impressions of all but II in the *Pilot* series. The compositions are identical in size with the exception of VII, which is slightly narrower than the others. They were printed in editions of twenty-eight black and white impressions and a further ten printed in colour of each one except, once again, VII, which exists only in monochrome. The subjects of the eight aerial views are as follows:

I: The Red Sea partly covered by cloud, taken from a satellite photograph

II: The outline of the coast of North Africa, an area particularly associated with Saint-Exupéry

III: The surface of the coastal landscape, brought into closer focus

IV: A storm moving over the surface of the earth

V: A diagonal view across the streets of Cairo

VI: A similar kind of view (like V) from a slightly different angle, across the urban network of New York

VII: A river valley in Sweden

VIII: Another close-up view (like III), mapping the earth's surface

Although von Schantz's images for this series have a rational context, there is also some affinity to the intense preoccupation with surface texture associated with the anti-rational artists of the postwar period in Paris, such as Wols, whose compositions could suggest planetary or urban structures subjected to intense scrutiny from afar, as for example in his painting of 1947 entitled *Manhattan* (Menil Collection, Houston).

Nils Stenqvist (born 1937)

Stenqvist, who for more than thirty years has divided his time between his studios in Stockholm and Gotland, succeeded Philip von Schantz as professor of printmaking at the Stockholm Academy from 1973 to 1983, having studied there himself from 1956 to 1961 under Harald Sallberg (p. 49) and Jürgen von Konow (p. 131). He respected Sallberg's technical expertise but also admired von Konow's lack of orthodoxy and the impetus he gave to experimentation, which ultimately had a greater effect on the direction of Stenqvist's own work. During his period as a student in Stockholm Stenqvist spent some time abroad in 1958 at the Royal College of Art in London, where he was taught etching by Alastair Grant and Julian Trevelyan, who had worked closely with Hayter (see p. 17) in the early 1930s. Stenqvist was introduced by Dick Fozard at the Royal College to colour printing, which he in turn incorporated into the programme of the Graphic School in Stockholm once he became professor, marking a decisive break with the black and white tradition laid down by the school's founder, Axel Tallberg.

Stenqvist's own printmaking has been in colour and black and white, concentrating for the most part on a combination of etching and aquatint, often executed on plates of considerable size. Since the early 1960s his subject matter has been drawn from a variety of natural phenomena, ranging from his early exploration of geological strata in 1961–8 to an interest in cellular and molecular structures and microscopy in the late 1960s, insect life in the following decade and then more recently to fossil forms and constellations, which have been incorporated into paintings and his designs for decorative art. A typical example of the latter interest is one of his prints in the British Museum's collection, *Fossil impression with William Herschel's illustration of the star system* (1985), in which the figure of Herschel (1738–1822) is denoted in terms of the subject of his studies.

The British Museum owns six of the artist's prints dating from 1961 to 1988.

Bibliography

Björn Håkanson, *Nils Stenqvist*, in the Konstnär i Bild series (Stockholm, 1991), surveys the artist's work as a whole and contains a full bibliography.

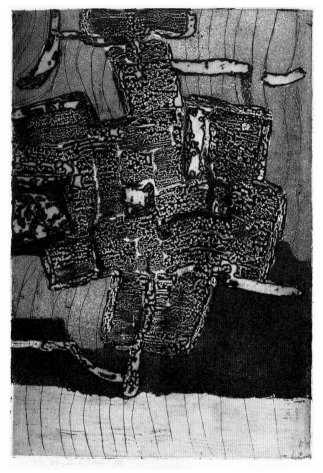

132

abstract configuration yet retained a referential purpose. It was part of the general vocabulary of postwar European art which assimilated the entomological, vegetative and cellular forms that preoccupied Stenqvist and his associates in Sweden. In Britain this was most notably articulated via the exhibition Growth and Form organised by Richard Hamilton at the Institute of Contemporary Arts in 1951, based on D'Arcy Thompson's book of the same title published in 1917. For Scandinavian artists there was another precedent in August Strindberg's experimental photographs in the 1890s capturing the effects of crystallisation, and his interest in perceiving the cosmos as a whole reflected in the artificially enlarged patterns of a microcosm.

Lennart Iverus (born 1930)

Iverus had a varied training as a printmaker, studying at Beckman's commercial art school in Stockholm from 1956 to 1957, at the Academy's Graphic School from 1957 to 1962, and at Atelier 17, Atelier Friedlænder and the Royal College of Art in London in 1959. It was Jürgen von Konow (p. 131) who encouraged his interest in pure line engraving as well as etching, which he has employed to vary the mood of his Piranesian architectural visions. Etching imparts a dreamlike quality to the compositions in which grandiose classical monuments subside into ruin, whereas the emphatic engraving line is used as a starkly expressive statement to convey a sense of violent and cacophonous dissolution. Since the late 1950s Iverus has returned many times to Paris to print at Lacourière's intaglio workshop.

132 *Primary rocks VI*, 1961

Colour etching and aquatint. Signed and dated in pencil, inscribed with title and numbered 30/30. 495 × 355 mm

1993-7-25-54. Purchased from the Rausing Fund

The subject of Stenqvist's series of seven prints from 1961 (the Museum also owns an impression of III) gave him ample opportunity to experiment with various etching techniques in order to achieve the desired differentiation of surface texture; the artist himself described his activity in preparing the plates in geological terms: 'I felt as though I was like a glacier moving over the rocks – the copperplates – scraping, scratching, hollowing out. In the dark reddish-brown of the copper I attempted to find the magic strength of the rocks' (Håkanson, *Stenqvist*, p. 12).

Stenqvist shared this fascination with geological material or the earth's encrustations with a number of other printmakers in Scandinavia, including his fellow member of the Group IX Philip von Schantz (p. 148) and the Dane Per Kirkeby (p. 166), who perceived the expressive possibilities afforded by subject matter that could be treated as an

133 *Falling building*, 1972

Engraving. Signed and dated in pencil, inscribed with title and numbered 5/30. 495 × 391 mm

1992-4-4-74. Purchased from the Rausing Fund

133

134

Sixten Haage (born 1926)

Born in Lund, Haage studied in 1945 at Isaac Grünewald's painting school in Stockholm where he was a contemporary of the artist and printmaker Maud Comstedt (1920–84), followed by two years at the Académie Julien in Paris from 1947 to 1949. His early work consisted principally of polychromed sculpture, but in 1968 he changed direction to concentrate on printmaking ranging across woodcut and screenprinting, lithography and a variety of intaglio techniques.

Haage's most distinctive contribution has consisted of urban and industrial architectural subjects executed on large plates using different combinations of drypoint, aquatint and mezzotint to create the depth of shadow on which he depends for the drama of his scenes. His choice of technique and interest in architectural subjects has been to a degree part of the heritage of Swedish printmaking from Axel Fridell (p. 35) onwards, but Haage's deserted vistas of 1976/7 (cat. 134), for example, are reminiscent of American urban imagery of the 1930s and 1940s as captured by contemporary printmakers and photographers such as Berenice Abbott. His industrial motifs have been taken from Belgium, Germany and Norrköping in Sweden, including a series of subjects from the Ruhr done in drypoint and mezzotint in 1979/80. Latterly Haage has lived in Brussels, where he has made a number of smaller 'portraits' of individual buildings.

Bibliography

Kim Nicklasson, *Sixten Haage*, Ur Vår Tids Grafik 8 (Kristianstad, 1989).

134 *Midsummer Day*, 1977

Etching and drypoint. Signed and dated in pencil, inscribed with title and numbered 30/150. 490 × 589 mm

1992-4-4-70. Purchased from the Rausing Fund

The British Museum's collection holds another of Haage's street scenes of this period, *Cyclists* (1976).

Jukka Vänttinen (born 1954)

Born in Finland, Vänttinen studied at the Forum Art School in Malmö, Sweden, from 1977 to 1980, and from 1980 to 1982 at the Graphic School with Bertil Lundberg (p. 125) followed by five years at the Academy in Stockholm. Just as Sixten Haage has concentrated on mysteriously deserted exterior views, Vänttinen has focused on the echoing spaces of empty interiors where the recession along dark corridors, up flights of stairs or across the floor of a room, accented by patches of light, provides the narrative thread to his work. This is particularly true of a group of aquatints from 1982 all of which refer to Raskolnikov, the central fig-

ure in Dostoevsky's *Crime and Punishment*: *Raskolnikov's door*, *Raskolnikov's window*, *Raskolnikov's stairs* and *Raskolnikov's attic* (an impression of which belongs to the British Museum).

From the mid-1980s onwards Vänttinen turned to mezzotint, a technique he first tried at the Graphic School in Stockholm where it had been practised by the founder, Axel Tallberg (who, like his compatriot Count Louis Sparre, had learnt it in London from Frank Short at the Royal College of Art). The main practitioner in Scandinavia, as far as interior scenes were concerned, was Peter Ilsted (p. 78), working in Copenhagen in the first three decades of the twentieth century, whose cool, spare monochrome rooms, like those of his brother-in-law Hammershøi, must have influenced Vänttinen; among the other former students at the Forum School, the Japanese artist Minako Masui (born 1940), who has lived in southern Sweden since 1962, also specialises in mezzotint. The intensely laborious nature of Vänttinen's printmaking has of necessity limited his output, which by 1992 amounted to around fifty subjects; some of the plates he used in the 1980s were over a metre in length, requiring the construction of a special press.

135

136

Bibliography
Kim Nicklasson, *Jukka Vänttinen*, Ur Vår Tids Grafik 32 (Kristianstad, 1994).

135 *After noon*, 1991

Mezzotint. Signed and dated in pencil, inscribed with title (in English) and numbered 20/100. 325 × 495 mm.

1992-1-24-29. Purchased from the Rausing Fund

This subject and its companion *Before noon* of the same size are views of the staircase inside a typical Malmö apartment house.

Ulf Trotzig (born 1925)

French influences have had a major role to play in the development of Trotzig's painting and printmaking, in common with many other Swedish artists. He was fortunate in being able to benefit from the cosmopolitan background of Endre Nemes (p. 119), who arrived to teach at the Valand Art School in Gothenburg in 1947, the year after Trotzig began his study there (1946–51). In 1951 he made his first trip abroad to Spain and to Paris, where he briefly helped in Zadkine's sculpture studio; then in the mid-1950s he went with his wife, the writer Birgitta Trotzig, to live at Villiers-le-Bel (where he later met Asger Jorn) and remained in France until 1969.

While he was at Valand Trotzig had made some prints, starting with woodcuts and a lithograph for the annual portfolio instigated by Nemes. In 1950 he began to experiment with copper-engraving, producing a number of nude female figure studies over the next five years. His interest in the medium burgeoned between November 1954 and 1957 when he was working in Friedlænder's studio in Paris. There he acquired the courage to combine a variety of intaglio techniques including mezzotint and to develop a fearless approach to the way in which he treated his plates which was the hallmark of Hayter's and Friedlænder's style. Trotzig's involvement was such that he thought he would devote himself entirely to prints, but the commemorative exhibition for Nicolas de Staël, held after the latter's suicide in 1955, inspired Trotzig to return to painting. This dominated his time from 1958 to 1960, when he developed an abstract style constructed like the work of Poliakoff and Estève, but becoming more freely gestural from 1960 onwards.

Between 1955 and 1960 he and his family lived in a conservatory belonging to the sculptor Jean Osouf, but in 1960 he resumed printmaking after a press had been installed in his newly acquired house at Villiers-le-Bel. Trotzig immediately executed a group of dynamic compositions whose centrifugal force was such that the lines often literally scour the surface (cat. 136). Despite the increasing abstraction of his style, Trotzig did on occasion attach literary and classical references to his work: for example, T. S. Eliot's *The Waste Land* in 1960, Thomas More's *Utopia* in 1973 and Ovid's *Metamorphoses* in the mid-1960s. There are clear hints of vegetative life in most of the compositions from the early 1960s onwards; over the next fifteen years these became more recognisably descriptive elements in a landscape.

Since 1960 Trotzig's painting, drawing and printmaking have been closely interwoven, with colour becoming of increasing importance to all three modes of expression. His first colour prints were lithographs executed from 1963 to 1967; then in 1968 he used colour in conjunction with pure

137

line engraving followed by a variety of etching techniques including soft-ground, aquatint and drypoint. His most monumental printed composition was *Travel and transformation* (1967), installed as a frieze in the booking hall of the railway station at Lund (where Trotzig has lived since the late 1960s), which was 10 m in length and involved the use of thirteen plates. Trotzig was again without a press for the first three years after his return to Sweden, but in 1972 he was able to revive his printmaking with a group of six colour etchings made in the recently opened workshop of Thormond·Larsen in Helsingborg in southern Sweden (cat. 137). During another stay in Paris in 1976/7 he availed himself of the services of the Lacourière-Frélaut workshop with which he has continued to collaborate as well as having his own press in Lund.

The British Museum acquired six of Trotzig's intaglio prints, one lithograph and one drawing, dating from 1960 to 1990, directly from the artist in 1991.

Bibliography

Thomas Millroth, *Ulf Trotzig: Måleri* (Åhus, 1988); Sven Sandström, *Ulf Trotzigs Grafik* (Åhus, 1988, with text in Swedish and French) contains at the back a checklist of all the prints.

136   *Dawn*, 1960

Engraving and etching. Signed and dated in pencil, inscribed with title (in French) and numbered 16/20. 439 × 560 mm

S.52

1991-1-26-14. Purchased from the Rausing Fund

137   *Colour etching I*, 1972

Etching and colour aquatint. Signed and dated in pencil and numbered 84/90. 495 × 600 mm

S.102

1991-1-26-17. Purchased from the Rausing Fund

Helmtrud Nyström (born 1939)

Helmtrud Nyström was one of the many students of Bertil Lundberg (p. 125) at the Forum School in Malmö, who has made her career as a graphic artist in southern Sweden. She was born into a German family from Hanover and went to Sweden in 1961 to work in the Bergianska Garden in Stockholm as part of her studies in landscape design. Later that year she moved to Lund, where she has lived ever since, and within the next few years her interest gravitated towards the fine arts, until in 1965 she joined the Forum School. After studying there for five years Nyström set up her own graphic studio in Lund with Mariana Manner (p. 161) in

1971, to be joined in 1974 by Olle Dahl (p. 161), another graduate of the same school.

The contrast between the three artists, who all concentrate on etching and aquatint, is a good example of the extreme catholicity of style embraced by the printmakers associated with the Forum School, where Lundberg's influence was less dominant than that of his model, S. W. Hayter, at Atelier 17. Nyström's earliest prints were black and white, but her work as a printmaker, draughtsman and painter has been mainly characterised by colour used in an intensely atmospheric way as part of her mysterious, elliptical narratives. These narratives are often rendered as elaborate pictograms, reflecting the influence of Paul Klee; sometimes they are set out in a schematised way reminiscent of a rebus. Then, more recently, graffiti-like marks have appeared like those in the work of A. R. Penck. Many of the prints incorporate ethnological motifs with reference to the culture of the Samma in Lapland and to a series of journeys the artist made during the 1980s – to the Yemen, Egypt, Iceland, the United States, Poland, France and India. One further aspect of her narrative construction is represented by cat. 138 in which Nyström's figures inhabit a mythological landscape; on occasion this evokes the paradisaical world of the Mughal miniature painters of the late sixteenth century.

According to the list of prints published by Thomas Millroth in 1990, the artist had executed some 360 works, of which the British Museum owns two examples, both acquired from the artist.

Bibliography

Thomas Millroth, *Helmtrud Nyström: Grafik* (Åhus, 1991; the text is in German and Swedish with a list of all her prints from 1968 onwards).

138   *Harvest celebration*, 1985

Colour etching and aquatint. Signed and dated in pencil, inscribed with title (in English) and numbered 7/125. 575 × 480 mm

1991-1-26-11. Purchased from the Rausing Fund

Illustrated in colour on plate 7

139   *Green man*, 1990

Colour etching and aquatint. Signed and dated in pencil, inscribed with title (in English) and numbered 11/60. 710 × 670 mm

1991-1-26-10. Purchased from the Rausing Fund

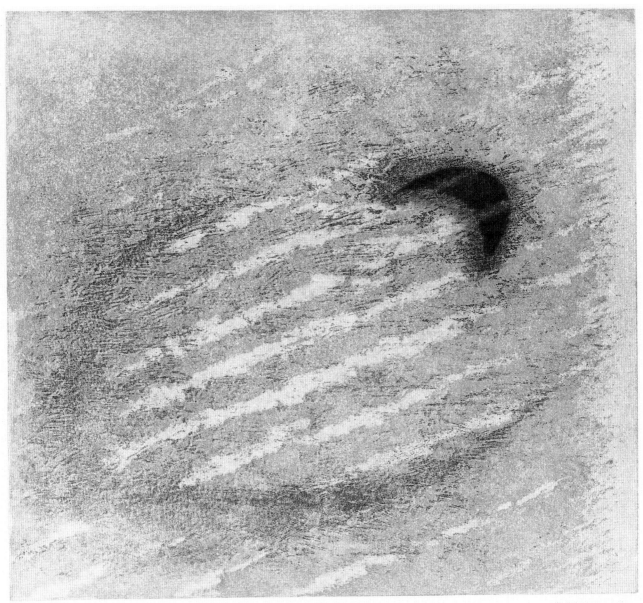

142

Mariana Manner (born 1943)

A printmaker, painter and sculptor, Mariana Manner studied first painting and then printmaking from 1965 to 1971 at the Forum Art School in Malmö, where she was a contemporary of Helmtrud Nyström (p. 158), with whom she and her future husband Olle Dahl were to collaborate in sharing a print workshop in Lund. (I should like to thank Mariana Manner and Olle Dahl for supplying information on their work.)

140 *Blue Nile*, 1992

Colour aquatint. Signed and dated in pencil, inscribed with title and numbered 113/150. 380 × 485 mm

1993-1-24-28. Purchased from the Rausing Fund
Illustrated in colour on plate 8

This subject has as its companion *Flood*, a profile of an ancient Egyptian head printed in an edition of 150 by Olle Dahl in three colours, evoking the sun beating on the desert, while the wave lines across the composition suggest the inundation referred to in the title.

Olle Dahl (born 1943)

Dahl, a painter and printmaker, graduated from the University of Lund in 1972, attending the Forum Art School in Malmö from 1972 to 1974, when he joined the print workshop in Lund set up by Helmtrud Nyström (p. 158).

In addition to the two prints catalogued below, the British Museum owns one other by Dahl, a close-up view of the masonry in a stone wall executed in 1983.

141 *Sombre*, 1989

Colour aquatint and drypoint. Signed and dated in pencil, inscribed with title (in English) and numbered 18/90. 331 × 485 mm

1993-1-24-27. Purchased from the Rausing Fund
Illustrated in colour on plate 8

142 *Stream I*, 1991

Colour aquatint. Signed and dated in pencil, inscribed with title (in English) and numbered 13/90. 259 × 284 mm

1993-1-24-25. Purchased from the Rausing Fund

Svend Wiig Hansen (born 1922)

A sculptor, painter and graphic artist with opera singing as a subsidiary interest, Hansen emerged as a powerfully expressive figurative artist from the mid-1950s onwards. Despite his rebellion against the prevailing academic discipline in Denmark, he was rapidly acclaimed and granted official recognition by senior figures such as Aksel Jørgensen (p. 81), who presented him with the Storm Pedersen Memorial Award in 1955. Other major awards followed in rapid succession, with a retrospective of 199 works at the Kunstforening in Copenhagen in 1959 and a further retrospective of 115 works (paintings, sculpture, drawings and prints) at the Venice Biennale in 1964, where he was chosen as the sole representative for Denmark. (It was his work, together with that of Francis Bacon, which aroused the Pope to denounce the Biennale for that year.) Between 1971 and 1976 he returned as a professor to the Academy in Copenhagen of which he had been so critical as a student in the late 1940s.

Wiig Hansen trained as a sculptor from 1946 to 1950, winning first prize for a *Monument to Liberty* in Roskilde that was never executed. His weighty sense of form and mass was influenced by work he saw in an exhibition containing Mexican pre-Columbian art in Stockholm in 1952, and by 1955 he had assimilated this characteristic into his painting and draughtsmanship to create figures whose violence of expression is akin to much that was happening elsewhere in the postwar period. The work of Wiig Hansen's compatriot Asger Jorn (p. 108) had an obvious bearing on the visual context in which he operated during the 1950s, but his figures are firmly rooted in the human form and lack the mythologising element so important to Jorn; a closer influence from the background of Danish art came from the early twentieth-century painter and printmaker Oluf Hartmann (1879–1910), whose work was readily accessible to him through the collection of the Statens Museum. Above all, Hansen's figures in their troubled isolation partake of the existential qualities expressed by the artists associated with *art brut* in Paris, by artists from North and Central America such as Rico Lebrun and Mauricio Lasansky and from Britain including Francis Bacon and Kenneth Armitage, whose work was assembled in New York in 1959 for Peter Selz's important exhibition at the Museum of Modern Art, New Images of Man. Henry Moore's spectral figures from his *Shelter* drawings of the early 1940s and Reg Butler's 'watchers' at the foot of his design for the *Monument to the Unknown Political Prisoner* of 1953, which like Hansen's *Monument to Liberty* was never realised, are further examples of near-contemporary work which was well known abroad and may have had some bearing upon Hansen's own development. Hansen himself organised an exhibition of the work of a group of Danish artists including Henry Heerup (p. 118) and Palle Nielsen (p. 91) who were committed to figurative as opposed to abstract expression under the

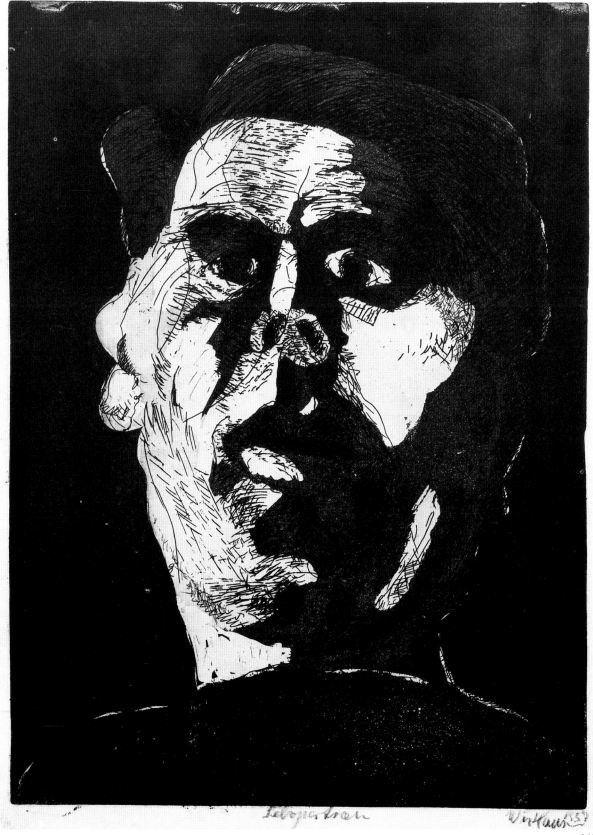

143

title The Human Being at Clausens Kunsthandel in Copenhagen in 1957.

Hansen's public breakthrough as a painter came with *The Searchers* of 1955 (Statens Museum for Kunst, Copenhagen), followed by an intensely productive period as a graphic artist. In 1957 he used one of his awards to finance a trip to Greece: eighty-eight of his subsequent ink drawings were published in book form in 1960, under the title *Greek Inspiration* with an introduction by Palle Nielsen, when the originals were presented to the Print Room of the Statens Museum. A similar series of calligraphic drawings was made in the autumn of 1960, in Rome, where the artist was a guest at the Danish Institute. These were exhibited the following year as Roman Fantasies and published in book form in 1968 (one of the original drawings was acquired by the British Museum in 1992). From the early 1960s Wiig Hansen's figures became more fantastical, their contours dissolved and the colouring of his paintings and pastels increased to such a pitch of intensity that the compositions became distillations of raw emotion. A similar effect was achieved in black and white alone, by his graphic work, which since then has been dominated by his drawing. At the same time, the scale of his compositions changed dramatically, influenced by his involvement in public projects that sometimes involved a dialogue with an immediate audience. For these he produced work in metal and ceramic clay, stained glass and glass mosaic, and drawings on aluminium sheets as well as paintings and drawings on canvas.

The British Museum's collection contains three drawings by Wiig Hansen, dating from 1960, 1985 and 1988, and seven etchings and one lithograph from the period 1957–69.

Bibliography

The most complete text is that for the catalogue accompanying the retrospective exhibition at Århus Kunstmuseum and the Statens Museum in 1989/90, *Svend Wiig Hansen: Klassik og chaos* (Århus, 1989), which is in English as well as Danish and contains a full chronology and bibliography. An anthology of his drawings from 1955 to 1991, with an introduction by Anne Christiansen in Danish and English, was published as the exhibition catalogue *Wiig Hansen: Spor fra en vandring* (*Traces of a Journey*), Kastrupgardsamlingen and Fyns Kunstmuseum (1994).

143   *Self-portrait*, 1957

Etching and aquatint. Signed and dated in pencil and inscribed with title. 310 × 229 mm

1991-4-6-50. Purchased from the Rausing Fund

This is one of Wiig Hansen's earliest prints. A later group of four self-portraits very similar to this was drawn in 1964 on four sheets of printed music joined together.

144

144   *Man on a chair*, 1957

Aquatint. Initialled and dated in pencil and inscribed 'ET'. 253 × 161 mm

1991-4-6-54. Purchased from the Rausing Fund

Of all Wiig Hansen's early subjects this haunting figure, like a living carcass, is one of those most immediately reminiscent of his Central American counterparts; the artist has used the very imperfection of his aquatint technique to enhance the expressive effect of the creature's ribbed and corroded outer surface.

145

145 *Bridled*, 1958

Etching. Signed in pencil, inscribed with title and numbered
14/50. 240 × 338 mm

1991-4-6-53. Purchased from the Rausing Fund

In 1961 Wiig Hansen executed a metal collage of the same
title based on the earlier print, measuring 220 × 280 cm
(Randers Art Museum).

146 *Portrait*, 1959

Etching. Signed and dated in pencil and inscribed with title.
160 × 144 mm

1991-4-6-52. Purchased from the Rausing Fund

Portræt   WHansen 59

146

Per Kirkeby (born 1938)

Among artists of Danish origin Kirkeby's diverse means of expression are most nearly comparable to the work of Asger Jorn (p. 108), with whom he has closely identified – to the extent of owning a house since 1979 on the same island of Læso off the coast of Jutland where Jorn had a studio towards the end of his life. Apart from painting, printmaking and sculpture which encompasses monolithic environmental sculptures in brick as well as work in plaster and bronze, Kirkeby has published more than sixty books of poetry and essays reflecting on his own work and that of others (for example Manet, Delacroix, Turner, Picasso and Gauguin in successive years from 1990 to 1994), and made both experimental and documentary films including one on Asger Jorn in 1976.

Like Jorn, he moved sideways into an artistic career after embarking upon training for something quite different; in Kirkeby's case this was geology, for which he was enrolled as a student of natural sciences at the University of Copenhagen from 1957 to 1964. For the last two years of his university education Kirkeby was engaged in experimental artistic activity which was to determine his future direction, but his early background in the study of Arctic quaternary geology (and the expeditions this entailed to Greenland and Pearyland) had a considerable effect on the whole course of Kirkeby's approach to art and his lifelong interest in exploration, description and classification. Scientific methodology informed aspects of his subsequent artistic practice: imagery culled from his geological experiences has surfaced time and again since his publishing debut in 1961 in the literary magazine *Hvedekorn* with an article and a woodcut related to one of the Greenland expeditions ('Nunarigsoq', *Hvedekorn*, VI (December 1961), pp. 202–3), while the geological processes themselves of stratification, sedimentation, erosion and fault lines have provided visual and literary metaphors for his work as a whole.

Crucial to Kirkeby's formation as an artist was the Experimental Art School which flourished as an informal meeting place and forum for discussion, improvisation and collective expression in Copenhagen from 1961 to 1964 under the aegis of the art historian Troels Andersen, the painters Poul Gernes (born 1925) and Richard Winther (born 1926), and the printmaker Jørgen Rømer (born 1923). Kirkeby became involved in the School from 1962, working with printmaking, drawing and film but above all with etching, with which Winther, Rømer and Gernes were all engaged. The first two were intrigued by the colour printing technique of the early seventeenth-century Dutch artist Hercules Seghers; Gernes had a wholly different approach, which amounted to a full-scale assault upon the plates with hammer blows followed by driving a car across them. The Experimental School was one of a number of sites for the type of spontaneous events and performances that characterised the Fluxus movement, which made its impact in

Europe through a series of festivals in 1962, including one in Copenhagen when Kirkeby contributed a performance of the nineteenth-century Danish artist Johan Thomas Lundbye's diaries, called *Time, Space and Place*. (For further information on Copenhagen and Fluxus see Elisabeth Delin Hansen, 'Flux Copenhagen Berlin', in *Head through the Wall: Collection Block* (Statens Museum for Kunst, 1992), pp. 94–106.)

Fluxus, and the contacts it brought for Kirkeby with Joseph Beuys in Copenhagen and Nam June Paik in New York during 1966/7 were an important catalyst for his own creativity because of the liberation they offered from conventional forms of expression, permitting an artist to escape narrow definition in terms of one medium or another. From the mid-1960s onwards Kirkeby diversified into environmental installations, paintings on interchangeable masonite panels, brick sculpture inspired by both Danish building traditions and the Mayan architecture he witnessed on a visit to Central America in 1971, and 'blackboard' drawings on masonite which came out of his preparation for a lecture on geological themes in 1976. These elements were often combined and their referential scope further enlarged by the inclusion of 'novels' of the artist's creation, either pictorial or textual in content. Since the mid-1970s Kirkeby through his painting and printmaking has contributed to a resurgent expressionism represented by the group of artists (Kiefer, Penck, Immendorff and Baselitz) associated with the Michael Werner Gallery in Cologne, Kirkeby's own dealer since 1974. This relationship and his two professorial appointments to German art schools, the first being at the Academy in Karlsruhe from 1978 to 1988 where he joined Georg Baselitz and Markus Lüpertz, followed by his current position at the Städel Art School in Frankfurt, have consolidated his position within the mainstream of European art.

Printmaking for Kirkeby has played an even more important role than in the work of the artist with whom he is often compared, Georg Baselitz, whose production has been documented with equal care. In Kirkeby's case his identity as an artist was forged through printmaking in the first instance; in his essay published in 1978, 'Naturens Blyant' (The Pencil of Nature, taken from Fox Talbot's title for his account of the discovery of photography published in 1844–6), he stated that all the ideas and experiences that surfaced in his later work had already been handled in embryonic form in the early etchings, which enabled him to move between recognisable motifs and abstraction. The first prints from 1962 reflected his interest in geology, and included a series of etchings of ammonites recalling some of Asger Jorn's work. These were followed by landscape compositions related to his visit to northern Greenland in the summer of 1963, one of the most recurrent themes in his work, which formed the subject of a group of performances he gave in Germany, Denmark and New York in 1967 called *Arctic I–III*. In 1976 he began to rework some of

147

his old plates of the Greenland expedition that had not been printed, overlaying the lines of fjords, cliffs and other landscape features with figures from his subsequent paintings and elements of urban life; this process created the kind of densely textured composition operating at several levels of execution, meaning and recollection that has characterised much of his two-dimensional work. More recently in 1993 Kirkeby has reverted to the same region, executing a series of forty small etchings, *Greenland journey*, printed by Niels Borch Jensen in Copenhagen. After the first geological references a completely different set of motifs emerged in the etchings of 1963/4, which were drawn from popular culture (see below) and set the agenda for Kirkeby's painting for the immediate future.

Although he made some woodcuts and linocuts, mainly in 1965, and also tried offset lithography, Kirkeby's principal allegiance as a graphic artist has always been to black and white etching; in the years up to 1984, the final date for the existing *catalogue raisonné*, he executed over four hundred

etchings. His practice diversified in the early 1980s when Maximilian Verlag in Munich became his publisher, starting with the three portfolios comprising *Erste Konzentration* (First concentration) in 1982, for which Kirkeby executed six large-scale colour prints in woodcut, linocut, lithography and etching alongside the work of Baselitz, Höckelmann, Immendorff, Lüpertz and Penck (see the catalogue for the series with an introduction by Alexander Dückers, Munich, 1982). They marked a transition to a more painterly use of the different media that he has continued to explore alongside the black and white etchings which remain of greatest importance to his process of recollection.

Bibliography

There is an extensive bibliography for work by and on Kirkeby in Danish, German and English, listed in the catalogues for all his major exhibitions of which the most recent example is *Per Kirkeby* (Kunsthalle Recklinghausen, 1994), which

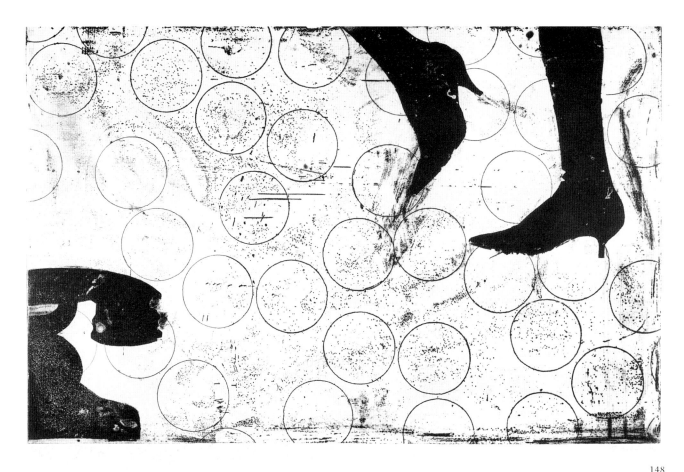

contains a full biography as well. The artist's collected essays were published in a German translation (Bern and Berlin, 1984) under the title *Bravura*. The only one-man shows devoted to his work in Britain have been *Per Kirkeby: Recent painting and sculpture*, ed. Nicholas Serota and Rachel Kirby (Whitechapel Art Gallery, London, 1985) and a retrospective at the Fruitmarket Gallery, Edinburgh in 1985, with an introductory text by Troels Andersen. The *catalogues raisonnés* of his prints are John Hunov, *Per Kirkeby: Oeuvrekatalog 1958–1977 over raderinger, linoleumssnit, traesnit* (Copenhagen, 1979) and Troels Andersen, *Per Kirkeby: Werkverzeichnis der Radierungen 1977–1983* (Bern and Berlin, 1986), followed by an exhibition catalogue, *Per Kirkeby Grafik 1978–1995* (Stadtgalerie Sundern, 1996). A good account in English of his early development is given by Lasse Antonsen in *Per Kirkeby: Early works* (Michael Werner Gallery, Cologne and New York, 1995).

147 *Various women*, 1964

Etching and aquatint. Signed and dated 63 in pencil and numbered 5/5. 372 × 493 mm

H.123

1996-4-27-3. Presented by the Asger Jorn Foundation in memory of Guy Atkins (1912–88; see p. 110)

148 *Telephone rings*, 1964

Etching and aquatint. Signed and dated 63 in pencil and numbered 5/5. 319 × 497 mm

H.130

1996-4-27-4. Presented by the Asger Jorn Foundation in memory of Guy Atkins

The two prints described here are part of a group of eleven duplicates presented to the British Museum from the Silkeborg Kunstmuseum, which had been reprinted in 1974 in editions of five by Brian Christiansen for the Asger Jorn Foundation. They form part of a larger group of more than twenty etchings that Kirkeby made in 1964/5 (not 1963 as he has dated the impressions) and exhibited at the Århus Kunstmuseum under the heading *Women of the times*. The

149

silhouette shapes of women's shoes and figures were those of fashion models copied out of magazines, made into templates and lined up or repeated within a grid structure for the prints and large-scale paintings on masonite that ensued; the patterns created by the rings from a telephone dial were used to greatest effect in the work reproduced here, but they reappear in fragmentary form as a decorative element in the paintings. (See, for example, the painting in the Statens Museum, *A romantic picture* (1965), reproduced in *100 Mesterværker* (Statens Museum for Kunst, Copenhagen, 1996), pp 206–7.)

Ole Sporring (born 1941)

Sporring was fortunate to become part of the circle of graphic artists in Copenhagen – including Palle Nielsen (p. 91), Jane Muus, Dan Sterup-Hansen and Svend Wiig Hansen (p. 161) – who were consistently supported by the dealer Viggo Clausen (see p. 17), whose premises he continues to use for studio space. His first one-man show there was in 1963, mid-way through his period of study at the Academy's Graphic School from 1961 to 1965, by which time he was already firmly established as one of the most prolific and inventive Danish printmakers and draughtsmen. From 1961 onwards there was a huge outpouring of activity on Sporring's part which resulted in some 360 prints by the end of 1964, to begin with mainly etchings on zinc to which Sporring would often apply sandpaper or aquatint to vary the surface textures. To these were then added prints executed in relief etching, linocuts and pictures created with rubber stamps, all teeming with a turbulent demotic imagery culled from films, comic strips and other aspects of contemporary popular culture, much of it derived from American sources.

I began to dream about eclectic art, an all encompassing landscape, the free use of my own elements and those of others, of bodies, reckoning, simplicity, chaos, dialectic, rationalization, injustice and truth. I dreamt of drawing a landscape from both sides of the paper at once, of drawing together with the landscape. A true partnership. What came of it was unfinished stumps. Souvenirs from otherwise undocumented journeys. (Ole Sporring in *Dinamarca: Danmark*, São Paulo Biennale, 1985)

Sporring continued to produce prints, though at a less hectic pace, after the mid-1960s, illustrating many texts in the same idiosyncratic style, but his printmaking activity has been largely displaced since 1985, the date of his professorial appointment at the Copenhagen Academy, by painting and drawing.

The British Museum owns seven of Sporring's prints dating from 1963 to 1986 and two drawings of 1986.

Bibliography
Hvedekorn, v–vi (October–December 1964) includes a complete list of Sporring's prints up to that point. The only other text to concentrate exclusively on his graphic work is *Ole Sporring* (Lommebog 25, Statens Museum for Kunst, 1983), with commentary by Jan Garff and the artist. I would like to thank the artist for supplying an explanation of the print below.

149 *Untitled*, 1977
Linocut and offset colour lithograph. Signed and dated in pencil and inscribed 'ET'. 340 × 432 mm
1991-4-6-44. Purchased from the Rausing Fund

During the course of the 1960s Sporring developed a liking for the linocut medium with its relative simplicity and lack of pretentiousness, which in this instance he has combined with offset lithography, another technique preferred by many Danish artists in the late 1960s and 1970s for its lack of preciosity. The virtues of linocut have been extolled by Sporring in the following terms:

A linocut is good in the morning. ... The picture is colourless in the fresh brown linoleum, reeking of work. It is absolute and yet without black and white and blue. ... The picture is an island. All else is sea. The coast goes through the knife. Outside lie all disturbances, windswept. The island is favoured, clear. It points the direction of longing. To and from. Wave scallops tear at the cliffs.

Printing takes no time at all. The whole surface at once – and it can be seen. The long time is suddenly fixed. The present and slow hauling. Printing is appearance and proof of the whole process. Several prints on top of each other create raw con-

frontation. The finished print is good in the evening. It folds up completely, and can be stuck in a pocket. So one has something to look at, when hunger for pictures strikes. On these conditions, linocuts are an island of collection and order, of great clarity, which even cleanliness cannot muddle. (*Dinamarca: Danmark*, São Paulo Biennale, 1985)

With reference to this particular print, the artist has explained that the offset printing used for the background was borrowed from a series made in 1969, *Listen now*, while the overlaying linocut composition was in turn adapted to a painting and linocut of 1980 and 1984 that 'had something to do with peace movements and pent-up love'.

Sigurdur Gudmundsson (born 1942)

Gudmundsson, the subject of a painting of 1986 entitled *The great Icelandic poet* by his friend the Norwegian artist Olav Christopher Jenssen (born 1954), has – like Jenssen, who works in Berlin – spent much of his career outside his native country, having been based in Amsterdam since 1970. Whether as a conceptual artist participating in 'situations' that he devised and captured in photographs between 1971 and 1980, or subsequently working as a sculptor, draughtsman and printmaker, Gudmundsson has rooted his work in his Scandinavian background, the barren Icelandic landscape and the frequent journeys between Reykjavik, Amsterdam, Berlin and southern Sweden which have been an essential part of his way of life.

Gudmundsson was born in Reykjavik, the son of a framemaker and art dealer whose gallery showed the work of contemporary artists including those from abroad such as the German Dieter Roth, who introduced the ideas of Fluxus (see p. 166) to Iceland, and the Dutch artist Anton Rooskens who was associated with Cobra. Gudmundsson's first visit to the Netherlands was in 1963, when he spent a year at an alternative art school, Académie 63, in Haarlem followed by two years working near Groningen. He returned to Iceland in 1966 to set up a group influenced by the work of Joseph Beuys and other artists connected with Fluxus which was instrumental in the opening of Súm, a gallery in Reykjavik intended to provide a forum for experimental art, and eventually in 1978 in the creation of The Living Art Museum. After settling in Amsterdam in 1970 Gudmundsson worked with poetry, installations and photography, changing to three-dimensional sculpture in 1981 after his return from a year in New York.

Since 1981, all aspects of Gudmundsson's visual work have been governed by the massive forms to emerge in his sculptural imagery, whose presence is often rendered all the more impressive by his use of pedestals and landscape settings. Parallel to the sculpture he began a series of large-scale pencil drawings in heavy iron frames, followed in 1985 by charcoal drawings entitled *With landscape* which chart the artist's journey through an imaginary landscape. These

150 (I)

150 (II)

150 (III)

led to his first etching, *Scandinavian fairy-tale*, incorporating a visual quotation from Munch, the pillared reflection of the moon in the sea which appears in many of the latter's compositions. Further prints by Gudmundsson have followed, closely related to his drawings and with the same monumentality as his sculpture, ranging from the *Park* series of 1986 (cat. 150) and *Urbilder, About art* of 1987 (*Palette, Atelier* and *Exhibition*), to *Landscape*, a woodcut of 1988 and *Sun stand still*, a portfolio of six etchings of 1989 whose title is taken from a poem of 1912 by Sigurdur Sigurdsson.

Bibliography

Gudmundsson's work has been shown in Britain as part of a travelling exhibition starting at Brighton Polytechnic in 1989 called Landscapes from a High Altitude: Icelandic Art 1900–1989 and in Border Crossings at the Barbican Art Gallery, London, in 1992. The principal source of information is the monograph accompanying an exhibition at the Kunstnernes Hus in Oslo, edited by Zsa-Zsa Eyck (1992), with text in English and Swedish.

150 *Park* series, 1986

Soft-ground etching, drypoint and aquatint printed in black against a beige background. Each signed and dated in pencil. 525 × 480 mm

I: *In the park*, numbered 6/25

II: *Park*, numbered 7/25

III: *Picture in the park*, numbered 7/25

1993-1-21-40 (–42). Purchased from the Rausing Fund

Technical Glossary

Aquatint A variety of etching in which tone is created by fusing grains of rosin to the plate and etching it. The acid bites in pools around each grain, and these hold sufficient ink to print a light grainy tone.

Drypoint A process similar to etching, except that the line is not bitten into the plate by acid but directly scratched in with a sharp needle.

Engraving A process using a metal plate. Lines are cut into the metal (usually copper) using a v-shaped metal tool called a burin. Pushed in front of the hand, this produces a clean and controlled incision. The plate is inked and printed in the same way as an etching.

Etching The artist draws the design through a waxy ground laid on a metal plate. The lines of exposed metal are then eaten away in an acid bath. After the ground is cleaned off, the plate is inked so that the ink lies only in the bitten lines, and the surface is wiped clean. The plate is printed by laying a sheet of paper over it and running both through a press under considerable pressure. *Relief etching* is achieved by using a resist for the main design so that only the background is bitten away by the acid.

Linocut An abbreviation for linoleum cut; the same process as for woodcut, except that linoleum is used instead of wood.

Lithography A method of printing from stone or zinc which relies on the fact that grease repels water. The design is drawn on the surface in some greasy medium. For printing, the surface is dampened with water, which settles only on the unmarked areas since it is repelled by the grease in the drawing. The surface is then rolled over with greasy printing ink, which adheres only to the drawing, the water repelling it from the rest of the surface. Finally the ink is transferred to a sheet of paper by running paper and printing surface together through a scraper press.

Instead of drawing directly on the stone or plate, the artist can use transfer paper, i.e. a sheet of paper which has been covered with a soluble surface layer. Once the design has been made with a greasy medium, the paper is placed downwards on the stone or metal plate and moistened until the soluble layer dissolves, leaving the greasy drawing to adhere to the printing surface. This is known as *transfer lithography*.

Mezzotint A metal-plate engraving process. The plate is worked over ('grounded') using a semi-circular spiked tool (a 'rocker') so that the entire surface is roughened. In this state, the plate will print a solid black. The lighter parts of the design are then created by scraping and polishing down areas of the plate so that they hold less ink in the printing. Any colouring is traditionally done *à la poupée* using stumps of rag to create the desired tones; no two impressions printed this way can ever be precisely similar.

Screenprint This is a variety of stencil printing. A mesh is attached to a frame and a design is either drawn on it in some impermeable medium or a stencil is attached to it. Ink is forced through the screen on to a sheet of paper with a squeegee.

Soft-ground etching A type of etching which uses a soft etching ground. By laying a sheet of paper on top of the grounded plate and drawing on the paper, the ground is made to adhere to the underside of the paper. A precise facsimile of the drawing is thus left in the ground and can be etched into the plate in the usual way. It can also be used for impressing any number of different surfaces to create a variety of textured effects in the final print.

Woodcut Using a block of soft-grained wood, the artist cuts away the background using knives and gouges, leaving the lines standing in relief. Ink is then rolled over the surface of the block, which is printed under light pressure on to a sheet of paper. Munch's technique with his colour woodcuts was to cut a single block into pieces around the main shapes of the design. He then coloured them separately and fitted them together again like a jigsaw for printing.

Wood-engraving A type of woodcut developed in the late eighteenth century using a hard-grained wood, such as boxwood, which is too hard to be cut with a knife; instead a v-shaped burin is used to incise lines into the block. As with a woodcut, the printing surface is provided by the areas standing in relief, so that the incised lines appear white against a black background in the final print. Sections of the block may also be lowered using scrapers to make them print as grey rather than black.

For fuller explanations see Antony Griffiths, *Prints and Printmaking: An introduction to the history and techniques* (British Museum Press, London, 1996).

General Bibliography

The emphasis, where possible, is on literature published either in English or with an English résumé. Modern Scandinavian material is not well represented in libraries in Britain, with the exception of the few universities with Scandinavian studies departments where the concentration is more on literature and history. Within London the best sources for information on nineteenth- and twentieth-century art are the library of the Department of Prints and Drawings in the British Museum, the National Art Library at the Victoria and Albert Museum and the library of the Tate Gallery. The general literary guides and biographical dictionaries are on the reference shelves of the British Library, and the Scandinavian section of the Library at University College London has a complete set of two of the main art periodicals, the Swedish *Ord och Bild* (1892–) and the Norwegian *Kunst og Kultur* (1911–).

This bibliography does not include the works on individual artists which are given at the end of their biographies. Dictionaries of artists and series (or parts thereof) providing a survey of the history of art are placed at the head of the appropriate sections, while other titles are arranged chronologically; exhibitions are listed under museums.

General biographical dictionaries

Dansk Biografisk Leksikon, ed. S. C. Bech (Copenhagen, 1979–84), 16 vols

Norsk Biografisk Leksikon, ed. E. Bull (Oslo, 1923–83), 19 vols

Svenska Män och Kvinnor (Stockholm, 1942–55), 8 vols

Svenskt Biografiskt Lexikon, ed. S. J. Boëthius (Stockholm, 1918–), 28 vols (not yet completed)

Scandinavian historical and cultural background

Virpi Zuck (ed.), *Dictionary of Scandinavian Literature* (Westport, Connecticut, 1990)

Alrick Gustafson, *A History of Swedish Literature* (Minneapolis, 1961)

Harald Naess (ed.), *A History of Danish Literature* (Lincoln, Nebraska and London, 1992)

Harald Naess (ed.), *A History of Norwegian Literature* (Lincoln, Nebraska and London, 1993)

T. K. Derry, *A History of Scandinavia* (Minneapolis and London, 1995)

Scandinavian art and design in general

The Macmillan Dictionary of Art, ed. Jane Turner (London, 1996), 34 vols (includes entries for individuals, general introductions to branches of fine and applied arts, and sections within national entries on collecting and dealing and museums)

Cooper-Hewitt Museum, *Scandinavian Modern Design 1880–1980* (New York, 1982)

Roald Nasgaard, *The Mystic North: Symbolist landscape painting in Northern Europe and North America 1890–1940* (Toronto, 1984)

Michael Jacobs, *The Good and Simple Life: Artists' colonies in Europe and America* (Oxford, 1985)

Hayward Gallery, *Dreams of a Summer Night: Scandinavian painting at the turn of the century* (London, 1986)

Neil Kent, *The Triumph of Light and Nature: Nordic art 1740–1940* (London, 1987)

Jennifer Opie, *Scandinavian Ceramics and Glass in the Twentieth Century* (Victoria and Albert Museum, London, 1989)

Kirk Varnedoe, *Northern Light* (New Haven and London, 1988)

Barbican Art Gallery, *Border Crossings: Fourteen Scandinavian artists* (London, 1992)

Richard Miller, *Cobra* (Paris, 1994)

City Art Centre, *From the Golden Age to the Present Day: Two centuries of art and craft in Denmark* (Edinburgh, 1995)

Danish art in general

Weilbach Kunstnerleksikon (3rd edn, Copenhagen, 1947–52), 3 vols, 4th edn 1994–5 (A–L, first 4 of projected 8 vols)

Henrik Bramsen and Knud Voss, *Dansk Kunsthistorie 5: Billedkunst og skulptur efter 1900* (Copenhagen, 1975)

Henrik Wivel, *Ny Dansk Kunsthistorie 5: Symbolisme og Impressionisme* (Copenhagen, 1994)

Hanne Abildgaard, *Ny Dansk Kunsthistorie 6: Tidlig modernisme* (Copenhagen, 1994)

Bente Scavenius, *Den Frie Udstilling i 100 År* (Copenhagen, 1991)

Marianne Barbusse and Nanna Hertoft (eds), *Danish Artists' Associations* (Copenhagen, 1996)

Danish printmaking

Jørgen Styhr, *Dansk Grafik 1500–1800* (Copenhagen, 1943)

Jørgen Styhr, *Dansk Grafik 1810–1910* (Copenhagen, 1949, reprinted 1970)

Erik Fischer, *Moderne Dansk Grafik* (Copenhagen, 1957)

Bente Irve, *Dansk Grafik* (Copenhagen, 1985)

Dansk Grafik i dette Århundrede (Copenhagen, 1989)

Statens Museum for Kunst, Copenhagen, *Lommebog* (pocketbook) series on different aspects of graphic art from the collections

Statens Museum for Kunst, *Den Danske Radeerforening 1853–1978* (Copenhagen, 1978)

Norwegian art in general

Norsk Kunstner Leksikon (Oslo, 1982–6), 4 vols

Norges Malerkunst, vol. 2 (twentieth century), ed. Knut Berg (Oslo, 1993)

Sigurd Willoch, *Kunstforeningen i Oslo* (Oslo, 1936)

Steinar Gjessing (ed.), *Kunstnernes Hus 1930–1980* (Oslo, 1980)

Frode Havercamp, *Oslo Kunstforening 1936–1986* (Oslo, 1986)

Norwegian printmaking

Olaf Willums and Eli Ingebretsen, *Om Grafisk Kunst* (Oslo, 1928)

Kristofer Sinding-Larsen, *Norsk Grafikk* (Oslo, 1941)

Rolf Rude, *Norske grafikere* (Oslo, 1973)

Jan Askeland, *Norwegian Printmakers: A hundred years of graphic arts* (Oslo, 1978)

Sidsel Helliesen, 'Norsk Forening for Grafisk Kunst', *Kunst og Kultur*, II (1984), pp. 102–25

Nils Messel, '100 år norsk grafikk, 1822–1922', *Norske Grafikere Jubileumsutstilling 1922–1987* (Oslo, 1987)

Sidsel Helliesen, 'Johan Nordhagen og opprettelsen av Radérklassen', *Kunst og Kultur*, IV (1988), pp. 226–50

Sidsel Helliesen, *Norges Malerkunst*, vol. 2 (section on prints), pp. 375-457 (Oslo, 1993)

Swedish art in general

Svenkskt Konstnärs Lexikon, 5 vols (Malmö, 1952–67)

Elisabeth Lidén and Sven Sandström, *Konsten i Sverige: 1900– talets bildkonst*, vol. 7 (Stockholm, 1975)

Sixten Strömbom, *Konstnärförbundets Historia*, vol. II (1891–1920) (Stockholm, 1965)

Ragnar von Holten, *Svenska Teckningar 1900–talet* (Stockholm, 1985)

Olle Granath, *Ett annat ljus: Svensk konst efter 1945* (Stockholm, 1986) (also published in English as *Another Light: Swedish art since 1945*)

Thomas Millroth and Pelle Stackman, *Svenska Konstnärer i Paris* (Stockholm, 1989)

Swedish printmaking

Gunnar Jungmarker and Harald Sallberg, *Svensk Grafik från Tre Sekler* (Stockholm, 1957)

Per Bjurström, *Tre Decennier Svensk Grafik* (Stockholm, 1976)

Jane Rothlind, *Svensk Svart-vit Grafik 1890–1990* (Lund, 1992)

Index of Artists